EDUCATION UNDER SIEGE

Why there is a better alternative

Peter Mortimore

First published in Great Britain in 2014 by

Policy Press
University of Bristol
6th Floor
Howard House
Queen's Avenue
Bristol BS8 1SD
UK
Tel +44 (0)117 331 5020
Fax +44 (0)117 331 5367
e-mail pp-info@bristol.ac.uk
www.policypress.co.uk

North American office:
Policy Press
c/o The University of Chicago Press
1427 East 60th Street
Chicago, IL 60637, USA
t: +1 773 702 7700
f: +1 773-702-9756
e:sales@press.uchicago.edu
www.press.uchicago.edu

British Library Cataloguing in Publication Data
A catalogue record for this book is available from the British Library

Library of Congress Cataloging-in-Publication Data
A catalog record for this book has been requested

ISBN 978 1 44731 132 4 paperback

Cover design by Andrew Corbett
Printed and bound in Great Britain by Short Run Press, Exeter

FSC
www.fsc.org
MIX
Paper from responsible sources
FSC® C014540

To Valentina, Sebastian, James, Peter and Adam – currently working their way through the English education system.

About the author

Peter Mortimore began teaching in 1964. He has worked as one of Her Majesty's Inspectors and was for six years Director of Research and Statistics for the Inner London Education Authority. He has been a professor of education at the universities of Lancaster, London and Southern Denmark. He was Director of the Institute of Education from 1994 to 2000. He has written widely on education issues.

Acknowledgements

I am very grateful to all who have helped develop my understanding of education. At the start of my career, countless pupils taught me how to teach. Later, Michael Rutter and Jack Tizard trained me to be a researcher and Peter Newsam instructed me in how government works. Since then, colleagues in the Inner London Education Authority and at the universities of Lancaster and Southern Denmark and from the 10 privileged years I spent at the Institute of Education, University of London, have generously shared their skills, knowledge and companionship. More recently my gym companion, Joe Collier, has been a source of potential titles and daily encouragement.

John Bangs, Michael Bassey, Melissa Benn, Clyde Chitty, Celia Dignan, Adrian Elliott, Anne Edwards, John Fowler, Ron Glatter, Sue Hallam, Mark Hartley, Alasdair Macdonald, Sue Roberts, Pam Sammons, Brenda Taggart and Pat Tunstall all contributed ideas on the strengths of the English system. John Fowler nobly volunteered to read an early draft and, as well as correcting many errors, contributed a number of important ideas to the book.

Emily Watt and her colleagues at Policy Press have been helpful and supportive.

Finally, Jo Mortimore has been critical friend, collaborator and frequent debunker throughout the writing of the book – as well as for the previous 50 years.

Peter Mortimore
July 2014

Preface

Education is important. It is the route by which society transmits its culture and its rules about how we live. It is also the means by which we each make sense of our world. It enables us to become our adult selves and shows us how to lead good lives. But to be effective, education needs good learners, good teachers and a good education system. Humans are born good learners and we have many good teachers. It is this third component – a good education system – that I believe is questionable in England today. This book is my contribution towards creating a better system.

We have each been to school and many of us have supported our children through their education so we all know something about education. I have also worked in the education system for nearly 50 years. I spent almost a decade as a classroom teacher and nearly two as a university researcher. I worked briefly as one of Her Majesty's Inspectors of schools. For seven years I was Director of Research and Statistics for the Inner London Education Authority and enjoyed a unique opportunity to explore schools' data. Then, as Assistant Education Officer responsible for secondary education in inner London, I worked with head teachers, teachers and governing bodies grappling with the challenges of inner-city work, albeit in a relatively well-funded authority.

My experience as a professor in two English and one Danish universities and my time as an international consultant have afforded ample opportunities to work with many schools around the world. As a school and college governor, I have also seen the education system from their viewpoints.

I was fortunate to work on one of the first studies of school effectiveness led by Michael Rutter, a distinguished child and adolescent psychiatrist. The study fostered my interest in research. It also evoked an interest in how the education system worked – from the classroom to the ministry – and encouraged me to consider its strengths and weaknesses. In various roles since then I have maintained this interest and observed, at close quarters, the relationship between politicians – at both central and local level – and practitioners.

I am not a particularly political person and have never stood for public office. I have always been of the Left rather than the Right but, during the years in which I held senior posts in universities, I did not think it appropriate to belong to any political party. Over my career I have observed 30 education ministers. Despite some political differences, the one I found most genuinely interested in improving education – and with whom I worked most harmoniously – was the Conservative education minister, Gillian Shephard.

After leaving the Institute of Education, I led international teams reviewing education in Denmark and Norway for the Organisation for Economic Co-operation and Development. Since then I have had the privilege of visiting the Nordic countries many times: observing in schools; meeting pupils, parents, teachers and education officials; and working in a Danish university.

Now, at the end of my career, I have taken the opportunity to reflect on the state of the current English education system in comparison to the various Nordic systems. This book is part history, part policy critique and part memoir. In it, I focus on what education means for individuals and for society. I consider the strengths and the weaknesses of the system and the features that can be either positive or negative and give my verdict on its overall effectiveness. I then discuss some of the characteristics of a more desirable system and propose a series of steps – distinctly different from the education market favoured by recent governments – through which the English system could be improved. Finally, I ask how, in a democracy, governments' insistence that there is no alternative to their way of thinking can be challenged.

I prepared for the paperback version of the book during the early summer of 2014. I have updated national and international data and added references to new relevant research. I have also endeavoured to note major policy changes that have occurred since the first edition of the book was submitted for publication in December 2012. Inevitably, more changes will have been announced by the time the second edition is published.

ONE

What is education?

Education in England is stressful. Children are pushed, pulled and stretched into line. The strains of keeping up with a national *expected level* or of competing for a scarce place in a popular school are immense. Time for pottering, observing the world or just 'being' has all but disappeared.

Many parents of pre-school children juggle the demands of seeking affordable childcare with managing their own employment demands. Those with primary age children help with reading, spelling and times tables. Those who can afford it send their children, from pre-school upwards, to an array of learning activities; those who cannot, watch other children move ahead.

Parents have to master elaborate gambling rules if they hope to secure a place for their child in a sought-after secondary school. Those with teenagers have to help their offspring cope with frequent examinations as well as supporting them through such adolescent stresses as bullying and the temptations of smoking, drugs, sex and alcohol.

The struggle for an education dominates life in our society to an ever increasing extent. Parents hope that education – no matter how much it will cost both in financial and in human terms – will help their children succeed. Yet many parents are unaware of how different education can be in other countries or of what it might be here. Our society has few mechanisms for debating such important questions, so we leave it to the state to decide. That allows politicians to indulge in whims.

Politicians are important. In a democratic society, in which millions of families depend for their livelihoods on a complex web of commercial enterprises, trade, services and benefits, policies have to be decided, rules created and resources distributed. But we should be wary of permitting politicians to impose their particular visions on our children. Two and a half thousand years ago, Aristotle argued that education must always 'be contestable'.[1] We – the people – should ensure that the debate is not closed. This book is my contribution to that debate. Drawing on my lifetime's experience in education, I have tried to make sense of the important issues involved in this engrossing topic.

Describing education is not simple. We still know far too little about how humans learn and, while we know more about teaching and can observe the way schools work, many education issues are far from straightforward. Some arguments are finely balanced; others – from hardliners of both Left and Right – often contain grains of truth amid much conjecture. I have tried to work through the issues – drawing on research evidence and my own experience – to form a balanced view of the worth of the current English system.

Education is both a personal development that we all experience during our lives – and a fundamental component of our society related to collective values, culture and history. And the personal has to mesh with the collective. I return to these issues throughout the book.

My focus is on schooling rather than on further, tertiary or adult education – not because these sectors are unimportant; far from it. In these days of life-long learning what happens between ages 18 and 80 is crucial. But my own experience is with primary and secondary schools, so my argument focuses on the initial opportunities which they provide. I will touch on some special education issues but will leave them for others with more knowledge to pursue.

I start with what we mean by the word 'education' and what most of us have in mind when we talk about 'an education'. I have not written specifically for academics (although I draw on research data, articles and internet sources) but for parents, teachers, aspiring teachers, interested older pupils, committed citizens and anyone else – including politicians – concerned about education today.

What does 'education' mean?

The exact derivation of the term is uncertain but three Latin words are related to education: *ducere* – 'to lead'; *educare* – 'to mould (into a particular shape); and *educere* – 'to bring out'. These three words illustrate a fundamental argument about education: is it active or passive? Is it about instilling knowledge into pupils' heads or about releasing their latent talents?

These questions too readily translate into a traditional versus a progressive, or a right-wing versus a left-wing, stance. Such divisions tend to polarise views and strengthen well-defined battle lines. For me, the answer is that education must be both and much more. It should instil knowledge, evoke natural talents and enable us to become who we want to be.

In seeking definitions of 'education' I have consulted three sources: Oxford and Cambridge dictionaries and – by way of a contrast – Wikipedia, which, as readers will know, has been created by thousands of voluntary contributors from around the world.[2]

The traditional dictionaries use terms such as: 'an enlightening experience', 'knowledge', 'understanding', 'skills', 'attitudes' and 'judgements'. Wikipedia, however, also emphasises education's dual role as both a public project for society and a personal process for individuals.

So, on the one hand, education is a vehicle – designed and overseen by the powerful in society – for influencing and controlling fresh generations by passing down prescribed knowledge and national culture. On the other hand, education – through its capacity to develop independent thinking – is also the means of freeing the individual from these very influences.

Drawing on elements from these dictionary definitions, and bearing in mind the perspectives both of those charged with managing education and of those experiencing it, I propose the following definition:

> Education is the process through which society transmits its accumulated values, knowledge, skills, attitudes and customs from one generation to another and influences how an individual thinks, feels and acts.

Applying this definition allows us to understand education as any act or process which influences us as individuals or as a society. It can be intended or incidental. It may be positive or negative. It affects both our national and our individual character. It determines much of *how* and *what* we think. Thus education – both good and bad – exerts a major influence on both how we wish, and how we are permitted, to lead our lives.

Let me get a few more definitions out of the way. In this book I use the term *information* for a basic fact or set of related facts. I use *knowledge* to characterize the use of that specific information in relation to all the other salient facts that we possess. Jean Piaget, a Swiss theorist,[3] provided a useful explanation of this. He used the term *assimilation* to describe the absorption of new facts and the term *accommodation* to describe the way this new information is subconsciously adapted and calibrated to fit with our existing knowledge. The second part of this process is essential. We have all met people – like David Brent (star of *The Office*) – who are always quoting *facts* but who appear incapable of relating one to another. I save *understanding* for a deeper appreciation of the significance of knowledge. Finally, I reserve the term *wisdom* to express the judicious use of knowledge in the right place at the right time.

Education, as the definitions make clear, also affects our attitudes and judgements. *Attitudes* are our normal ways of thinking, 'settled ways of thinking or feeling about something'.[4] Lacking the time and energy to consider carefully each aspect of every object we encounter, we create a generalised view – a 'default option'.

Judgement is the ability to form opinions and make decisions – an essential life skill. We make hundreds of judgements every day. Some can be delayed while we sum up the advantages and disadvantages of different options. Others have to be decided in an instant and we have to rely on our intuition as a guide.

It is impossible to assess the amount of knowledge an educated person possesses, but, given the range of topics and events that touch peoples' lives, it is likely to be vast. Some individuals – like Chris Hughes, a London taxicab driver and past winner of BBC's *Mastermind* – have a remarkable capacity for storing and organising knowledge, coupled with highly desirable (especially for pub quiz enthusiasts) instant recall. London taxicab drivers are believed to have excellent memories as a result of their learning 'the knowledge'.[5] Researchers have suggested that the hippocampus area of the cab drivers' brains develops to a greater extent.[6]

Of course, much of our education is not planned. It takes place under many different guises at different times in our lives. Key opportunities occur serendipitously.

There is a tendency in discussions of English education to downplay its more noble side. Yet it is this aspect of education that German and Nordic societies value in their culture. It is called *bildung*.

What is 'bildung'?

The word is used to characterise education in its most pure and noble form. According to Klaus Prange, a German philosopher of education, 'bildung … is associated with liberty and human dignity … something to do with the spiritual and/or aesthetic side of our lives … a value in itself'.[7] This lifts our gaze from the mundane to the profound. Education is seen as worthwhile both for individuals and for their societies. Its instrumental importance – for example, for career development – is predominant in England. But the concept of *bildung* should also remind us that there is more to education than the chance of getting a good job.

Before considering what a personal education means for an individual, I want to comment on the relationship between society and education.

Society and education

Many writers have stressed that an education system fulfils a series of roles on behalf of society in addition to its role in relation to individuals. John Amos Comenius,[8] a 17th-century Czech Protestant priest and educational reformer, was one of the first to recognise this dual role when he wrote his 'Brief Proposal', advocating reform of Bohemia's society through its education system. He was influential in many European countries and was invited to England, where, among other ideas, he suggested that Parliament establish an international college. Unfortunately this notion was overtaken by the outbreak of the English civil war in 1642. Comenius addressed many questions to do with teaching methods – including writing a book for mothers to use[9] – and was enthusiastic about the use of Latin as a common European language.[10]

Centuries later John Dewey, a 20th-century American professor,[11] elaborated the function of schooling in a democracy. He suggested that the school had a role in transmitting the dominant culture of the society, though he also stressed a different role – 'as an agent of social progress'[12] – in changing that culture, a point to which I will return later.

Transmitting the culture (a set of shared values, attitudes and practices) of a particular society from one generation to another occurs through the passing on of laws and conventions, an agreed history, a language and a generally accepted 'way of doing things'. The culture is woven into pupils' education through many curriculum subjects, but particularly through history – where versions of the events chosen for study will be those which reflect the way each country wishes to view its past. As two of Julian Barnes' characters in his novel *A Sense of an Ending* claim, history can be seen as either 'the lies of the victors' or 'the self-delusions of the defeated'.[13] Culture will also be reflected in citizenship studies, in which collective attitudes towards other countries and topics will be explored, and in how enthusiastically foreign languages are taught.

In the Nordic countries there is a strong tradition of preparing children for democracy. This entails teaching them about their duties and rights. It affects the way schools are organised and ensures a strong non-conformist pupil voice.

Is conformity a good or a bad thing? While it is easy for a school to focus on conformity as a means of ordering institutional life, this can be overdone. Of course, schools need to be orderly places and every member of the school community (children and adults) deserves to be treated with respect. But this does not necessitate the imposition of a military-type regime. In the schools I have known, most pupils have conformed to reasonable rules. However, once teachers begin to measure the length of skirts, the width of trouser legs or the type of hair style, it seems to me that the school's priorities are shifting from learning to conforming. And, as many teachers will know, pupils pushed into a corner over uniform can react with creative flair, damaging stubbornness or both. An obsession with control and the need to achieve total conformity in a school can stem from the insecurity of the head teacher. I have seen an entire school marching in and out of assembly several times in a morning because a few pupils had broken the imposed rule of silence. It was, of course, a foolish strategy which handed to the least responsible the power to disrupt the maximum number.

One of the education system's traditional tasks is to prepare future generations for the occupational roles needed by society. In the past this was more straightforward: outstandingly able children were educated to undertake necessary functions for the gentry as doctors, lawyers or administrators, or trained as skilled craftspeople. The vast majority of the population, destined for low-status and limited-skill tasks, were deemed to warrant only the most rudimentary education.

Following the Industrial Revolution, the country required a more efficient – though not much broader – education for a greater proportion of the population. The country needed workers with some bureaucratic and technical skills. Once the traditional pattern of children following in the occupations of their parents and learning all that was necessary from them was no longer sufficient, schooling became necessary for everyone rather than a diversion for the privileged.

A further reason for the growth of schools was that political reforms had brought about an increase in the number of people permitted to vote. The political elite worried about this. In the words of Robert Lowe, an important 19th-century politician: 'From the moment that you entrust the masses with power, their education becomes an absolute necessity'.[14]

In England, emerging schools were modelled loosely on a mixture of the existing village 'dame schools' and the grammar schools (provided by voluntary and religious bodies, but later publicly funded). No one wanted to spend too much on schools for the poor – as the same Robert Lowe made clear in his introduction to the Revised Code of 1862: 'if it is not cheap it will be efficient; if it is not efficient it shall be cheap'.[15]

In nations emerging from revolutions or territorial changes, schools were needed to form 'a cohesive citizenry out of these heterogeneous populations particularly in immigrant nations such as the USA'.[16]

The 'common school' was entrusted with the task of how best to make a common people. Today, many nations seem to be stuck in a quandary as to how 'common' a school they actually want. Do they want a fair system in which everyone – according to his or her talents and level of dedication – can develop? Or do they really want to retain a system which still favours the children of those already advantaged? This is a key question for many countries – including England – and one to which I will return throughout the book.

The relationship between a society and its education system is, of course, two sided. Today, when governments often force reforms on schools, it seems that the education system must be the servant of the state. Future citizens, however, will be influenced by the schooling they have received and, in turn, may use their voices to bring about radical changes to the education system that they have experienced. Just as children can react by rejecting their parents' values and espousing radically different ones, a similar process can happen in society.

If, for example, the majority become conscious of issues to do with racism, then there is hope that society will – in time – become less racist. If the majority learn to value democracy, then its preservation becomes more likely. Although the 1988 television film *A Very British Coup*, based on a novel by former Labour MP Chris Mullin – which depicts a left-leaning prime minister brought down after attempting to take on 'the British establishment' – illustrates what a tricky process questioning existing privilege can be, for even a legitimately elected government.

Social change can work the other way too. If, for instance, there were to be a significant increase in the number of comparatively well-off people using private schooling, there would obviously be fewer pupils left to attend state schools. This might marginally reduce the cost of state schooling but it would also reduce the range of pupils and parents involved with it. The country would develop a polarised system – with pupils from reasonably wealthy families attending schools worlds apart in resource levels and quality of environment from those attended by their less well-off peers.

Such a situation would mean that pupils would lack the opportunity to mix with people different to them. This, in turn, would affect society by perpetuating the existence of different 'tribes' living parallel lives – suspicious of each other and unhappy at having to mix. This would be another step towards a land of gated communities and ghettoes.

In Chapter Thirteen I discuss the implications of such a situation and what can be done about it. In the meantime, I will turn to some of the issues to do with personal education.

When does our education start?

Education begins at birth. The initial responses of new-born babies are stimulated solely by hunger and pain. Yet, within weeks, babies have learned to use their limited powers. Their capability is astonishing. They absorb concepts about the world while simultaneously developing their own brains. Within two or three years the vast majority have learned to feed themselves, walk and manage their bodily functions. They have also acquired a great deal of knowledge about how the world works.

All young children (except for those with the most severe learning problems) acquire naturally the language in which they are raised, no matter how complex its grammatical structure. Psycholinguists argue about how exactly this happens: whether it is gained through listening and imitating others or whether babies are born equipped with (what linguists call) *a language acquisition device*.[17] Either way, it is an amazing achievement. A young child's enthusiasm for learning is precious. The sight of two- and three-year-olds 'gobbling up' information through play is truly impressive.

The definition of education discussed earlier included *values*. These lie at the heart of education, although the education process itself treats them more neutrally. For instance, it is possible to describe the schooling, university courses and professional training of a solicitor to uphold the law as *an education*. It is equally possible to use the same term to describe the training of an apprentice in a criminal gang overseen by a modern-day Fagin.[18]

In her memoir – parts of which were adapted into a film (*An Education*) – the journalist Lynn Barber recounts how, as a schoolgirl, she gained an education through her relationship with an older married man involved in shady criminal pursuits. The message of her book is that education can take many different forms. She reflects that, although she succeeded easily in her academic education and ended up studying at Oxford, she also gained a different, negative education through this relationship.

> What did I get from Simon? An education – the thing my parents always wanted me to have ... but there were other lessons Simon taught me that I regret learning ... I learned to suspect that anyone and everyone is capable of 'living a lie' ... It made me too wary, too cautious, too ungiving. I was damaged by my education.[19]

Is education active or passive?

In the past, learning was often seen as something to be forced on children. Many autobiographies stress the passive role of a pupil: having facts beaten into them or being punished for failure. Witness Winston Churchill's experience of one of his early schools:

> How I hated this school, and what a life of anxiety I lived there for more than two years. I made very little progress at my lessons, and none at all at games. I counted the days and the hours to the end of every term.[20]

While passive learning can be forced on another person through punishment, the best kind of learning is active and needs to be embraced by the learner.

Of course, school pupils are passive in the sense that they usually have little control over how their time is spent. They can be ordered to carry out a particular task and can undertake rote learning – such as memorising a poem. But deeper understanding will be limited without the pupil's more active involvement. A smart but disruptive pupil, recognising this reality, can lay down the gauntlet to a teacher 'well, you teach me then!'

Lynn Barber could have declined the education described in her book. She chose not to, even if, in time, she came to regret some aspects of it. Churchill, too, despite his miserably passive experience of school, eventually actively educated himself.

Life-long learning

Today almost all adults in developed countries have experienced years of schooling. Some will continue formal studies into adult life. England has a worthy tradition of local authority adult education classes and organisations such as the former Mechanics' Institutes or the Workers' Education Association. For over 100 years Birkbeck College has specialised in providing degree courses in the evenings for part-time undergraduate and post-graduate learners.

Since the 1960s the Open University (OU) has offered the chance to gain a degree and has thus enhanced the lives, career prospects and self-esteem of tens of thousands of people. In the words of the performance poet Matt Harvey, 'OU, we owe you'.[21] The 1983 film *Educating Rita*[22] follows the life of a young hairdresser discovering, through her interaction with a sensitive OU tutor, a new world of learning. She slowly realises that she, too, has a right to enter what she had always seen as an inaccessible world. Many others will continue their education through life experiences gained in their families, their employment and – in difficult economic times – perhaps even through their unemployment.

My point is that education is a life-long process for all of us, provided we make the most of the opportunities. But, of course, we have to want to do so. We can just as easily reject such opportunities and even celebrate our lack of education.

Whether we choose to be life-long learners will depend, in part, on our early school experiences. If we have decided – with or without the help of our teachers – that we are no good at learning, like Willy Russell's Rita we will need to change our opinion of ourselves. If, however, our schooling has given us a positive view of our potential (whatever we actually achieve at the time) and stimulated our curiosity, imagination and capacity for sustained learning, our scope as life-long learners will be boundless.

Conclusion

Education is both the process by which a society renews itself and a long-term course for an individual's all-round development. These two functions are entwined within schools. They provide the opportunities for individuals to make something of themselves and, through their community ethos, they shape future generations. Unlike most other institutions, schools are compulsory. They carry huge expectations and are frequently scapegoated for society's problems. In Chapters Eight to Ten, I discuss their strengths and weaknesses.

In my view, a good education must encompass the development of society and of every aspect of an individual's life. It should be about fostering a good society as well as enabling learners to find the life they want to live and acquire the skills to do so. This is much more than the education that I experienced. But it is what I want for my grandchildren. In the next chapter I focus on the crucial question of what we hope educated people will be like.

TWO

Desirable outcomes

People surely hope that their children will live in a society both peaceful and fair. We like to think that our children will be good people, living reasonably happy lives. We want sufficient opportunities for them to earn a good living, have the chance to explore their interests and bring up our grandchildren safely. We hope that their environment will not have been ruined by the exploitations of our generation or by the geo-political feuds that we have bequeathed them.

Realistically, other than taking action to protect the environment (which, collectively, we seem loath to do) we are likely to have little influence over our grandchildren's world. We need only think of the way technology has developed within our lifetimes to see how difficult it is to predict, let alone influence, future developments. Political alliances and disagreements are also notoriously difficult to foretell, although perceptive writers like George Orwell (predicting the use of CCTV to control people's behaviour[1]) and Graham Greene (picking out future trouble spots such as Vietnam and Haiti[2]) clearly managed.

What we can do is consider the qualities and attributes we would like future generations to possess. Such an exercise can be dismissed as utopian. But this is to miss the point: it should be utopian. If we want a better world for them we have to aim high. Events, no doubt, will knock the shine off our ideas but we need to start in positive mode. Our children and grandchildren will rightly take the initiative and adapt the system we leave to suit their times – but we can give them a good start: an education system that, in addition to providing them with the necessary qualifications to earn their living, will imbue them with positive values to help foster a future society built on similar values.

A common view about the kind of education system we would like to give to our children and grandchildren would provide a template against which new proposals can be tested. In this way educational reform should become less haphazard. I recognise that consensus is silence when the other person is speaking but engaging with what they have said and responding in a balanced exchange of ideas.

Young people lead the way when it comes to communicating with their friends via Twitter, Facebook or other new modes of social networking. Emailing currently relies on the acquisition of keyboard skills (until sound-sensitive computers become common). Traditionally only taught to (mainly female) commercial students, typing skills have become universally beneficial. Texting has rapidly developed not only its own rules of syntax but also its own fingering technique. Because of the size of most mobile phones, it is manageable by children – who have small thumbs – and many become amazingly proficient.

Reading

We read for many different reasons: to search for information, follow instructions, absorb new knowledge or share an experience – as well to enjoy different forms of literature. Reading a novel takes one into a different world in which, although not physically present, one can share the hopes and disappointments, failures and triumphs of a host of imaginary characters in different environments. Young people also need to be able to comprehend analyses and savour description. Crucially, they need to be able to discriminate between factual reporting and commentary – a difficult task, thanks to the skilful work of spin doctors, lobbyists and advertising companies.

Writing

Composing formal business letters, memos or reports, writing poetry or prose, personal letters, keeping diaries and even 'to-do' lists – are important, despite advances in IT. In my experience, being shown how to write, and daily practice throughout the years of schooling, does not necessarily lead to success. Some people seem to learn to write well only when their jobs require them to produce regular reports.

Due to its irregularity, English spelling presents a particular problem. Those without strong visual memories or who suffer from dyslexia are seriously disadvantaged. Thankfully, the advent of computer spell-checks enables them to produce less error-strewn products.

surroundings and solving problems. Drawing on my experience as a teacher and researcher, I want to build on this definition.

Broadening the concept of ability

People seem to me to vary greatly in the possession of the following abilities.

Absorbing and recalling information

This draws on the efficiency of both parts of one's memory – being able to store and organise information so that it relates to other knowledge – and the distinct skill of being able to recall it rapidly. Efficient recall is the hallmark of successful examination candidates. It is also a valuable asset in dealing with a plethora of crucially important user names and passwords.

Comprehending how one's world operates

This is the ability to understand our historical, geographical and social contexts. It also includes basic scientific principles (such as how electricity can be used and its dangers), as well as the increasingly complex financial arrangements involved in contemporary life – from buying a mobile phone to taking out a mortgage.

Engaging with complex thinking

Examples include understanding the principles of advanced forms of mathematics, mastering the grammatical structures of foreign languages and reading philosophy.

Weighing alternatives

At its simplest level, this concerns which of several garments suit us best. It also applies to important, life-changing decisions such as the choice of jobs, partners and homes.

Taking a long-term view

This concerns our ability to adopt planning strategies and tactics, as opposed to acting impulsively. But, somewhat paradoxically, it can also include the ability to grasp that, in a particular situation, one's customary cautious approach may not be appropriate and that one has to seize the moment.

Balancing the big picture with the detail

Again, this involves a somewhat contradictory approach – managing two different thought processes. One is concerned with the impact or consequences of an action; the other is concerned with the detailed steps necessary to execute the action, for example, dealing with its logistics.

Integrating one's capabilities

This overarching ability is what – I think – distinguishes the 'highly able' from the rest of us. The ability to match the correct way of thinking to the particular circumstances: to see beyond the obvious, to cope with complexity, manage tactical and strategic choices while maintaining the ability to grasp the rare opportunity if it arises. These are enviable skills.

Edward de Bono, a Maltese doctor who has, over many years, specialised in teaching thinking skills,[12] argues that a truly intelligent person is one who uses his or her strengths in order to compensate for their weaknesses. Someone, for example, who tends to panic, should avoid being pushed into taking rushed decisions. Given time to reflect on the issues, he or she may be capable of great wisdom.

Holding this somewhat broader view of ability also encourages a certain humility: in some situations it is sensible to seek help or call for advice. It also offers a more realistic view of very able people. Some of those who appear good at everything – the polymaths – may, in fact, be more limited but, because they have learned coping strategies, give the impression that they find everything easy. This is encouraging, because most people are not good at everything. Some parents of exceptionally lively children know. For those diagnosed with attention deficit hyperactivity disorder (ADHD), the problem of too much energy can be severe.[22]

Curiosity

Curiosity has been described by an American research team as 'a desire for learning and knowledge'.[23] As yet, little is known about its biological basis, though it is obviously a driving force in a great deal of our behaviour. Researchers have found that their subjects' memories appeared enhanced when their curiosity was aroused. Curiosity seems to vary a great deal, with some people displaying very little and others showing high levels. Strict education regimes – such as were common in Victorian England and still persist in some countries – tend to dampen down pupils' curiosity and their questioning behaviour, implying that 'children should be seen but not heard'. Not a good recipe for active learning.

Motivation

Motivation is another powerful driving force that pushes us to do particular things. It can be intrinsic – promoted by curiosity, anticipated enjoyment or, alternatively, a fear of failure. It can also be extrinsic – driven by the prospect of a reward (money or fame) or, alternatively, by the threat – or experience – of punishment. Some circumstances, such as being in a competition, may evoke both intrinsic and extrinsic motivations.[24] For parents, particularly, extrinsic rewards (ie bribery) may seem a good idea and, in some circumstances, work well. But if parents are not careful they may rear offspring who are, for example, conditioned to help with the washing up only if the reward is sufficiently worthwhile! Ultimately, it is intrinsic motivation that drives people to outstanding efforts.

Enthusiasm

This overlaps with motivation but appears to me to have a slightly different meaning. It is possible to be motivated to do something –

perhaps because of the promise of a reward – without necessarily being enthusiastic. The ancient Greeks thought an enthusiast was someone possessed by a god, and both Catholic and Protestant writers have discussed enthusiasm as applied to religion.[25] Today, though, we are more likely to use the word to describe a blogger, a football fan or an allotment keeper.

Stamina

This is the ability to maintain mental or physical exertion for a long time. It is similar in its meaning to endurance – often used to describe the experience of hardship or pain – but frequently drawn on in connection with those training for sports competitions. Athletes seek to increase their stamina through the use of aerobic exercises. In the context of education, undertaking a long or difficult course, particularly on a part-time basis alongside family and employment demands, requires considerable stamina.

Perseverance

Though related to stamina, perseverance, to me, expresses a mental rather than a physical determination to keep at something when the going gets rough. Of course, it can be overdone. People can sometimes stick at a task without the faintest hope of achieving it. Psychologists term this 'over-perseverance' and encourage people to make more realistic assessments about the limited chance of a 'pay off' from further effort. Sometimes, however, that extra effort brings a reward – even in the most unpromising circumstances. This is where a learner's judgement comes in: deciding the relative risks of wasting further effort and the potential gains of succeeding against the odds.

Resilience

In simple terms, resilience can be seen as the ability to cope with stress – a topic that has generated a considerable body of scientific research.[26] In an educational context, resilience is demonstrated by those who are able to bounce back after failure. It is also used to and, accordingly, would be highly likely to do well in their classes. Test results demonstrated this to be the case. This self-fulfilling prophesy was termed the *Pygmalion effect*, after Ovid's account of the sculptor who fell in love with the statue he had constructed. Although the precise results of this experiment have never quite been replicated, a number of researchers argue that 'When teachers expect students to do well and show intellectual growth, they do'.[43]

As many teachers know from their own experience, pupils' own expectations can also influence their results. Succeeding once does seem to make later success more likely, just as a history of failure does the opposite. For many teachers, trying to change the mind of a pupil who is convinced that he or she cannot succeed can be frustrating. Expectations also feed off each other. If parents, pupil and teacher all share positive expectations, the prognosis for success will be high, and, conversely, where they share low ones, success is likely to be elusive.

In the 1980s I was involved with a research study of 11-year-old pupils of the Inner London Education Authority. The research team encountered a disturbing example of low expectations stemming from latent racism. We were following the pupils' transition from primary to secondary schools. As part of the process, pupils completed an anonymous verbal reasoning (ability) test and were independently rated on their school performance by their primary class teachers.

Our research team was given confidential access to the pupils' identities. We could, therefore, compare the pupils' scores on the tests with the ratings awarded by the teachers (who were unaware of the test results). We found that, overall, there was a close correspondence between the two sets of data; teachers' judgements and the test results were generally similar. But there were exceptions. With two groups of pupils there was a tendency for teachers to express lower ratings than the test scores.

Which were the two underestimated groups? One group was Caribbean boys. Unfortunately, the groups were too small for tests of statistical significance. But there was a clear tendency for some pupils, predicted to be in the top band on the basis of test scores, to be assigned to the middle band by their teachers, and for those predicted to be in the middle band to be assigned to the lowest. And these were inner London teachers who were, at that time, probably more aware than many of their colleagues elsewhere in the country of the dangers of unconscious racism.

The other vulnerable group consisted of children who were young in relation to their school year – those born during the summer months. This group had experienced one or two terms' less schooling than their classmates and were up to 12 months younger than the oldest in the age range. The test scores benefited from a built-in age correction but the teachers' own judgements did not. It appeared that some had forgotten that these children were summer-births and had assumed that they were less able. Since that time there have been many other studies drawing attention to the continuing disadvantage faced by the youngest pupils in each year group.[44]

Importance of hard work

Some people like to give the impression that they seldom have to exert themselves over their learning, probably because they believe it is not 'cool' to be seen to work. This bravado is probably exaggerated but it can have an undue influence on impressionable friends and colleagues who, believing what they are told, may reduce their own efforts – and may, as a result, pay a heavy price. In my experience, learners who work hard usually reap the benefit of their labours. The phrase 'Genius is one per cent inspiration and ninety-nine per cent perspiration', ascribed to Thomas Edison (the self-educated inventor of many applications of electricity), illustrates the point. It is also emphasised by Malcolm Gladwell, who calculates a work time of 10,000 hours needed for success, citing examples as diverse as the Beatles and Bill Gates.[45]

Conclusion

It would be helpful to have a simple way of defining ability. Unfortunately, I have not yet found it. The following is the clearest description I can manage:

> A person's ability is made up of their intellectual, social, emotional, physical and artistic capabilities, skill in using luck, capacity for hard work, resilience and sense of strategy.

This description recognises that, while we are all different and some people have been dealt a better hand than others, we all have the opportunity to develop and expand our capabilities. And, crucially, that the ability to learn easily is only part of one's total ability. Like de Bono, I see the strategic skill of making the most of one's strengths in order to overcome one's weaknesses as supremely important.

So, if ability is such a multi-faceted concept – how best should we employ it? This question takes us directly into the world of learning and teaching.

FOUR

Learning

Everyone knows that the process of education involves two distinct activities – learning and teaching: two sides of the same coin, different but (hopefully) connected. Those doing the learning are children. Those doing the earliest teaching are parents, siblings and friends. The process continues with professional teachers and trainers until we leave school or university. Or this is how we used to see education. Today we are more likely to recognise that learning never stops, including for those who do the teaching. In this chapter and the following one I discuss what we know about these related activities.

What is learning? In the simplest of terms it is the process of gaining knowledge or skills. John Abbot, an English former head teacher now working in America, defines it more elaborately as:

> That reflective activity which enables the learner to draw upon previous experience to understand and evaluate the present, so as to shape future action and formulate new knowledge.[1]

As I stressed in Chapter One, early childhood is a time of particularly intense learning as babies and young children struggle to make sense of the world. They appear to learn unselfconsciously – absorbing information from their interactions and experiences. They seem to realise that it is in their interest to learn to walk and to speak so that they can become active little people rather than dependent babies.

In pre-school, too, young children continue to learn through the experience of play. This form of early learning seems particularly powerful. Findings from an on-going study into the effects of pre-school experiences show that 'high quality pre-school has lasting benefits even after 10 years'.[2]

It is in school, when they are expected to undertake formal learning as opposed to learning from experience, that problems can develop. There, children are fed lots of information and expected to engage in learning activities within a competitive situation – even if this is underplayed by the teacher – in a structured and relatively constrained environment.

Advocates of learning through experience, such as John Dewey,[3] Paulo Freire[4] and Maria Montessori,[5] always stressed the limitations of school learning removed from the daily life of the child. The American academic David Kolb founded a company to promote experience-based learning.[6]

Are some of the difficulties encountered by new pupils caused by the switch from learning-through-experience to the more formal school learning? Or is it the constraints of the environment, pressure of competition or the intensity of the situation? Or could difficulties be caused by the introduction of formal teaching? This is a challenging thought for people like me – who have worked in education all their life.

Unfortunately, we do not know the answer. Learning cannot be directly observed because the brain's activity in absorbing and organising information is hidden. Whether pupils have learned – absorbed new information, made sense of it and stored it sufficiently well to be able to recall it appropriately – has to be inferred from their responses or their subsequent behaviour. Moreover, it is impossible to judge the impact of particular teaching on specific learning, as there may be a time lag between the teaching and the learner's reaction.

Not many of us find school learning as easy as Kimberley, the young Chinese heroine of Jean Kwok's novel *Girl in Translation*, who begins her story by relating that: 'I've always had a knack for school; everything that was taught there. I could learn: quickly and without too much effort.'[7] Lucky girl!

Teachers know how easily children learn the things that interest them. Football fans are like sponges, absorbing details of matches, teams and even specific goals. Pop music fans are the same – seemingly effortlessly absorbing details of their idols' lyrics, lives and loves. As I discuss later, this is the kind of learning that young people exhibit in relation to digital toys, telephones, televisions and computers. But it is quite different from school learning – which some find particularly difficult.

Some pupils seem to need longer than their peers to master the same tasks or acquire the same skills. Unfortunately, in our pressured system, slow starters often fail to catch up. Data published by the Department for Education (DfE) show that 'three-quarters of children in England who make a slow start in the three Rs at primary school, fail to catch up by the time they leave'.[8]

I was painfully reminded of the difficulties of school learning when I was living in Denmark and attempting to learn Danish (as I noted in Chapter Two). The fact that I was 35 years older than my classmates and, unlike most of them, was not living with a Danish partner, did not help. But I found learning the different sound/letter combinations of everyday Danish words, to say nothing of the intricacies of counting and time-telling, extremely difficult. It was a salutary reminder of the plight of so many pupils for whom failure and potential humiliation in class is a daily routine.

Learning processes

Traditionally, the process of learning was studied through either philosophy or theology until, in the nineteenth century, Wilhelm Wundt, a German doctor at the University of Leipzig, began a series of scientific investigations into human consciousness, using the introspective ability of volunteer subjects. Thus was born the study of experimental psychology.

Watson and the behaviourists

The value of introspection was dismissed by the founder of behaviourism, John B. Watson,[9] in his work on consciousness. Watson and his fellow behaviourist, B.F. Skinner,[10] argued that learning theory must be related to the motivation to learn and that this could come only from the promise of reward. The most famous behaviourist experiment involved the Russian psychologist Pavlov transferring his dog's salivation from the sight and smell of food to the sound of a bell previously paired with the food.[11]

Using a similar technique, researchers conditioned various animals to learn unusual skills (like pigeons playing table tennis). The researchers were successful within a limited repertoire of learning tasks. Conditioning is still used as the basis for training dogs and circus animals. But it is viewed by animal rights supporters as cruel and by most psychologists as too limiting to shed much light on human learning.

Vygotsky

Lev Vygotsky,[12] a Russian psychologist born in Belarus in 1896, is probably best known for his work on the relationship of thought and language. He took learning theory in a different direction by focusing on the mental processes of perceiving, remembering and reasoning. For many years his pioneering work, carried out from 1925 to 1934, remained untranslated and largely unknown in the West. He died tragically early in 1934. Vygotsky's work emphasises the social context of learning. His theory of what he called 'the zone of proximal development'[13] identifies how children, working alongside their teacher or more advanced pupils, can learn and achieve at a level way beyond their current competence.

Some readers – whose children have struggled to produce acceptable school projects for their homework – may have been inveigled into helping them. The bad news is that assessing the projects is extremely difficult, since it is impossible for the teacher to know just how much has been contributed by the parent and how much by the child. It is also unfair, as those with parents or friends with relevant skills or knowledge will benefit significantly. The good news is that children may have been extended far more than if had they worked alone – just as Vygotsky's theory predicted.

Piaget

Jean Piaget was born in the same year as Vygotsky (though he lived 40 years longer). He was a Swiss philosopher-turned-developmental psychologist who studied the intellectual development of his three children and devoted his life to studying the origins and acquisition of knowledge (known as genetic epistemology[14]). Piaget's theory of children's cognitive development involves four stages of increasingly sophisticated kinds of human learning (sensory-motor; representational; concrete operations; and formal operations).[15] As I noted in Chapter One, Piaget coined the terms *assimilation* and *accommodation* to describe how children deal with information. Like the American academics John Dewey[16] and Kurt Lewin (remembered for his aphorism 'There is nothing so practical as a good theory'),[17] Piaget considered that learning takes place mainly as a result of experience.

Bruner

Jerome Bruner,[18] an American psychologist born in 1915, who spent the 1970s at Oxford, is generally recognised as one of the most important of today's psychologists. He uses the terms *scaffolding* and *spiralling* to describe ways in which teachers can transfer responsibility for learning to their pupils. Much of his work is based on the theory that learners 'construct knowledge from their experiences, mental structures and beliefs'.[19] Through Bruner's contributions, work on learning moved to a constructivist set of theories. Constructivists generally see learning as active rather than passive and as much more open to social and cultural influences than had been envisaged by the previous theorists.

Theory of mind

What has been termed a 'theory of mind' has developed from philosophical thinking. It is the ability, possessed even by young children, to recognise that other people – just like them – also have minds which express intentions, desires and beliefs. This enables them to understand and even anticipate other peoples' behaviour towards them and provides a strategy for some kinds of learning.[20] Simon Baron-Cohen draws on this idea in his work on the difficulties faced by people with autism.[21]

Learning styles

In 1981 David Kolb (the American academic I noted in relation to experiential learning) proposed a new theory about the way children learn. He argued:

> Because of our hereditary equipment, our particular past life experiences, and the demands of our present environment, we develop a preferred way of choosing. We resolve the conflict between concrete and abstract and between active or reflective in some patterned characteristic ways. We call these patterned ways learning styles.[22]

The idea of different styles of learning was welcomed by teachers who began to seek ways of adapting their practice in order to fit Kolb's different learning styles: 'converger', 'diverger', 'assimilator' and 'accommodator'.[23] The first two terms have an intuitive appeal. We all know people whose thinking seems to fit with others, and those who march to the beat of a different drum. The last two terms are clearly drawn from Piaget's work – those who just take in information and those who can relate it to other knowledge they possess.

Researchers further adapted Kolb's work to include such styles as 'theorist', 'activist', 'reflector' and 'pragmatist'.[24] These titles suggest useful distinctions between the ways different people tend to think (actively or reflectively) and, indeed, how they tend to behave (pragmatically or in accordance with a principled position).

Another adaptation of Kolb's work focused directly on the modes of absorbing information as a 'visual learner', an 'auditory learner' or one predominantly geared to 'kinaesthetic' or 'tactile' learning.[25]

Learning styles – and the innovative applications that Kolb's theory inspired – seemed to offer an important breakthrough for teachers. They would be able to group their pupils into those using different learning styles and then focus their teaching to suit the different groups. It seemed that learning theory had finally produced some practical guidance for the classroom.

Unfortunately, despite the intense interest these styles aroused, systematic evaluations have produced little evidence that learning styles are consistent, and eminent critics have lined up to attack the theory.[26] It appears that while we might, in some circumstances, receive information in different ways, what we do with this information – in relation to our previous knowledge, understandings and attitudes – is much more complex than can be explained by reference to learning styles. So, sadly, this theory was not able to provide concrete help for teachers.

The promise of neuroscience

The developments in neuroscience may – in time – provide new opportunities. Gerald Edelman, an American physiologist who was awarded a Nobel Prize in 1972, has claimed: 'We are at the beginning of the neuroscientific revolution. At the end we shall know how the mind works.'[27] He sees the brain as a jungle in which systems interact continuously in a chaotic fashion, but one in which learners thrive. He believes that children have a natural inclination to learn and understand. (As I noted earlier, this appears true with regard to learning-through-play and digital learning.)

With any new field there is always the opportunity for 'pseudo-scientific fads' to be confused with vital knowledge.[28] (I suspect that the obsession with children drinking lots of water – in the hope that it will enhance their brain development – will turn out to be one such fad.) We are still waiting for a neuroscientific breakthrough. But breakthroughs take time and it might be some while before we understand learning sufficiently to be able alter classroom practice with confidence.

The investigation of the brain, of course, is not new. In 405 BC a Greek physician and writer, Alcmaeon of Croton, concluded that the brain, rather than the heart, was responsible for the body's sensations and was the likely seat of intelligence.[29] In the 11th century one of the first people to be acknowledged as a scientist, Ibn al-Haytham of Cairo, was endeavouring to understand the nervous system.[30] During the 15th century, Leonardo da Vinci (noted in the last chapter) was trying to make sense of the traditional view of the soul and new ideas about the links between the senses and the brain.[31] By the 19th century, techniques had been invented to allow brain cells to be stained and studied, and the Spanish Nobel Prize-winning doctor, Santiago Ramón y Cajal, demonstrated that the brain was composed of a mass of interconnected cells.[32] But strange ideas also persisted. For example, Franz Gall studied the brain by feeling bumps in the head and measuring the positions of facial organs.

The brain injuries produced by the terrible wars of the 20th century provided revealing data about the way the organ functioned and about its relation to speech and movement. Emerging technology also provided new ways to study the brain. Science writer Rita Carter recounts how the 1970s brain-imaging technology made it possible 'for the first time, to observe a living, working brain and to match its processes with the sensations, thoughts and behaviour of its owner'.[33]

Brain scanners, using methods such as positron emission tomography (PET) and magnetic resonance imaging (MRI), have, for instance, revealed patterns in the billions of neurons active in a person's brain. Frank McNeil, an educational researcher who has explored this field, notes how a PET scan revealed the different kinds of brain activity between a depressed Romanian orphan and a child who had not experienced difficulties in early life.[34]

Digital learning

Today, children and young people have a new way to learn – through the digital media. Diana Laurillard, an expert in information technology, argues that different types of media 'can be used to support guided discovery'.[35] Children from a very young age, as I have noted, seem to have a natural ability to handle the aspects of technology that interest them. Many of my friends rely on their grandchildren to show them how to use the latest telephones and computers (as the cartoon I described in Chapter Two illustrates). But, despite the number of computers in schools, I am not convinced that the teaching of, for instance, mathematics and science has changed that much.

The mobile phone has undoubtedly revolutionised the way people communicate by providing a new mode – the text message. Social networking has altered the way many young people relate to each other, though schools are having difficulties in finding ways to use this tool for learning purposes.

Schools face similar questions over whiteboards – interactive displays linking computers and projectors. These are now essential pieces of classroom equipment and provide teachers and pupils with techniques to browse the web, show software or amend and save notes. They can also be used to poll different opinions and display feedback. For a teacher of my age – used to struggling with stubs of chalk and dusty board rubbers – they are magic. But do they enable more learning to take place in the classroom?

The answer from research remains ambivalent. An evaluation of their use conducted by the Institute of Education in London found little evidence of their benefit to learning in secondary schools.[36] But a different study of primary education found what the authors term 'significant gains' – especially in schools where teachers had grown familiar with the technology.[37] Another specialist media researcher comments:

> Technology is believed to motivate learners in and of itself – particularly 'disaffected' learners, who in contemporary debates are almost always implicitly defined as boys … technology is seen to provide guaranteed pleasure and 'fun' in a way that older methods simply fail to do.[38]

The danger is that the 'wow factor' disappears as teachers and pupils get used to the innovation. Might pupils then lose their increased motivation? Perhaps – as the above quotation makes clear – we expect too much of technology. It has, within a short time-scale, so revolutionised the way people work that we assume it will revolutionise the way we learn. The internet offers enormous scope, but learners, perhaps, need to adapt ways of learning in order to utilise it more effectively. We will see if the work of people like Sugata Mitra, who is pioneering 'the school in the cloud' based on his 'hole in the wall' experiment, can revoutionise the way people learn.[39]

Autodidacts

Autodidacts are self-taught. Such people learn without the benefit of a teacher or formal education. Notable autodidacts include Leonardo da Vinci – whom I have already noted and who, although trained in drawing and painting, taught himself architecture, engineering and the sciences;[40] John Clare – the early 19th-century English poet and thinker;[41] and Arnold Schoenberg – the Viennese composer who invented atonal music.[42]

Is this a clue to how people learn most effectively – by teaching themselves? As I noted earlier, many children's difficulties with learning start only when they experience formal school teaching. The autodidacts are too small a number on which to base any argument, but maybe those of us who are teachers need to think harder about whether our teaching always assists pupils to learn.

Conclusion

Although numerous investigations have been undertaken by countless researchers over many years, we still know little about the way learning actually takes place. As I have noted, and as advocates of experiential learning argue, there is a danger that our usual methods of teaching – at least for some children – inhibit their natural learning.

I have suggested that computers and other high-tech gadgets may, at some stage, help to promote better learning. Developments in neuroscience may reveal the key mechanisms by explaining the meaning of the various electrical and chemical changes that take place in the brain. Such developments may give us a sounder understanding of how learning can be aided so that it will be possible to design more efficient ways of teaching and, perhaps, easier ways of learning.[43]

In the meantime, teachers still have to use their best judgement about how to help children learn. And we must never forget the value of all the incidentals that pupils pick up during their time in schools. A former BBC education correspondent, the late Mike Baker, reported how, since being diagnosed with terminal cancer, he had re-evaluated his schooling. His list of 'worthwhile learning' favoured poetry, classical music, creative writing, nature walks, debating, sport, dance and craft skills over all the more conventional subjects.[44]

FIVE

Teaching

In contrast to learning, teaching is observable. But whether it is effective and pupils are actually learning remains a judgement rather than a fact. As I remember from my days as a school inspector, deciding whether a pupil staring out of a classroom window is thinking purposefully or day-dreaming is quite a challenge.

Teacher education

Teaching as a profession does not have a long history in England. It is only since the mid-1970s that most new entrants to teaching have been graduates. Prior to this, while private schools usually employed people with MAs from Oxford and Cambridge (see Evelyn Waugh's *Decline and Fall*[1] for an amusing parody of recruitment procedures), the majority of teachers were recruited from training colleges, many founded in the 19th century.[2]

Today, teachers have to study a specialist subject plus pedagogy to degree level, or undertake a postgraduate certificate of education (PGCE) after completion of a degree in a relevant school subject, or train on the job in a school. Government guidelines about teacher education became more specific after the James Report of 1972.[3] These have steadily become more directive.

The Council for the Accreditation of Teachers, established by a Conservative government in 1983, was superseded by the Teacher Training Agency in 1994. This was then converted into the Training and Development Agency for Schools in 2005 by the Labour government, which also established the General Teaching Council. Modelled on the General Medical Council, this body rested on the (luke-warm) support of the teachers' unions. Its brief was to 'contribute to improving standards of teaching and the quality of learning, and to maintain and improve standards of professional conduct among teachers, in the interests of the public'.[4] Its responsibility for teachers in England was abolished by the Coalition government in 2012, together with the Training and Development Agency. A new body – the Teaching Agency, an executive agency of the DfE – now has responsibility for the supply and retention of teachers and the regulation of teachers' conduct on behalf of the Secretary of State.[5]

Despite this growing control – limiting all but minor scope for university staff in charge of teacher education – recent governments have nonetheless expanded routes into teaching that avoid higher education. These routes include a one-year, salaried graduate training programme in any school prepared to take an untrained person and both paid and unpaid courses under the government scheme 'Teach Direct'.[6]

In addition, since 2000, an initiative by an educational charity has organised a two-year, salaried scheme, 'Teach First', designed to attract high-flying graduates who might not have thought of becoming teachers. The scheme is dedicated to lifting the standard of entrants into teaching – in its own words: 'Transforming exceptional graduates into effective, inspirational teachers'[7] – at least for a few years.

I believe that all this top-down control of teacher education has stifled much innovation. In my experience, the university staff with responsibility for teacher education are generally highly competent and experienced school heads and teachers who, after successfully working in schools, entered universities and often added to their qualifications and understanding of pedagogy. Instead of treasuring this resource, governments have sought to destroy it.

Under the Coalition government, permission has been given for free schools to employ unqualified teachers. As Chris Husbands, the Director of the Institute of Education,[8] has commented, this even "contradicts the Government's own White Paper". Entitled *The Importance of Teaching*, the White Paper states that the best education systems 'train their teachers rigorously at the outset'.[9]

In reality, it appears that ministers believe teaching is best learned on the job: 'Teaching is a craft and it is best learnt as an apprentice observing a master craftsman or woman.'[10] While it is undoubtedly true that some of what teachers do is a craft, best learned in this fashion, many other aspects of the job are more of an art and a science.

Topics such as how children develop, how humans learn, how subject knowledge can be adapted for children of different ages, how pupils with special needs can best be supported and how to evaluate one's work as a teacher, together with an awareness of the latest research on learning and the history of how education has developed are, I believe, best studied in university. Francis Gilbert, an experienced teacher, thinks that the motivation for permitting untrained teachers is the minister's dislike of 'the educational establishment' and his wish to de-professionalise teaching, as well as to prepare the way for businesses to run schools for profit.[11]

The situation is very different in Nordic countries, where ministries provide general guidance but the content of courses is delegated to the universities. In Finland all teachers – primary and secondary – take education programmes lasting five to seven years and qualify at master's level. Furthermore, universities do not charge fees and students can often claim funds for living costs. The critical difference seems to be that, in the Nordic countries, those responsible for teacher education are trusted, whereas, sadly, in England, they are not.

Andreas Schleicher, an Organisation for Economic Co-operation and Development (OECD) education expert, argues that it is possible:

> to elevate teaching to a profession of high-level knowledge workers, who work autonomously and contribute to the profession within a collaborative culture.[12]

What does teaching involve?

All around the world teachers are expected to provide moral leadership, impart knowledge, foster understanding, train their pupils in appropriate skills and manage the behaviour of classes. There have been attempts to identify the characteristics of sound teaching[13] and the Office for Standards in Education (Ofsted) website offers examples of good practice drawn from school inspections.[14]

Academic books on pedagogy (briefly described as the art and science of teaching)[15] seldom manage to capture the full scope of classroom teaching. One possible reason for this is that there are so many different facets to being a teacher. We can all remember teachers who were nice to individual pupils but hopeless at controlling the class, or those who, while they could be unpleasant to some pupils, exerted a welcome authority over the rest. Talented teachers manage to address the whole class while convincing each pupil that they are speaking directly to them.

In September 2012 the government elaborated teachers' tasks into a formal set of standards.[16] These provide a template against which the performance of teachers will be judged.

Following a preamble that states that teachers must 'make the education of their pupils their first concern and are accountable for achieving the highest possible standards in work and conduct', the standards lay down what a teacher 'must' do:

- Set high expectations which inspire, motivate and challenge pupils.
- Promote good progress and outcomes by pupils.
- Demonstrate good subject and curriculum knowledge.
- Plan and teach well-structured lessons.
- Adapt teaching to respond to the strengths and needs of all pupils.
- Make accurate and productive use of assessment.
- Manage behaviour effectively to ensure a good and safe learning environment.
- Fulfil wider professional responsibilities.

A coda about 'personal and professional conduct' extends the standards to teachers' private lives.

I remain undecided about the value of these standards. On the one hand, I applaud them for aspiring to the highest possible levels. On the other hand, I question whether excellence can be mandated by diktat. The authors fail to recognise that effective teaching is always an interaction with learners. It is not something that even the most excellent teacher can guarantee.

The addition of a phrase such as 'should strive for …' would have made the standards more plausible. I wonder how many other occupations would welcome being measured against such a standard of perfection. (Would politicians and civil servants be happy to be judged by equivalent standards?)

According to one of the teachers' unions (the Association for Teachers and Lecturers), the standards 'betray a view of teacher professionalism which impoverishes the profession and learning. They imply a didactic model of teaching based on a supposedly unproblematic relationship between what teachers do/say and what pupils learn'.[17]

They also fail to catch the excitement – and exhaustion – of teaching. They contrast vividly with Frank McCourt's account. The author of *Angela's Ashes*, and a New York teacher for 30 years, he describes what life in the classroom can be like:

> I was more than a teacher. And less. In the high school classroom you are a drill sergeant, a rabbi, a shoulder to cry on, a disciplinarian, a singer, a low-level scholar, a clerk, a referee, a clown, a counsellor, a dress-code enforcer, a conductor, an apologist, a philosopher, a collaborator, a tap dancer, a politician, a therapist, a fool, a traffic cop, a priest, a mother-father-brother-sister-uncle-aunt, a bookkeeper, a critic, a psychologist, the last straw.[18]

I remember my days as a classroom teacher, getting to know hundreds of pupils over the years: the talented and those with difficulties, the well-behaved and the miscreants. I recall the delights and frustrations of helping them learn, as well as listening to home problems. Even the amateur detective work was important. (On one occasion, following a hint from one of my class, I was able to retrieve a stolen wallet from its hiding place and return it to the teacher from whose jacket it had been taken – before he had even missed it.)

There are also sundry unglamorous tasks for teachers and teaching assistants, such as washing infants who have been sick, removing graffiti and bus stop supervision. This real world of schools seems far removed from the clinical words of the 'Standards' document.

Teachers' conditions

Few teachers will have chosen their career because of the likelihood of high pay. Even so, pay varies considerably between different countries.

OECD figures[19] show teachers with at least 15 years' experience at lower secondary level annually earning approximately £7,764 in Estonia but well over £62,849 in Luxembourg. In the Nordic countries Danish teachers earn £31,024; Finns £24,975; Norwegians £22,225; and Swedes £21,298. Similarly experienced teachers in England earn the equivalent of £27,254. Teachers' pay obviously needs to be 'reasonable', so that able people are encouraged to enter the profession. According to TALIS – the latest OECD international survey into the conditions of teachers working in the lower years of secondary schools – 73% of teachers in England felt that their profession was underpaid.[20]

A common public perception is that teaching is a cushy number – with long holidays and short working days. Those who have actually done the job tend to see it differently (I know that I used to be exhausted at the end of a long term). Many teachers work much longer hours than are required by their contracts – marking work, preparing lessons and writing reports in their evenings and at weekends. In terms of formal commitments, the number of teaching hours also varies considerably between countries. The OECD average for state primary schools is 782 hours per year. The range stretches from just over 500 hours in Poland to more than 1,000 in the United States. The Nordic figures are: Danish 650; Finnish 680; and Norwegian 741 (no data for Sweden). The figure for England is 684.[21] The pattern in many countries of three uneven terms in an academic year is curious. My own preference would be for the school year to be divided into five terms of equal length so that learning and holiday weeks were more evenly spaced. But resistance to such an idea, as I discovered some years ago when I championed it, remains strong.

Since 1988 there has been an expansion of various kinds of teaching support. Teaching assistants not only prepare teaching materials but also mark some work and support pupil groups. This assistance has provided much needed help to busy teachers, enabling them to focus on their main pedagogical role. According to TALIS, teachers in England have considerably more assistance than their counterparts in other countries. But such innovations seldom come without problems. A study with which I was involved identified a number of 'grey areas' to do with lack of adequate training, tensions with teachers over the limits of the assistants' roles, weak career structures and potential exploitation of a mainly female workforce.[22] Some of these issues remain.[23]

Class size

OECD statistics[24] show that, while the average number of pupils in a state primary education class is 21.3, in Japan it is 27 and in Luxembourg only 15.3. The data are not available for Norway and Sweden but the figure for Denmark is 19.9 and for Finland 19.4. The average class size for the United Kingdom (data for England were not available in the same form) is much larger – 25.8.

Another way of measuring class size is through the number of pupils for every teacher – the pupil–teacher ratio. Those with the lowest ratios have the most staff resources to use in the school. The latest OECD figures for state lower secondary schools show that the average ratio across countries is 13.5 : 1. The highest (least favourable) ratio is in Mexico, where it is 35.5 : 1, and the lowest (most favourable) is in Belgium, where it is 7.5 : 1. The ratios for the Nordic countries are: Denmark 11.3 : 1; Finland 9.8 : 1; Norway 9.9 :1; and Sweden 11.2 : 1. The ratio for the UK, in contrast, is 17.3 : 1.

The OECD data also show that, of the 32 countries with both state and private schools taking primary age pupils, the UK has the smallest average class size for private, but the ninth-largest for state schools. This is the largest gap between private and state schools in any of these countries.

The question of whether the size of a class actually makes a difference to the standards achieved by pupils has been much debated.[25] The most thorough English research undertaken to date shows that small classes have a positive and long-lasting impact on the learning of the youngest children. However, the same research also shows that the positive effect is much less conclusive with older children.[26]

The teachers' unions have constantly argued that smaller classes are the key to improvement. This is also the view of the proprietors of most private schools, where the average class size is approximately one third that of those in state schools. (This is seen as one of the key selling points of English private schools.)

Whatever the research conclusions, however, many parents feel happier with their child in a smaller class, where the child should get more attention from the teacher and the atmosphere will probably be less daunting.

With older pupils, the size issue is less about the number of people on roll – a formal presentation to a group need not vary, whether the size is 20, 30 or more – than about time allocation. The smaller the group, the greater the time available for teachers to analyse and reflect on each pupil's progress, and to provide detailed individual feedback – leading to richer learning.

Chris Husbands – the current Director of the Institute of Education – in his comments on the TALIS study of teaching notes that 'there is evidence that disciplinary environment improves in smaller classes'.[27]

Class control

There are many different ways in which control can be exerted. Bluster and bullying may appear to work initially, but smart pupils will soon discover the cracks. As a researcher, I once observed a class on the pupils' first day of secondary schooling and then revisited the same class – being taught by the same teacher – six weeks later. The teacher had clearly relished the opportunity to impress the nervous new pupils with his rather grand behaviour. He had shown off and taken advantage of their (temporarily) unnaturally restrained behaviour. Six weeks later, having seen through the bluster, an emboldened class was directly challenging his shaky authority.

More successful than bluster, though crueller, is sarcasm. The teacher who can put pupils in their place by singling out an unfortunate individual with a comment designed to make the class laugh is implicitly warning everyone of what might befall them. Today's pupils are probably better than when I was a pupil at matching fire with fire. As a result, there is probably less 'dark sarcasm in the classroom' (to cite the immortal line from Pink Floyd).

Good teachers control classes without recourse to bluster, sarcasm or the threat of dire punishment. They do it by exhibiting a natural authority stemming from their own experience and self confidence. Somehow, a confident teacher expecting pupils to be polite and well-behaved seems to make this more likely. Sadly, the opposite is also true: a teacher signalling to the class that they are expecting trouble will seldom be disappointed. Teachers without this natural authority have a hard time. It is often difficult to help them, as sending pupils to senior colleagues for punishment serves to highlight their weakness.

Managing pupils' behaviour is particularly difficult for new teachers. How can they transmit a natural authority when they have no experience and may be scared stiff by the sight of their classes? They need to have observed successful teachers, modelled their behaviour, studied the social psychology of classrooms and developed positive attitudes. Even so, it will be daunting. And modelling the behaviour of experienced practitioners may not always help.

As a young teacher, I saw a colleague produce instant order among what looked like a mob of angry pupils, simply by issuing, sotto voce, an instruction. The next week, in a similar situation, I modelled this behaviour. But the pupils still ignored me. I had yet to learn that it was not the low tone of voice that produced good order but the respect enjoyed by the older teacher.

Fear is a bad master. Teachers who are afraid of their classes will always find them difficult. But it is hard to overcome fear when you are a novice. As a new teacher I felt extremely nervous facing notoriously difficult classes, knowing that if I were unable to control my pupils I would be despised by them and pitied by my fellow teachers. An 'occasional holiday' once saved me from teaching just such a challenging class. I had celebrated the free day by taking my own toddlers to the London Zoo, only to be shocked by encountering the very same class, taken there by another (more generous) colleague. Initially horrified, I was amazed to be greeted like an old friend and to witness some of the most difficult pupils playing affectionately with my little ones. Situations like this convinced me that the fear came from my insecurity rather than from their malevolence. Once I had grasped this insight, I learned to manage my classes.

I also learned how generous and loyal inner-city pupils could be. They could provoke you, challenge you and push you to the limit in the battle for control. But if you passed their exacting tests and they accepted that you had their interests at heart and did not patronise them, they trusted you.

Sadly, not all teachers get to this stage. Teaching is not suitable for everybody. A former colleague, after years of humiliation, went into school one Saturday and leaped to his death from a top floor window. Perhaps he wanted to make clear to his pupils and his colleagues (who may have tried to help – but not enough) that his pain had become unbearable.

Asking questions

Questioning absorbs much classroom time.[28] Socratic questioning, named after the techniques developed by the Athenian philosopher,[29] is used for a number of distinct purposes – motivating pupils to think, testing whether a concept has been understood, probing to stimulate connections to other knowledge or to develop critical faculties. It is also used as part of the teacher's repertoire of control – to wake up a soporific class, to demonstrate teacher superiority or to recapture the initiative.

Observing classes, however, has made me aware of how often teachers direct questions to the most overtly responsive pupils. Less confident – or idler – pupils may fail to raise their hands, and thus forgo the opportunity to answer. Some boys may be content to let more articulate female classmates answer questions. This is an aspect of pedagogy that could benefit from a new approach – perhaps using information technology to allow everyone in the class simultaneously to formulate an answer.

I have also noticed how teachers vary in the time they leave for some pupils to answer questions. This can be a powerful signal of whether the teacher thinks a correct (or an interesting) answer is likely. Yet pupils who are naturally hesitant or have difficulty in articulating their thoughts will be at a disadvantage. Those only allowed a brief moment before the question is transferred to a peer are likely to interpret this as a sign of their teacher's low expectation. The teacher, however, may be concerned that long delays or too hesitant an answer may dissipate the momentum built up in a rapid question and answer session. Willy Russell, whom I have cited before, tells a story about low expectations, based on his own schooldays. His teacher asks the class 'What is the greatest invention ever?' Willy, hand up, thinks he knows the answer. But the teacher declines to ask him until everyone else has failed to answer it correctly. When, finally, Willy is permitted to answer 'The wheel!' the teacher, instead of heaping praise on him, as Willy expects, demands 'Who told you?'[30]

This raises the awkward question of favouritism. As in any other walk of life, teachers relate better to some people than to others. But if a teacher allows this to show and cultivates favourites – asking them to do jobs in the classroom or giving them privileges – this can poison the class atmosphere, infuriating those who feel excluded and embarrassing even 'the chosen ones'.

Assessing pupils

Assessment is another crucial pedagogical role for a teacher. It ranges from correcting an answer in the classroom, via marking a piece of written work, to the formal grading of a school report or test. It also includes the provision of feedback to the pupil about how their work might be improved, and to parents on their child's progress. In the past, this assessment role was sometimes neglected: comments on written work limited to one-word exclamations, reports using hackneyed or ambivalent phrases – 'Gary (or Jade or anyone else) is trying' – raising a smile in the staff room but providing little information on how the child could improve.

English newspapers had a field day reporting how, in 1949, the Eton school report for John Gurdon, winner of the 2012 Nobel Prize for medicine, had commented:

> His work has been far from satisfactory … I believe he has ideas about being a scientist. On his present showing this is quite ridiculous.[31]

Today, partly due to the focus during the 1980s and 1990s on how assessment worked,[32] and particularly on what was called pupil profiling,[33] assessment and feedback to both pupils and their parents are taken far more seriously. Many of the criteria or 'rules of the game' used to judge pupils' work, which previously had remained implicit, to be guessed at or available only to the initiated, have been made explicit. The downside is that detailed reports to parents can read as if they have been assembled (as they sometimes have) from a computer phrase bank.

I was once involved in a discussion about assessment with a group of teachers of English in a large secondary school. It quickly became apparent that, while each teacher had clear criteria for their pupils' work, they had never before shared them or compiled a common list. Once this had been hammered out, their pupils were able to see the criteria by which they were being judged and to see what merited an 'A' rather than a 'C'. Whether a pupil could bring his or her work up to an 'A' would depend on their learning ability, motivation and the amount of time available, but at least they would know what was required.

With young children there is a tendency to give very positive reactions to their work as encouragement and as a way of demonstrating high expectations. As children mature, such reactions need to be calibrated by real-world standards, or pupils can rightly complain that they have been misled. I have met pupils who felt that they were given 'real-world' feedback only when they had finished their course and it was too late for them to work harder.

Outstanding teaching

The elements that make a particular teacher outstanding are not always easy to analyse. Thorough knowledge of one's subject is often cited as crucial and teachers with, for example, first-class degrees are highly esteemed. Such a degree provides an excellent foundation for teaching – but is seldom sufficient. Many people will remember clever teachers who were unable to understand their difficulties and to pitch their teaching to an appropriate level. I once listened to a world expert at a famous museum deliver a deadly boring talk, followed by a non-specialist curator (but an experienced teacher) who enthralled her audience.

Paradoxically, some of the best teachers I have observed are people who have experienced difficulties and can identify with their struggling pupils. One was a swimming teacher who had been terrified of water until, in her forties, she learned to swim. Pupils knew of her earlier fear and trusted her to understand theirs and to look after them in the water.

Pupils like 'characters' that excite their interest and stimulate their imaginations. Literature is full of Jean Brodies[34] or John Keatings,[35] characters whose flamboyance appeals to their pupils or who, in contrast to their more conformist colleagues, have a rebellious attitude to the school management. However, the best (and one of the most-loved) teachers I ever encountered was the opposite of flamboyant. He was a slight non-graduate who had taught for over 40 years in the same part of London. He commanded the respect of the toughest pupils – not because he, too, was 'hard', but because he was competent, reliable and fair. His pupils knew that he cared about them and worked hard for their success. He achieved excellent results, solved most of the school's petty crimes and spent every Saturday coaching the district football team. He continued to work in the school on a voluntary basis for years after his official retirement.

In the view of Shirley Lawes, an expert in the teaching of languages, an outstanding teacher is someone:

> Who knows more than how to deliver effective lessons, who can rise above the perceived imperative of examination results, league tables, Ofsted inspections and a micro-managed school culture because they have principled views on education that come from theoretical and professional knowledge, and expert knowledge of their subject discipline.[36]

Although it might be difficult to predict with any accuracy the characteristics of good teachers, there is little doubt about the value of their work. The McKinsey Report on education systems claims that 'there is no more important empirical determinant of student outcomes than good teaching'.[37]

Teachers' critics

Disgruntled pupils like nothing more than 'slagging off' their teacher. And some parents, perhaps still carrying a grudge from their own school days, seem happy to join in. But it is a pity that politicians are so critical and that so many newspapers and television programmes echo them. In a *Daily Mail* interview with James Chapman,[38] the minister said that he wanted 'parents to go into classrooms to assess how well children are being taught'. He was also reported as saying that he wanted bad teachers sacked 'in weeks'. No one wants bad teachers, but many parents would find it difficult to judge how good a teacher is. They will know how well or badly their child is progressing, but whether this is due to teacher or child is another question. As to sacking 'in weeks', teachers – like all citizens – should be subject to well-thought-through employment laws, not to an arbitrary judgement.

In England there is still a tendency for the teaching profession to be looked down upon by older-established occupational groups. The comment by George Bernard Shaw, 'He who can, does; he who cannot, teaches',[39] still holds sway.

I know, from my years in schools, how difficult a job teaching can be. I also know that there are some bad teachers. I once encountered a colleague on his way into school on a beautiful spring morning. His response to my cheery greeting was 'Good morning? … what do you mean – it won't be good morning until 4 o'clock this afternoon'. But, thankfully, such miseries are rare.

Conclusion

England has thousands of teachers who have devoted their lives to promoting learning in a profession all too often patronised and unfairly criticised by those in better-paid but less demanding occupations. Some years ago the *Times Educational Supplement* ran a series on 'My best teacher' in which famous people recalled a teacher who had made a difference to their life. Some of those described sounded truly exceptional: most did not. They were *ordinary teachers* who had believed in the student's potential and done their best for them. And, thankfully, there are people who remember to express their gratitude. Albert Camus, winner of the Nobel Prize for literature in 1957, wrote thus to his former primary school teacher:

> Dear Monsieur Germain
>
> I have let the excitement around me these last few days die down somewhat before writing to you – from the depths of my heart. I have just been given a great honour – one I neither sought nor solicited. But when I heard the news, my first thought – after my mother – was for you.
>
> Without you – without the affectionate hand you held out to the small poor child that I was, without your teaching and your example none of this would have happened.
>
> I don't want to make too much of this sort of honour. But at least it gives me an opportunity to tell you what you meant – and will always mean – to me and to assure you that your work and the generous heart that you put into your effort is still alive in one of your pupils who, despite his age, has not ceased to be a grateful one.
>
> I hug you with all my might.
>
> Albert.[40]

So it is not all criticism. I now turn to discussion of the place where the teaching and much (but by no means all) of the learning takes place – the school.

SIX

Schools

Schools are an important part of our lives. Whether we love or hate our school days, we seldom forget them. Schools are where we spend much of our childhood and adolescence, form friendships, gain knowledge and understanding and start to become our adult selves. For all of us, except those whose intrepid parents exercise their legal right to provide home-schooling,[1] schools are where we encounter formal teaching.

Origins of schools

Schools probably came about because of the development of writing. This is thought to have taken place about 5,000 years ago in Mesopotamia, Egypt, China and Central America.[2] With commonly agreed conventions of writing and calculating, some form of organised teaching was needed to pass on the newly developed skills.

Much later, the sacred writings of the Torah (the book of Jewish law) were taught in some system of schooling. It is also believed that Confucius (551–479 BC) was involved in a kind of educational training[3] and in 4th-century Athens Plato had established his 'Academy' (387 BC)[4] and Aristotle the 'Lyceum' (334 BC).[5] The first English schools were started by the Romans in order to train a cadre of people to undertake local administration. With the Romans and their Viking successors departed, the church needed schools to train its priests. Boys from rich families were given collective tuition in 'chivalry' (their sisters were taught suitably 'female' activities at home).

The subsequent story of schooling in England is a complex mixture of private initiatives and progressive Acts of Parliament. Those wishing to learn more about this story should consult former head teacher Derek Gillard's excellent historical account – complete with links to all the relevant documents.[6] The following is a very brief note of the most significant events.

During the 19th century a series of faltering steps were taken towards the establishment of a national system. Successive British governments were unwilling to commit public money to help poor people. They were happy to let the assortment of voluntary and religious bodies continue until it became evident that an aspiring country needed something better. Even then, efforts to build a national system were half-hearted. According to comparative education specialist Susanne Wiborg, the laissez-faire principles that had encouraged individuals to promote industrialisation with such great success became a barrier to national development.[7]

The 1807 Parochial Schools Bill made provision for 'the labouring classes', and by 1840, a parliamentary grant had been established for 'the education of the poor'.[8] The Newcastle Report (1861) recommended a system for 'sound and cheap' elementary education and the Taunton Report (1868) proposed a national system of secondary education. Forster's 1870 Act made elementary schooling compulsory up to age 13 (though it needed the 1876 Elementary Education Act to establish committees to promote attendance).

After this piecemeal development, the bare bones of an English system were finally put in place with the creation, in 1899, of the Board of Education and, in 1902, of local education authorities. The shape of primary schooling was determined by the Hadow Report (1931) and of secondary schooling by the 1944 Education Act (the Butler Act). This combination established the form of English education for the next 50 or so years.

The 1944 Education Act did not specify the type of secondary school to be provided: it left that to local authorities to decide.

Local authorities were charged with securing providing primary and secondary schools

> sufficient in number, character, and equipment to afford for all pupils opportunities for full time education offering such variety of instruction and training as may be desirable in view of their different ages, abilities, and aptitudes (Section 8(1)).[9]

Many Labour Party supporters had hoped that the Ministry of Education would establish a universal comprehensive system. They were disappointed. The government, under privately educated Clement Attlee, baulked at such a radical step. Instead, grammar school-educated minister Ellen Wilkinson used a ministry publication, *The Nation's Schools*,[10] to promote a tripartite system of grammar, secondary modern and – in theory – technical schools. (For reasons of cost, few technical schools were actually established.)

This divided education system became the standard for the country as a whole. Selection of pupils was undertaken through the 11-plus examination. This consisted of tests of intelligence (discussed in Chapter Three) and attainment in English and arithmetic. Overall, about 20% of pupils were educated in selective grammar schools (in some areas it was as high as 40% and in others it was as low as 10%). About 76% of the remaining pupils were educated in secondary modern schools and about 4% in technical schools.[11]

The Attlee government compounded the situation by refusing to allow secondary modern schools to enter pupils for public examinations and rejecting proposals from several local authorities to introduce comprehensive schooling.[12]

At the time of the Education Act 1944, R.A.B. Butler had the opportunity of thanking religious schools for providing a service prior to the creation of a national system and standing them down. But, instead, he shoehorned them into the new, publicly financed system as voluntary-controlled or voluntary-aided schools.

Until 1990 most religious schools were Church of England or Roman Catholic, with only a small number of Jewish, Methodist and Christian non-denominational schools. The last Labour government, however, began to use the term 'faith school' and encouraged Muslims, Seventh Day Adventists and other faith groups to open state-funded schools.

This action surprised many people. Aware of the recent history of Northern Ireland, many considered that encouraging sectarian division was not a good idea in an English society already stratified by social class and still engaged in conflicts in the Middle East. According to a YouGov poll, reported in the *Observer* in 2011, 80%

were against the plans for the expansion of faith schools, and only 11% in favour.[13]

Faith schools, nevertheless, were allowed to expand, on the grounds that they would be popular with parents. Many religious bodies have responded to the opportunity of opening a faith school under the free school legislation. As Melissa Benn, writing in 2011, noted: 'In London's Waltham Forest ... there are currently ten plans to set up free schools, seven of which would be faith-oriented.'[14]

Schools today

In England in 2013 there were 418 state-funded nursery schools admitting over 38,000 pupils below five years of age. There were nearly 17,000 state-funded primary schools admitting over four million 5- to 11-year-olds and over 3,000 secondary schools admitting over three million 11- to 19-year-olds.[15]

Pupils generally move from primary to secondary at age 11, although, where there are middle schools, the age of transfer can range from 9 to 13 years. This transition is a potentially stressful event in a child's life. Some stress is due to the uncertainties of the system (as I will argue in later chapters), but some is simply the result of the fear of leaving a small, friendly school and moving to a bigger one, full of unknowns. For most pupils, however, this anxiety is short lived. In a research study looking at primary/secondary transfer my colleagues and I found pupils nervous about the change – influenced both by their primary teachers' anxiety on their behalf and by the many myths about maltreatment. In fact, they quickly settled into their new environment. The few pupils who found the transition traumatic were the particularly vulnerable ones who had also experienced difficulties in the primary school.[16]

In England, 88% of state secondary schools are mixed; 7% are all-girls' schools and 5% are all-boys'.[17] (Some parents want a single-sex school for their daughters but a mixed one for their sons.)

Types of schools

There is an astounding variety of secondary schools in England. The range includes: private – some of which are boarding schools; grammar schools; faith schools of many different religions and denominations; voluntary-aided and voluntary-controlled schools; middle schools – with varying age limits; foundation schools; trust schools; community schools; sixth-form colleges, tertiary colleges (sixth-form colleges with open entry, a broader range of post-16 courses and additional adult classes); city technology colleges; technology schools; specialist schools; academies – including technical academies; free schools; studio schools; and the newly inaugurated university technical colleges; and the proposed university training schools.

Some types of schools have been transient. Grant-maintained schools existed for just 10 years. They were introduced by the Conservative government as part of the 1988 Education Reform Act, ostensibly to create greater diversity in provision, but also to reduce the educational influence of local government. Governing bodies (or even groups of parents), after a parental ballot, were allowed to remove the school from the local authority's control and receive funding directly from the ministry. With enhanced funding came powers over admissions and semi-independent status. Grant-maintained status was abolished in 1998 by the incoming Labour government. Schools either reverted to their former type or became voluntary-controlled or foundation schools (retaining much of their former independence). Even with extra funding and much cajoling, the majority of governors declined to go down the grant-maintained route (only 19% of secondaries and 3% of primaries did so[18]). One of the reasons for forgoing the extra funding and enhanced status was an unwillingness to damage collaborations under the local authority.

Private schools

Private schools are funded by pupil fees, gifts and charitable endowments. They do not receive state funding (although they claim charitable status, with associated tax advantages) and are free of much, though not all, state control. Approximately 7% of pupils attend about 2,400 private schools. Ten per cent of private schools are part of the Headmasters' and Headmistresses' Conference[19] and – paradoxically – call themselves 'public schools'. Some have boarding facilities. The oldest are The King's School, Canterbury (founded 597), St Peter's School, York (founded 627) and Sherborne School, Dorset (founded 710).

Grammar schools

Grammar schools also have a long history (the oldest is The King's School, Rochester, founded 604). The schools were initially established for the teaching of Latin but, over time, broadened their curriculum. During much of the 20th century, grammar schools (as noted earlier) provided the academic component of the tripartite system. With the widespread introduction of comprehensive education in the 1970s and 1980s, most became all-ability schools. There are currently 164 grammar schools admitting pupils on the basis of their performance in entrance tests.

Middle schools

Middle schools were championed by Alec Clegg (the pioneering chief education officer of the West Riding of Yorkshire), who created schools that crossed the traditional primary/secondary divide. The number of middle schools reached a peak of 1,400 in 1983. But within five years the introduction of the National Curriculum Key Stages made middle schools less popular. By August 2012 there were only 199 such schools, spread across 20 local authorities.

Faith schools

At the beginning of this chapter I described the role of religious schools in the history of English education and their recent growth as faith schools.

and others have been accused of excluding less able students from examinations in order to boost their school's results.

The aims of schooling in the Nordic countries:

> were to develop social justice, equity, equal opportunities, participative democracy and inclusion, as those were pivotal values in Nordic welfare state thinking.[31]

Nordic countries generally divide schooling into a combined primary and lower secondary course in the *folkeskole* (usually in the same premises), followed by a three-year course in an upper secondary school. Traditionally, the Danes have preferred their teachers to teach all subjects to the same group of children over several years. But today there is specialist teaching, particularly for the older pupils. In Denmark, upper secondary schools are still divided into academic gymnasia,[32] technical schools[33] and commercial schools,[34] though many of the old differences have been phased out. Curriculum reforms have also brought about integrated approaches to subject teaching.

A unique feature of Danish education is the optional Year 10 in an *efterskole*. The first *efterskoles* were founded in the 19th century by educationalist Kristen Kold and Danish folk hero Nikolaj Grundtvig – poet, philosopher and Protestant clergyman. These men dedicated themselves to creating schools that would provide not just academic or vocational training but enlightenment for life.[35] The Year 10 is a voluntary year undertaken by pupils between the comprehensive *folkeskole* and the three-year courses of the more diverse upper secondary schools. Some pupils choose to use the year to increase their competence in basic skills. Others want longer to decide which of the academic, technical or commercial upper schools to attend. Many, however, simply wish to broaden their learning. Half the curriculum of the *efterskole* is devoted to Danish, mathematics and English; the rest is open to choice, depending on the specialism (often particular sports) offered by schools. One in three Danish pupils currently takes advantage of Year 10. Many of these spend the year as boarders in schools in other parts of Denmark or even abroad, for which some financial assistance is provided by the state.

After the Second World War, Norway established a centrally directed, but regionally administered, education system. A large country with a small population, it overcame many problems to establish a sound national comprehensive system. Norway's values emphasise participation, equity and the preparation of young people for life in a democracy (possibly influenced by its experience of German occupation during the Second World War).

Norway sees its head teachers as 'first among equal professionals', and schools tend to have flat, rather than hierarchical, management structures. The Norwegian system is similar to the Danish, although its upper secondary schools are comprehensive, combining academic and vocational courses. Following the second Programme for International Student Assessment (PISA) results of 2003,[36] a national assessment system has been introduced.

Swedish education policy, throughout most of the 20th century, sought to create an equal society. To this end it established a centrally directed system of comprehensive schooling up to the age of 16. Both the Liberal–Conservative Coalition and the Social Democratic party have experimented with the promotion of choice, increased citizen participation and decentralisation. Parents have been encouraged to select schools for their children and 'independent schools' – though still publicly funded – have been promoted. However, the current Liberal–Conservative Coalition government (in power since 2006), perhaps alarmed at the social divisions appearing in the country, has reverted to more centrally driven policies, including the formation of a school inspectorate, aimed at pursuing equality.

In Finland, 'education is seen as a public good and therefore has a strong nation-building function'.[37] The Finnish system has evolved over 20 years. It includes free day care and pre-school provision as well as free lunches for all full-time pupils. Schools are comprehensive and have no setting or streaming. Teaching is considered an important vocation and all teachers study at university for at least five years. They are trusted to do a good job – there are no inspections or national test programmes. Pupils who experience difficulties in learning to read are provided with individual help in a special reading programme. According to Finnish education expert Pasi Sahlberg, 'Unlike many other contemporary systems of education, the Finnish system has not been infected by market-based competition and high-stakes testing policies.'[38]

There are, of course, many differences between the Nordic systems. Whether there is an overarching Nordic style (as in architecture, police, crime stories and cuisines of the countries) is an on-going debate.[39]

Further afield, in Singapore, education is seen as vital for economic growth as well as for social cohesion.[40] The education system, traditionally, has been centralised and highly competitive. In recent years, however, Singapore has been moving towards a more diverse system, in the hope that allowing pupils more choice over what and how they learn will give them greater ownership of their learning. The intention is 'to nurture young Singaporeans who ask questions and look for answers, and who are willing to think in new ways, solve new problems and create new opportunities for the future'.[41]

Countries have diverse approaches towards the education of pupils with special needs. For example, Spain has relatively little special provision – 'It is a widespread policy to educate these pupils alongside their peers in mainstream schools'[42] – whereas in Germany, 'The main form of provision is special schools'.[43]

Countries also vary in how they group pupils. In most education systems children born within 12 months of each other are grouped together. Some countries – like England – also stream or set pupils according to their perceived ability. Others – like Finland – do their utmost to keep pupils in mixed-ability classes for most of a pupil's schooling.

Which is best? I will return to this topic and suggest an answer in Chapter Ten.

Universal features of schools

The basic structure of schooling is similar worldwide. In general, schools are divided into age-related classes; knowledge is divided into subject areas; and the school day is partitioned into a series of timed lessons. Of course, there are exceptions. Some schools have longer hours, while others employ a shorter 'continental day' to avoid lunchtime problems (even if this causes afternoon problems for parents); some use IT more than they use teachers; some, in developing countries, have little physical presence (perhaps meeting under the shade of a tree), and progressive or free schools (in the pre-Gove model), such as A.S. Neill's Summerhill,[44] allow pupils to choose whether or not to attend lessons.

Willy Russell, whom I quoted earlier, recounts a story about visiting Summerhill as a student teacher. While moving about the building he observes an angry pupil purposely break a window. Not knowing how best to react, he is relieved to discover that the incident has also been seen by the head teacher. He is amazed – as is the pupil – to see A.S. Neill pick up a stone and break another window – with the presumed aim of shocking the culprit into realising the damage of vandalism. It works. The pupil expresses heartfelt regret for his action. Willy is impressed and adds this technique to his repertoire. On a subsequent occasion, when he sees a pupil engaged in vandalism, he knows exactly what to do. But, sadly, his vandalism achieves a markedly different reaction to that enjoyed by A.S. Neill – with pupils rushing to follow Willy's example.[45]

During the decades following Neill's death, Summerhill experienced difficulties in justifying its progressive stance. However, following an unsympathetic television programme and hostile Ofsted inspections, it emerged in 2011 with the best inspection report of its 90-year history.[46] According to Ian Stronach, Professor of Education at Liverpool John Moores University, 'Inspectors were particularly impressed by its continuing excellence in relation to pupils' spiritual, moral, social and cultural development'.[47]

Despite the success of Summerhill, the majority of schools have remained stuck in a 19th-century mould and would probably be recognisable to Edwardian teachers (although they would be surprised at how few pupils there were in each class).

In most developed countries, the law requires children to start school by about the age of six. In England children enter schools earlier – usually in the September of the academic year in which they are five. This means that those born in July and August are barely four when they start 'big school'. In contrast, in the Nordic countries, children will not start school until they are six or seven,

unlimited freedom over working inside or out of doors, going to the lavatory and even over whether or not to attend classes. Extremely traditional schools have taken another route involving strict discipline and an insistence on total compliance.

Most English head teachers do not favour either of these solutions. Rather, they seek to establish order based on good community sense. They provide their pupils with the security of reasonable boundaries and resist the overly strict discipline that can lead to rebellion or unquestioning conformity.

Classroom roles

As happens in all social groups, children adopt, or are forced into, different groups and roles in classes. Some individuals are dominant – leaders with their 'court' of supporters. Another might be a class comic (the court jester) and, in too many cases, there will be one or more scapegoats. This miserable role is often assigned to a pupil who is different physically or is socially inept or who comes from a different cultural background. Whether the background is considered by their classmates to be superior or inferior ('posh' or 'chav') does not seem to matter. Using data from British longitudinal studies, researchers from the Institute of Education have found that bullying is the most serious concern of pupils with disabilities.[50]

Despite anti-bullying policies, unpleasant treatment of scapegoats still takes place and makes life a daily misery. Pupils who are obese and those who are unsure about their emerging sexuality are particularly vulnerable. Shy children can have their reticence reinforced by the presence of especially confident peers. Well-behaved pupils can feel aggrieved if the behaviour of boisterous colleagues brings collective punishment. But being part of a subgroup or of a class can provide opportunities for learning social skills and the development of empathy.

Misbehaviour

Bad behaviour in school is not a modern problem. Eton suffered a pupil rebellion in 1768 and there were five separate uprisings at

Winchester between 1770 and 1818 as well as mutinies at Harrow, Charterhouse, Rugby and Shrewsbury.[51]

As I have noted, the basic organisation of a school, plus its rituals, encourages pupils' conformity. Some schools set strict uniform rules and suspend anyone who does not comply with them. A London paper ran a story about a 13-year-old boy being taught in isolation because his Mohican-style haircut was judged by the school's head teacher to be 'inappropriate'.[52]

Is taming pupils and inducing compliant behaviour a good or a bad thing? In some obvious ways calming unruly behaviour is unquestionably good. A large group of children running wild can descend into a mob. In his novel *Lord of the Flies*, William Golding (a former school teacher who apparently would permit his classes to read so that he could get on with his own writing) provides a dramatic story of what happens without adult supervision.

Undoubtedly many parents are grateful to schools for the way they induce more compliant behaviour in their offspring – especially when even toddlers have gained so much power through skilful negotiation, training their parents to 'do deals'. In other ways, however, using the years of compulsory schooling to produce compliant people is more questionable. Do we not need – to use a current expression – people who can think 'outside of the box'?

There is a balance to be struck between a system of compliance from which all creativity has been purged and the frustration of trying to live in an institution where conventions – created in the interest of all – are flouted by inmates and where daily life resembles a struggle for the survival of the fittest. Good teachers strive to inculcate in their pupils the skill of judging which behaviour is appropriate in different settings.

Today, thankfully, classroom riots are rare. But many teachers still have to wait for pupils to quieten down before lessons can begin, and aggressive behaviour can still flare up in classes. Tragically, a 61-year-old teacher - Ann Maguire – was stabbed to death by one of her pupils in a lesson in a Leeds secondary school in April 2014. This was the first recorded murder of a teacher by a pupil in a classroom in England.

There have been two major government-sponsored reviews of school behaviour in England in the last 25 years: the Elton Report in 1989 and the Steer Reports of 2005 and 2009. Elton emphasised two points:

> We find that most schools are on the whole well ordered.... [and] [t]eachers in our survey were most concerned about the cumulative effects of disruption to their lessons caused by relatively trivial but persistent misbehaviour.[53]

It was not the big, publicity-achieving pupil challenges to teachers that were the real problem, but the stream of relatively trivial incidents constantly interrupting the class's work.

Elton's review was carried out over a quarter of a century ago. But his main findings were echoed in Alan Steer's 2005 report:

> Our experience as teachers, supported by evidence from Ofsted, is that the great majority of pupils work hard and behave well, and that most schools successfully manage behaviour to create an environment in which learners feel valued, cared for and safe.... Incidents of serious misbehaviour and especially acts of extreme violence remain exceptionally rare and are carried out by a very small proportion of pupils.[54]

This view was reinforced by Steer's 2009 report of pupil behaviour, drawing on work undertaken between March 2008 and February 2009: 'I remain confident that standards are high in the large majority of schools.'[55] A more recent report by a former Chief Inspector for England found that 'Pupils' behaviour was good or outstanding in 87% of schools'.[56] So, in the view of these experts, bad behaviour in schools is not a major national problem, even though in the TALIS survey, one in five teachers said they had to wait 'quite a long time' for classes to quieten down.[57] Bad behaviour can still be a daily problem, however, for some teachers, as a head teacher's blog about dealing with a particularly difficult primary pupil illustrates:

> This child has extreme reactions when he is reprimanded in any way. He feels very bad if he has done something wrong and his emotional resilience is so low that even the most minor of reprimands, 'please don't do that', can result in a firestorm of flying stuff and verbal abuse. More often than not this includes all the displays being ripped off the walls too.[58]

The effect of drugs on pupils' behaviour can be unpredictable and make school life extremely difficult for fellow pupils and teachers. A different problem is the 'turbulence' factor. By this I mean pupil mobility, with pupils who stay for only a few months or those who – for complicated family reasons – come and go. Unlike schools with more settled membership, those coping with turbulence might, after four or five years, end up with a significantly different group of pupils in the same year group.[59]

Some pupils with behaviour issues attend pupil referral units. These are 'mini-schools' away from the main site. They are usually staffed by experienced specialist teachers. In January 2012 there were over 400 such units, with a total of over 13,000 pupils (predominantly boys) of secondary age. Thirty six per cent of the pupils in these units were eligible for free meals (compared to less than 15% in schools overall).[60]

Some years ago I was involved in an evaluation of similar units.[61] We found that the relationships between the teachers and the pupils were generally positive – a parent told me that this was the first time his son had ever 'got on' with a teacher. But they do not solve all problems. We found that approximately one-third of pupils went back to the mainstream school and prospered; another third re-encountered the same problems that had caused their referral and tended to drop out of school once they returned; and the final third remained at the unit.

If a teacher and a class are unable to relate well together, the dominant atmosphere of the class is likely to become one of conflict and unpleasantness. Of course, in such circumstances pupils will continue to learn – about group dynamics, conflict and the power politics of strong individuals – but not necessarily about the subjects that they are supposed to be studying.

Competition

Whether or not all living things are naturally competitive is the subject of much debate among evolutionary psychologists.[62] Certainly most of us seem to have a streak of competitiveness, though its strength varies from those who are intensely competitive – the alpha males and females of the outfit – to others who bend over backwards to avoid taking advantage of anybody.

For many of us, an element of competition produces extra adrenalin,[63] which can fire us up to do better. Daily competition between individual pupils in classrooms has a long tradition in many schools and can enliven the class atmosphere. But it needs to be handled with sensitivity, or it may put off as many pupils as it encourages.

Yet, in recent years, ministers have upped the stakes by insisting that teachers differentiate between even quite young pupils, thus setting an individualistic and highly competitive tone in our classes. This approach is not followed in Nordic countries, as a little-known Ofsted Report of 2003 on six-year-olds in England, Denmark and Finland illustrates.

> In Denmark and Finland, whole-class interaction was less tightly structured and more open and speculative. The English children were less confident speaking in whole-class settings, while in Denmark especially the strongly collective ethos encouraged rather than inhibited their contributions.[64]

The pressured English approach contrasts with the more patient Nordic promotion of class cooperation.

Public nature of classrooms

Unlike a number of other occupations carried out in private settings or among workmates (in offices, studios and factories) teaching is always performed in a semi-public setting. In this arena a difficult interaction with a stroppy pupil – perhaps one determined to humiliate the teacher – will be witnessed by all present. Teachers who fail to cope with these situations will feel their authority leaching away.

As I noted in Chapter Five, skilled teachers learn to manage these difficult public situations, using their personality, humour or social and pedagogical skills to create positive learning environments. But this is challenging and requires careful preparation, sensitive awareness of their pupils' needs – and considerable stamina. It is particularly hard for young teachers endeavouring both to establish their authority and to develop their pedagogic skills.

In the hours I have spent in classrooms, I have seen many highly skilled teachers creating a positive atmosphere and hard-working pupils responding to it. I have seen superb demonstrations of how to cope with a pupil's extremely difficult behaviour while managing a class. And I have seen the opposite – pupils moving from one teacher to another and changing their personality from reluctant to eager learners or, more colloquially, from devils to angels.

School leadership

One aspect of schooling not yet discussed is the leadership role of the head teacher. From the earliest days of English schools the head has wielded considerable power. Today, heads also oversee many administrative and business functions. Some 'super heads' hold responsibility for a federation of several schools.

I am not convinced that a super head overseeing several schools is a good idea. In my experience, schools benefit from hands-on leadership. Each school is an institution in its own right, with its own culture. Head teachers are key players and if they are not 'resident' they cannot fulfil the role adequately. Francis Beckett, an educational writer, calls such people 'hero heads' and asks 'Is the concept of a "hero head" – a charismatic leader who comes in and sweeps away all the dead wood – either useful or relevant?' There is a tendency, he suggests, 'that, in order for him or her to shine as bright as possible, the school's past has to be painted as black as possible'.[65]

On the whole, I think the delegation to heads of many administrative functions under Local Management of Schools (LMS) has been helpful. But a balance needs to be struck. The necessity for the head of a very small school to negotiate over building contracts and deal with many ancillary duties seems unwise if they are to maintain a focus on learning and teaching. Where the school size does not allow for the employment of suitable trained staff for such non-pedagogical roles, it seems to me better for the local authority to retain these duties.

Some countries, such as the Netherlands, give less power to heads – even at times filling the position through an election – and delegate more power to the teachers. Again, there is a balance to be struck. Teachers need to be recognised as professionals and accorded proper responsibilities. But school-wide coordination is also important. Heads can act as overall planners and galvanise the collective energy of the school community. This is a role akin to that of an orchestral conductor – able to give prominence to skilled players but responsible for keeping the ensemble together.

I am not a fan of the Ghengis Khan school of tough leadership. Like most of us, I can be impressed with obvious charisma, but find that it quickly loses its attraction if accompanied by arrogance or the failure to delegate. I prefer consensus builders, able to judge when a decision needs to be shared by all the staff – or, at times, by the whole school community (including the pupils) – and when it is imperative that it is taken from the front, by the leader.

I have seen the different approaches of many heads. One I interviewed some years ago appeared deeply impressive. He was charismatic and had developed a sound philosophy of education. He wanted the best for his pupils and he cared about the lives of his colleagues. Yet his writ ran only as far as his office door. Once you passed through it and entered classrooms you realised how little influence this head actually had over the life of the school.

Another – who appeared far less charismatic – always led from the front. She would not dream of asking a colleague to take on anything which she would not do herself. She consulted widely and was a hard-working model for both staff and pupils. She called herself the 'head learner' rather than the head teacher and was far more effective than the charismatic male I described earlier.

Can a school make a difference to pupils' achievement?'

Since the mid 1970s educational research has explored how much difference particular schools are able to make to the behaviour and achievement of their pupils – the field of school effectiveness. Much of my own research has been concerned with this topic.

One of the first studies followed groups of pupils as they progressed through a number of London secondary schools.[66] This research found that, rather than schools being the same, some promoted better attendance, behaviour and examination results and seemed better able to protect their pupils from delinquency, even when allowance was made for their different socioeconomic backgrounds. We found that the most effective schools were more ambitious, used rewards more than punishments and were more inclusive. We suggested that the effective schools had a more positive ethos than the others. These findings were controversial and arguments about the methodology and scope of the study have persisted over many years.[67] Since then there have been hundreds of articles and books addressing aspects of the research.[68]

I subsequently worked with a number of colleagues on a five-year study of primary schools, exploring whether significant differences in pupil outcomes could be identified with a younger age range. Using newly developed statistical techniques, such as multi-level modelling, and an increased number of outcomes measures – including many more to do with attitudes and behaviours – we largely replicated the findings of the secondary school study.

It was clear that some primary schools promoted more positive outcomes in attendance, in behaviour and on a range of academic measures. We also found that there were differences in pupils' attitudes to school and in their views of themselves as learners. As with the study of secondary schools, teachers in the schools that were most successful had more positive attitudes and a clearer focus on their role.[69]

But controversy about school effectiveness has not diminished. In my view, this is partly because of the way that politicians reacted to the research. It took successive British governments 20 years to absorb the lessons from the secondary school work and 10 years to absorb those to do with primaries.[70] But, having finally done so, ministers applied the lessons indiscriminately, expressing a view that if one school could buck the trend, they all could do so. The result has been to give school-effectiveness research a bad name and encourage a backlash against its findings.[71]

Social disadvantage

The research also identified the benefit for a school of having a proportion of pupils who find learning relatively easy. In the discussion of ability, in Chapter Three, I note how some pupils, for a variety of reasons, find learning extremely difficult. This is often related to family circumstances. Some pupils come from homes deprived of many of the things that other children enjoy, while others have experienced every advantage that money can buy – as well as what is termed 'cultural capital' (positive attitudes towards learning, 'taken for granted knowledge' and understanding of how the education system works).[72] These two characteristics – ability to learn easily and advantaged home backgrounds – are often elided.

When I first started teaching I was shocked to hear teachers questioning whether progress was possible 'with poor pupils like these'. On the other hand, I now react with caution when I hear ministers declare that 'poverty is no excuse for failure'. It isn't. But it is, nevertheless, related to it.

In every country that measures performance, pupils with advantaged social and economic family backgrounds generally outperform those from disadvantaged family backgrounds in competitive tests or examinations. The reasons for this are not hard to detect. Consider two children of the same age, sex and ethnic background. The first has benefited from stable and well-paid parental employment, good healthcare, excellent diet, comfortable housing, the availability of toys, books, stimulating outings and numerous other educational experiences, including, increasingly, private coaching. She or he will have grown up with confident parents living in networks of similar people who know how to make things happen and they will be expected, and will expect, to do well in the world.

The second child may have lived a life punctuated by crises. She or he will have had fewer toys, books or additional educational or cultural experiences and no chance of private tuition. There will be far less certainty – or expectation – of success in life by parent or child.

Yet these two young people will take part in the same highly competitive tests and examinations. Can anyone be surprised that the first child is more likely to do well than the second? The real surprise is that some exceptional pupils buck this trend and succeed against all the odds. Some people – undoubtedly a number of readers of this book – manage to cope with disadvantage and even to thrive on it. It is a tribute to human nature that this can happen. But do not be deceived: such people are the exceptions. Most disadvantaged pupils achieve less well than their more advantaged fellows. So, although poverty should not be used as an excuse, it is a major component in the achievement gap.

Moreover, according to the National Equality Panel, led by John Hills, since the 1970s the share of total income going to the richest 1% of people in the country increased from 4% to over 10%, and the richest 10% ended up 100 times better off than the poorest.[73]

So the role for schools is important. Teachers' reactions to the achievement gap are crucial. It is no use shrugging shoulders and accepting it. Doing all that one can to reduce the gap is vitally important – this is how the positive exceptions occur. On the other hand, teachers need a lot of help if they are to succeed – extra resources, more time for their most needy pupils and, most important of all, a balanced intake to their schools.

School improvement

Over the years I have observed many attempts to improve schools. One approach involves a new head radically altering the school's existing, but inadequate, approach. This may entail identifying better methods of teaching, installing more effective systems of assessing, providing greater learning support, finding new ways to improve pupils' experience of school life or working with parents and the local community. Of course, some of the least effective teachers or other staff may move on – with or without encouragement from the head – and new blood helps. However, many of the former staff will remain and, with support, can adapt and provide continuity as they improve in the new, more positive culture of the school.

This method usually takes a number of years, entails much hard work in envisioning what the school could be like, and planning, implementing and modifying (because they seldom get it right first time) strategic changes. No head teacher can do this alone. Their role is to inspire colleagues, model new approaches, re-invigorate those who have flagged and galvanise wider support for the school.

Another method involves making different changes: of pupils, teachers and examinations. Changing the pupils can be achieved by expelling those with behaviour issues and persuading other 'energy-consuming' pupils to leave. The school's intake can be changed by attracting more advantaged pupils (other things being equal, they are likely to raise the school up the league tables).

Changing the staff provides an opportunity to bring in new blood, and there are situations where this is the best solution. But these two methods also entail the rejection of many staff and pupils – some of whom could perhaps have been transformed by the first method. In one of the most impressive cases I have seen, a new head transformed a previously failing school by inspiring and retraining existing staff, who then recaptured the interest and motivation of their disaffected pupils.

Changing the examinations taken by pupils (since results are used as the key judgement of the school) can also help to lift the reputation. Until recently, it was possible to enter pupils for some equivalent courses leading to multiple grades equivalent to up to four GCSE subjects. (I discuss 'equivalence' in Chapter Nine.) Of course, I understand why this method was used – it could dramatically improve a school's position in the league tables. But it should not be confused with genuine school improvement.

I have described these approaches to make the point that, even though the head is in a pivotal position, she or he cannot by themselves 'turn around' a school. They can inspire colleagues, galvanise efforts, create a positive culture and be a good model. But, ultimately, it is the individual teachers working with classes of pupils who will determine the success or otherwise of the improvement efforts.

Value-added analysis

Some researchers have criticised the statistics employed in school studies, often condemning the use of what became known as 'value-added analysis'.[74] But the use of such a technique is crucial for a comparison of schools with contrasting pupil intakes. Regrettably, there is as yet no commonly agreed method for calculating value-added scores. This means that different methods will produce slightly different results. Statisticians can claim that, had marginally different variables been used, a school might have fared better or worse. For this reason, some researchers have argued that value-added cannot be used and that the ordinary (raw) results have to suffice.[75]

Whether or not to use value-added techniques depends on the question being asked. If, for instance, parents want to know how their *child* is performing in any test or school examination, they will not need to use value-added data. The 'raw' results will tell them how their child performed in that test relative to other children locally or nationally. But if the same parents want to know how their child's *school* is performing in relation to other schools, then the raw results will not be sufficient because of the different intakes to schools. A fair comparison will require an examination of the value-added results.

If a particular school which routinely takes a high proportion of pupils with disadvantaged family backgrounds is regularly bucking the trend and achieving good results, the school is 'adding value', and we need to analyse how it has done this. This gives rise to several questions.

Is the school one of the new types which ministers wish to promote and which has received extra funding? If not, is success due to harder work by the teachers and other staff? Have they adopted a different approach to teaching? Have staff provided a more effective structure for learning, perhaps with more 'scaffolding' (the learning support discussed in Chapter Four in relation to Bruner's learning theories)? Have they provided extra classes or additional in-school coaching sessions? Have they provided more detailed feedback for their pupils? In some schools, staff clock up many hours of extra work. This is deeply impressive but can create problems with their partners, children or other dependants. (I know one head teacher who regularly leaves home before 6 am each day and seldom returns before 9 pm – as well as devoting all Sunday to school work!)

If it is not extra hours, have the staff managed to inspire pupils to work much harder? This would be impressive – particularly if it occurred with each successive year group. Or is it something completely different? I have come across schools that advocate fish oil or extra vitamin pills or have even given examination candidates a banana in the hope that extra energy will improve their performance.

Perhaps the staff have involved the parents so that, together, they have formed a united, exceptionally powerful influence on the young people? Or could it be that a large proportion of parents are paying for extra coaching for their children outside of school? This growing practice deserves comment.

Coaching

Coaching is an elephant in the room in many discussions about school effectiveness. No one knows how much the position of schools on the league tables depends on the prevalence of private tuition. In 2011 the Sutton Trust reported that 23% of pupils between 11 and 16 had received private tuition. This figure had increased from 18% in 2005.[76] Right on cue, as I am writing this, through my letterbox has dropped a pamphlet advertising 'Maths tutoring on Saturdays: fun and friendly'.

When parents are seeking places for their children in a market of popular schools, it is easy to understand the motivation for seeking this kind of advantage. But the more the practice spreads, the more the disadvantaged families that cannot afford it fall behind. This kind of coaching can also have a powerful effect on the rest of the education system – as I witnessed a few years ago in Mauritius. In this small country in the Indian Ocean, private coaching has become so endemic that even poor families feel they must struggle to meet its costs. Mark Bray, an international authority on coaching, draws attention to its pernicious impact – particularly when it is undertaken by regular school teachers.[77]

Pressures to get into particular schools are now strongly felt in China. An article in the *Oriental Morning Post* reported that some parents in Shanghai had paid the equivalent of £10,000 for a summer school course which claimed to teach speed reading by touch and to develop 'special abilities' in the children.[78] It was, of course, a scam.

Any plausible explanations for schools bucking the trend need to be investigated and disseminated. My own experience leads me to believe that, while there are no silver bullets, exceptional heads and school staffs can achieve exceptional success against the odds. The *Times Educational Supplement* has highlighted a school in Islington (with 99% of its pupils eligible for free school meals and 75% with a first language other than English) that had 90% of its 10- to 11-year-old pupils making the 'expected progress'.[79] This was an excellent outcome for which head teacher, teachers, pupils and parents all deserve congratulations. But maintaining this success will be difficult and, as I have noted, comes at a price for the families of those staff involved. The crucial point is that a successful education *system* cannot be built on such exceptional models.

Future of schooling

Educationalists in a number of countries have been engaging in 'futurology' – considering how schools might develop in the years to come. Drawing on this work, the OECD has published six contrasting scenarios based on current trends and developments.[80]

Scenario 1 builds on the continuation of the current model of schooling. Its authors project strong bureaucratic control and uniformity. They see the influence of current vested interests (satisfied parents as well as conservative teachers) as powerful enough to overcome any demands for radical change. This scenario can be characterised as a strengthened version of the status quo.

Scenario 2 formulates the idea of an extended education market. Its authors suggest that what they term 'widespread dissatisfaction' will force a move to more 'demand-driven' provision, supplied by a mixture of professional and non-traditional teachers. They note that such a model is likely to lead to greater inequality. This scenario can be characterised as the status quo model – but in an exaggerated form.

Scenario 3 sees schools develop into community resources as a bulwark against social fragmentation. The authors see such institutions being strengthened by a powerful sense of 'education as a public good'. They recognise, however, that schools would need to be released from the current burden of what they term 'credentialism' (an excessive focus on providing qualifications). This scenario can be characterised as one version of a re-schooling model.

Scenario 4 anticipates schools becoming 'focused learning organisations' using the latest IT equipment and networking with international experts. The authors, however, seem to doubt whether the necessary supportive media facilities and essential financial resources are possible. They also question whether teachers would be willing to cultivate a less authoritarian role. This scenario can be characterised as a second version of the re-schooling model.

Scenario 5 projects a negative picture of current schooling. The authors anticipate increasing dissatisfaction, leading to a collapse of education systems and the evolution of fragmented 'learning groups' based on shared interests, social groupings and business connections. They foresee this leading to major problems of inequality. This scenario can be characterised as a de-schooling model.

Scenario 6 leads to chaos. The authors see teachers becoming so frustrated and dispirited that they leave the profession in such numbers that schools have to close. Although teaching continues in some quarters and the situation provides scope for innovations, the education system experiences 'meltdown'. This scenario can also be characterised – though for different reasons – as a de-schooling model.

Walo Hutmacher, a Swiss sociologist who has focused on education issues concerning equity,[81] and participated in OECD meetings to discuss them, found a broad measure of agreement among the group of education experts that the most likely scenario was one of the re-schooling models (Scenarios 3 and 4). But this may, of course, have been a case of wishful thinking.

My view is that, while it is sensible for futurology to be studied so that societies are not caught napping, the message of these six scenarios is that there is as yet no clear alternative to schooling as we know it. Our best response, therefore, might be to prepare pupils, schools – and the education system as a whole – to be adaptable.

This means encouraging innovative ways to teach and to support learners. As Andreas Schleicher, an OECD education expert, argues:

> Schooling now needs to be much more about ways of thinking, involving creativity, critical thinking, problem-solving and decision-making. For an inclusive world, we also need people who can appreciate and build on different values, beliefs and cultures.[82]

Conclusion

Classes and schools have been organised in much the same way since the earliest days of schooling. Given the OECD scenarios, some readers may well be wondering for how much longer education should be organised as we now know it. But, as I have suggested, the traditional school still seems to be the only practical model. But we need to experiment with different ways of organising learning within schools – especially in the light of the developments in neuroscience and information technology.

Let me end this chapter on a positive note. Ernest Barker– a former Principal of King's College, University of London – grew up in a poor family in the north of England in the late 19th century. In his autobiography he acknowledged that he had never sufficiently thanked his school for what it had given him. So he penned – too late for his particular teachers – this testament of his gratitude.

> My school taught me to work, to read and to think. It gave me great friendships. It filled me entirely and utterly for nearly the space of seven years. Outside the cottage, I had nothing but my school; but having my school, I had everything.[83]

SEVEN

Quality control

Two ways of judging the quality of what goes on in schools are assessing the progress of individual pupils and inspecting the work of teachers. In this chapter I will describe how these different processes work and the results that they produce. I reserve criticisms of the two methods for Chapter Nine.

Assessment

How can we find out if we have learned something except by testing ourselves – repeating, applying or developing it on paper, the screen or in front of someone else? Testing enables us and our teachers to track how much we have learned. At least that is the theory. It actually works best when what we are attempting to understand is simple and factual. More complicated skills, involving analysis, critique or synthesis of advanced knowledge, are much harder to test and to generate a result that will be both valid and reliable – in other words, give us results we can trust.

If we are competitive by nature and know that we are going to be tested, we tend to push ourselves harder. Doing well in the test is also reinforcing – making us feel good about ourselves. But for some people too much testing can have negative effects, particularly when a group of pupils are being tested to identify which one is the winner. The remainder can easily see themselves as 'losers'.

Competition works best when everybody has some chance of winning. This is why some sports use a system of allocating handicaps to the best players. But – as discussed in the section on ability in Chapter Three – we know that some children will be more mature than others (remember, those with September birthdays will be almost a year older than those in the same school year who were born in August). We also know that the ability to learn varies and changes during maturation. Social and economic backgrounds, while not determining progress, seriously influence it. So, in most cases, competition will not be between people who have an equal chance. This has implications for the way assessment is used in the education system.

Teachers daily assess pupils through questioning or informally testing whether they can remember information, understand concepts or undertake specific skills. Through such techniques, they build up an account of how pupils are progressing (and, for the more reflective teachers, of how well they themselves are teaching). This daily activity, however, is a long way from the formal assessment procedures that successive governments have built into our system.

The assessments used in schools today have a complicated history. By 1858 both Oxford and Cambridge universities – influenced by an experiment at the University of Exeter[1] – had introduced 'locals' to examine and issue certificates to pupils. This was rapidly followed by a similar scheme launched by London University and several schemes by bodies such as the Royal Society of Arts, the City and Guilds of London Institute (the precursors to our current vocational examinations) and the College of Preceptors. Thus began a long line of school assessments.[2]

A different kind of assessment appeared in 1862 as part of a 'Revised Code'[3] in which school pupils were individually tested by an inspector in reading, writing from dictation and arithmetic. In one of the first performance-related pay schemes ('payment by results'), teachers were paid only if the pupils were deemed by the inspector to have reached the required standard. The Code was criticised on the grounds that it restricted the curriculum and that teachers – who resented it – focused almost exclusively on the age groups to be tested and it took no account of pupils' backgrounds (does any of this sound familiar?). The Code lasted for 30 years, during which time it was continually modified, before being abandoned.

In English schools today, assessment starts with the, relatively informal, Early Years Foundation Stage profile. This requires teachers to describe each child's level of attainment at the end of the pre-school stage and to identify the child's learning needs in communication and language, physical development and personal, social and emotional development.[4] Later come the standard assessment tests (SATs), the GCSE, AS and A levels and a range of vocational diplomas.

Standard assessment tests and tasks

Standard assessment tests (and tasks) were introduced in 1991 to test seven-year-old students at the end of Key Stage 1 of the National Curriculum. A second set of tests was later added for 11-year-olds at the end of Key Stage 2. A third set, for 14-year-olds at the end of Key Stage 3, was introduced in 1998 but was subsequently dropped in 2009. The results of all the sets of SATs are expressed in levels 1–8 (with variations) to show attainment in terms of the National Curriculum. From these results, school league tables are drawn up and published widely in the media. It is no exaggeration to say that they dominate life in many primary schools and are closely scrutinised by parents.

The General Certificate of Secondary Education (GCSE)

The GCSE is the examination currently taken by 16-year-old pupils. The first formal examination for this age group was the School Certificate (known as 'Matriculation'), inaugurated in 1918. In order to matriculate, the top 20% of the ability range of pupils (assumed to be in either grammar or private schools) had to pass mathematics, English and three other subjects, including a foreign language.

In the early 1950s, the School Certificate was abolished in favour of the General Certificate of Education Ordinary Level (GCE O level).[5] What was different from the old Certificate was that passes were awarded for each subject separately. This allowed pupils who, for instance, had a problem with one of the subjects, still to obtain certificates for the others that they passed.

The raising of the school leaving age from 14 to 15 in 1947 increased the number of candidates, even though pupils in secondary modern schools were still not allowed to be entered for the GCE examinations. The next rise in the school leaving age, requiring pupils to stay until they were 16, was implemented in 1972, so another (different) examination was needed. The Certificate of Secondary Education (CSE)[6] was aimed at the 40% of the ability range below the 20% already covered by the GCE. There was some overlap in that the top CSE grade was deemed to be 'at least the value of a

GCE grade C'. There was no school-leaving examination for the remaining 40%.

The new CSE provided the chance for many more pupils to have their achievement recognised. But, despite the overlap in grades, the side-effect in the growing number of schools with comprehensive intakes was further to subdivide pupils between 'academic' and 'non-academic' streams.[7]

In order to overcome this problem a merger between the two examinations was approved in 1984, after much soul-searching by Conservative education minister Keith Joseph. The GCSE was taken by the first candidates in 1988. Although it has no specific pass grade, the old pass standard of the GCE was incorporated into the top three grades of the new examination. A new grade – the A-star (A★) – was added from 1994. In 2012 the GCSE was sat by over half a million 16-year-old pupils, entered for over 5 million examinations.[8]

Some of the GCSE's subject papers are 'tiered' – meaning that the grades are limited. Thus, candidates for English, science or most modern languages may be entered either for the 'foundation tier', in which the best grade they can achieve will be a C, or for the 'higher tier', in which grades range from D to A★. Mathematics has three tiers.[9] The examination is set and marked by a number of examination boards[10] regulated by the Office of Qualifications and Examinations Regulation (Ofqual).[11] Ofqual is a non-departmental public body 'sponsored by' the DfE.[12] It was established in 2012 to replace the previous regulatory body, the Qualifications and Curriculum Development Agency.

The prime task of the GCSE is to provide valid and reliable assessments of year 11 (16-year-old) pupils. But it is also used by government to monitor national standards and as a key indicator of every secondary school's accountability.

In some forms of assessment, candidates are simply ranked from best to worst and the top grade is allocated to, say, the top 10%, the second grade to the next 10%, and so forth down to the lowest grade. This is sometimes termed 'norm-based' assessment. It means that the proportions obtaining grades remain the same from one year to another, thus providing consistent results. But, of course, if the performance of a particular year group is significantly better or worse than others, this will go unnoticed because the apparent consistency will mask the change.

Norm-based assessment was used in the heyday of the 11-plus tests in England (late 1940s to mid-1960s), when the proportion passing was related directly to the number of grammar school places available. Border-line candidates were either lucky and passed or unlucky and failed, depending on how good was the particular cohort of candidates in any given year. Since there were more grammar school places for boys than for girls, it was easier for them to pass. Such capping of places was finally deemed unfair and stopped. (A Twitter group of head teachers feel that capping grades is still an issue in examinations today.[13])

An alternative model of assessment tries to reflect what the results actually show. So in some years all the candidates may reach the stipulated pass level and (in theory at least), in others, none may do so. This model can describe all fluctuations in results over time. It is sometimes termed 'criterion–referenced' assessment. It is similar to the driving test, in which a successful candidate has to undertake a series of pre-ordained manoeuvres. Passing them all leads automatically to success. (The graded music examinations are similar, differing from the driving test only in that the scores of candidates are aggregated. So it is possible to make up for failing one part of the test by an excellent performance in another.)

The GCSE was originally designed to spread candidates out in a 'normal distribution' of grades in the shape of a bell,[14] as in the intelligence test described in Chapter Three. In an attempt to maintain constant standards and to be fair to candidates, the GCSE providers have, in recent years, combined the norm-based and criterion-referenced assessment models. But getting this right is a difficult task, even for highly skilled assessment experts (see Chapter Nine).

In September 2012, the minister announced to the House of Commons his intention to replace the GCSE by 2015 with a new examination – the English Baccalaureate (EBacc). Gaining this would require pupils to pass English, mathematics, a science, a language and a further subject from the humanities. Initially, it looked as if not all pupils would be expected to sit the new examination.[15] The minister suggested that the attainments of pupils not eligible for an EBacc would be reported in a Record of Achievement. The similarity to the examinations available during the middle years of the 20th century will not have escaped readers. The one clear finding from the research I undertook on Records of Achievement was that, for them to have any credibility with employers, they would have to be for *all* pupils and not just the lower-achieving ones. The minister's speech gave former Children's Laureate Michael Rosen the impression that the principal aim was to reduce the pass rate as proof of the increased 'rigour' of examinations: 'make the exams harder in order to get more students failing'.[16]

However, following criticisms by the House of Commons Education Committee[17] and reported comment by Ofqual that the ministerial ambitions for EBacc '*may exceed what is realistically achievable through a single assessment*',[18] the minister made a statement in the House of Commons on 7 February 2013. He reported that he had changed his mind and that the GCSE, rather than the EBacc, would remain the principal qualification for 16-year-old pupils although other reforms to the examination system would continue.

The minister made a further statement about the future of the GCSE on 11 June 2013.[19] He announced the publication of draft details of new GCSE content in seven subjects. He stated that the new specifications were more 'challenging, more ambitious and more rigorous' than those in current use. According to the *TES*, the changes – which apply only to England – include:

- 'A★–G grades replaced with grades 8–1 and tougher pass marks.
- The end of the modular system with all exams taken at the end of two-year courses.
- A drastic reduction in resit opportunities, with all sittings in the summer except for English language and mathematics.
- A reduction in coursework.'[20]

Such changes rarely occur without unintended consequences but my initial response is to urge caution. They risk creating an assessment system which favours pupils who absorb information easily and who are good at one-off examinations. Other kinds of pupils – no matter how able – may be seriously disadvantaged.

Advanced levels (A levels)

The examination for sixth-form pupils, the Advanced Level General Certificate of Education (A level), also has a history. It developed out of the Higher School Certificate awarded between 1918 and 1951. In its early years, A level grades were awarded on a strict norm basis (10% got As, 15% Bs, 10% Cs, 15% Ds and 20% Es). This marking scheme was abandoned in 1987 and new grades, including the N (nearly passed), were introduced. Over time the A level has continued to change.[21] It is currently a modular course with examinations – Advanced Subsidiary (AS) levels taken during the first year of study. Pass levels go from Grade E to Grade A and, since 2010, to A* for the most successful candidates. A levels are pitched approximately at university entrance, so that those passing well can expect to proceed to a degree course.

Vocational examinations

As more and more pupils have chosen to remain in education, A levels have been supplemented by a series of other diplomas and certificates. In addition to the examinations provided over many years by the City and Guilds and the Royal Society of Arts, there have been the Qualifying and Further examinations (Q and F), the Normal and Further (N and F), the Certificate of Extended Education (CEE), the Certificate of Pre-Vocational Education (CPVE), National Vocational Qualifications (NVQs), General National Vocational Qualifications (GNVQs), Business and Technology Education Council Certificates (BTECs) and assessed courses provided by the Business Education Council (BECs) and the Technical Education Council (TECs). From this alphabet soup of acronyms it is clear that no recent government has been able to design and successfully implement a satisfactory group of courses providing progression for 16- to 19-year-old young people. The courses that have got off the ground have generally been accompanied by severe criticisms. Experts from the LSE commented in 2006 that:

> Many of the newer vocational qualifications have very little labour market value, suggesting that they have not been successful in drawing young people into high quality learning that leads to successful labour market outcomes.[22]

Two attempts to bring order to courses for this age group have each been abandoned by different governments. In 1988 a committee chaired by the Vice-Chancellor of Southampton University, Gordon Higginson, proposed that a five-subject structure should be adopted for A levels.[23] The Conservative government rejected the recommendations on the day the proposals were to be launched.

In 2004 a committee chaired by Mike Tomlinson, a former Chief Inspector of Schools, proposed that academic and vocational qualifications should be merged into a single structure to replace A levels and GCSEs, within an overarching baccalaureate-style diploma.[24] This report was also rejected, this time by a Labour government.

In 2011 a report on vocational courses compiled by Alison Wolf was published – and accepted by the government. Among other measures, Wolf recommended that the nature of courses and qualifications available to older pupils be clarified and that changes to funding and accountability regimes be made, in order to:

> remove the perverse incentives which currently encourage schools and colleges to steer young people into easy options, rather than ones which will help them progress.[25]

But the minister has indicated that, in his view, current academic courses are too easy and fail to prepare students adequately for university. He has suggested that universities should 'dictate' the content of A level papers:

> Leading university academics tell me that A-levels do not prepare students well enough for the demands of an undergraduate degree.[26]

He has asked the regulatory body, Ofqual, to consult, with a view to requiring A levels to be strengthened by allowing only one resit and by replacing modules with end-of-year examinations. According to examination experts Bethan Marshall and Margaret Brown, mathematics A level was purposefully made more difficult by a committee of university mathematicians and examination board examiners in 2000. The result was 'a much higher failure rate followed by a significant drop in the participation rate for mathematics A and AS courses'.[27]

The proposals for greater involvement by universities have been attacked by a Cambridge academic, Priyamvada Gopal. She accepts that current A levels do not prepare students well for university or 'equip them to engage intelligently with the challenges of a complex world'. But she argues that 'education cannot be overhauled in this typically top-down manner with a select minority of institutions running the show at the expense of the sector as a whole'.[28] Nevertheless, the minister has announced that the Russell Group of the most elite universities has been asked to review current A levels and to be involved in an annual check. My initial reaction to this announcement is also to urge caution. The Russell Group may well produce examinations suited to serve as a university entrance test but this may not serve the education system well.[29]

This brief discussion illustrates how difficult successive governments have found it to design an appropriate assessment scheme for school pupils. I return to this topic in Chapter Nine and in Chapter Eleven I discuss the growing body of international assessments.

Inspection

Her Majesty's Inspectors

Formal inspection of English schools began in 1837 with the appointment of two 'Her Majesty's Inspectors' (HMI) in order to approve the new publicly funded elementary schools. From the start of the 20th century the role was expanded and other HMI were appointed to undertake full inspections of secondary schools. Over the 155 years of its existence, HMI exercised a strong influence on the education system – contributing to numerous policy initiatives and producing many publications.

From its inception, the role of HMI has been complex. Inspectors were expected to make independent judgements about standards. (Robert Lowe, whom I noted as one of the architects of the early education system and the creator of a scheme of 'payment by results' for teachers, was forced to resign for threatening this independence by (allegedly) editing HMIs' comments[30]). Yet HMI also acted as the eyes and ears of ministers, reporting back to them. What inspectors saw and heard used to play a full part in the policy making of the education ministry. HMI also worked closely with local authorities, chief education officers and their own teams of local inspectors.

It would be difficult for any one body to do one or two of these tasks without experiencing a conflict of interest – let alone all of them. With a remit guaranteeing its independence, HMI sometimes found itself passing critical judgements on government policies. As a result, ministers were often wary of the Inspectorate – possibly seeing inspectors more as 'turbulent priests' than 'standard bearers'.[31] Between 1968 and 1983 ministers had HMI reviewed no less than nine times. Most of the reviews, however – including the final Rayner Report[32] – were extremely positive.[33] Despite all these positive assessments, HMI was 're-organised' into the Office for Standards in Education by the Conservative government in 1992.[34]

Office for Standards in Education (Ofsted)

This new body was given a duty to inspect all schools on a regular basis. It has a small permanent staff – with a number of inspectors still titled HMI – supplemented by teams from two private companies. These companies compete for contracts to inspect batches of schools.

Ofsted's founding Chief Inspector, Stewart Sutherland, held the post part time, combining it with the vice-chancellorship of the University of London. He resigned in 1994. His successor, Chris Woodhead, proved controversial. He dominated media headlines with frequent attacks on teachers and widened his scope to include educational research and chief education officers of local authorities.

During his tenure, Ofsted developed a reputation for an aggressive approach and inspections became greatly feared. Even the House of Commons Select Committee called for measures to curb the Chief Inspector's 'intemperate' style.[35]

There was sometimes a kernel of truth in Chris Woodhead's criticisms but, all too often, in my view, this was exaggerated beyond justification and served mainly to sabotage confidence in the system. A number of reports about education produced by Ofsted also proved highly controversial.[36]

Mike Tomlinson, a former HMI, became Chief Inspector in 2000. He and his successors, David Bell (2002–06), Maurice Smith (acting from January to October in 2006), Christine Gilbert (2006–11) and Miriam Rosen (acting from July until December 2011) were less controversial in office, though inspections continue to be a difficult issue. It remains to be seen how Michael Wilshaw (appointed in 2012) will be judged. His first annual report concluded that while schools were getting better, 'there is a long way to go before the nation catches up with the best in the world'.[37]

I return to the role of inspection in Chapter Nine.

Conclusion

Assessment of pupils and inspection of teachers are the means by which the governments seek to monitor what happens in education. Many other countries use one or other method, but few use both in such extreme forms.

In the next chapter I begin my review of the strengths and weaknesses of the English system.

EIGHT

Strengths

In this and the following two chapters I consider the strengths and weaknesses of the English education system as I have experienced them over my working life. The conclusions of these chapters may be too obvious for some readers – they will have lived the story – but for others there may be a few surprises.

In seeking to judge strengths and weaknesses I have compared England (but sometimes specific data for England are not available and so it has had to be the UK) with the countries with which I am familiar. I use data from international bodies, such as the OECD, and other research evidence and my own knowledge and experience.

I have arranged my material according to what I see as: clear strengths, ambiguous features and obvious weaknesses. Strengths are readily understandable, as are weaknesses. But my middle category – ambiguous features – is less obvious. In Chapter Nine I deal with those parts of our system that have the potential to be either positive or negative, depending on how they are implemented.

Throughout these three chapters I will be seeking answers to the following questions:

- How worthwhile are the aims of the system?
- How appropriate are the structure and governance?
- How adequate is the funding?
- How satisfactory are the buildings and equipment?
- How wise have been the major policies of the last 25 or so years?
- How good are the administrators?
- How inspiring and competent are head teachers?
- How skilled are teachers?
- How well does the system work for pupils of different ages?
- Does the system generate well-qualified, intellectually curious young people?
- Does the system bring about happy and well-adjusted young people?

I will summarise my answers to all these questions in Chapter Eleven.

Let me begin with my impression of the strengths of the English system – both the major factors and some that are minor, but also important.

Aims and aspirations

I found it difficult to identify the formal aims of our education system. Since it has evolved over 150 years, I did not expect to find aims clearly stated at its start. But I did expect some of the milestone Education Acts to include a statement of general aims for the system which their parliamentary drafters were seeking to change. Instead, I found a system with confused aims – frequently shifting between the three Rs and broader ambitions.

According to the educational philosopher John White, statements of national aims need to be accompanied by a *raison d'être* that indicates 'why items in a list have been chosen … [and] … how the items fit together in a unified vision'.[1]

This implies that aims need to be clearly thought through and justified. White argues that this is a task for politicians rather than to be left to teachers, but that teachers need to be involved in the planning for how the aims are to be realised in everyday life in school.

The Newcastle Commission on the state of education in England published its six-volume report in 1861. It included the statement: 'The duty of a state in education … is to obtain the greatest possible quantity of reading, writing and number.'[2] This was seen as far too limited by HMI (and poet) Matthew Arnold. Nine years later, the 1870 Elementary Education Act stressed the provision of buildings. Section 5 states: 'There shall be provided for every district a sufficient amount of accommodation in public elementary schools.'[3] But drafters of the Act failed to state the purpose of what would go on in the buildings. The 1944 Education Act, the basis of much of our current system, provides details of the various powers of the minister and of how property is to be dealt with. But, again, it is curiously silent on the purpose of the education system. However, some aims were included in the 1943 White Paper 'Educational Reconstruction' and in R.A. Butler's comments to the House of Commons.[4]

The 1988 Education Reform Act does not provide aims for the system as a whole, though it does stipulate a 'broad and balanced curriculum' and the requirement that each school should:

- promote the spiritual, moral, cultural, mental and physical development of pupils at the school and of society; and
- prepare pupils at the school for the opportunities, responsibilities and experiences of adult life.[5]

These two statements recognise that education is about more than just the three Rs and that it is to serve both individuals and society as a whole.

The revision of the National Curriculum undertaken by Ron Dearing in 1993, however, retreated to the limited aim of the Newcastle Commission: 'The principal task of the teacher … is to obtain the greatest possible quantity of reading, writing and number.'[6]

A similarly narrow aim was emphasised in the 1997 White Paper, *Excellence in Schools*, produced by the incoming Labour government: 'The first task of the education service is to ensure that every child is taught to read, write and add up', although it also stated: 'but mastery of the basics is only a foundation'.[7]

In a subsequent revision to the National Curriculum, undertaken by the Qualifications and Curriculum Authority (QCA) in 2007, educational aims were broadened to helping young people become:

- successful learners who enjoy learning, make progress and achieve;
- confident individuals who are able to live safe, healthy and fulfilling lives;
- responsible citizens who make a positive contribution to society.[8]

These aims, of course, need to be translated into practical actions via the National Curriculum and the general organisation of schooling. But at least they provide three worthwhile goals for the system and, by implication, for society.

Finally, in the introduction to the Coalition government's 2010 Education White Paper, *The Importance of Teaching*, the minister drew attention to the problem of the achievement gap: 'our schools should be the engines of social mobility'. But, in outlining the thrust of the White Paper, he emphasised – whether consciously or not – the importance of the political process rather than of education itself: 'Education *reform* is the great progressive cause of our times.'[9]

It is a pity that the statements about 'aims' appear so insular. They contrast poorly with, for instance, the aims of the Norwegian education system. In its School Law, Norway stresses the need for the education system to:

> Combat all forms of discrimination … (and foster) … respect for human dignity and nature, intellectual freedom, charity, forgiveness, equality and solidarity … and open doors to the world … (through) knowledge and understanding of the national cultural heritage and our common international cultural traditions.[10]

The aims of any education system must remain contestable (as Aristotle advised), and two English academics, Robin Alexander of Cambridge University and the philosopher John White of London University, have set out detailed rationales for sets of aims more suited to a modern world.[11]

Despite obvious limitations, I accept that British ministers, from both the current and recent governments, have genuinely wished to improve the education system that they inherited. These positive aspirations deserve to be acknowledged.

Both the last Labour government and the Coalition government emphasised the issue of the gap between the school achievement of the advantaged and of the disadvantaged. This is not just an English problem. It can be seen in many countries – even in those ostensibly performing well. There is, however, a greater gap in the English system than in many others. Of course, this is not a new problem. People have been concerned about the achievement gap for many years.[12] I discussed the most likely reasons for this gap in Chapter Six and I will make some suggestions for how best to address it in Chapter Thirteen. At least the matter is now on the national agenda and, for this, the ministers responsible deserve praise.

Adequate functioning

Without doubt, the English education system functions adequately. There is a named senior minister overseeing it – a Secretary of State – and a number of junior ministers, together with political advisers and a professional civil service. All state (and some private) provision is financed by the Exchequer from taxes. Every child of school age is entitled to a place in an age-appropriate institution dedicated to learning and teaching. Teachers and support staff are recruited, trained and deployed. They are generally well qualified and receive regular payments. There are well-established assessment, supervision and disciplinary procedures. Pupils – and their parents – enjoy an entitlement to adequate provision.

Pupils' special needs are recognised and systems have been put in place to diagnose problems and provide appropriate provision wherever possible. (However, parents of such pupils may feel that insufficient attention and resources are devoted to this part of the education system and may be extremely worried about the changes that the Coalition government is seeking to make.)

Information about the education system is publicly available and, for the most part, subject to Freedom of Information regulations. So, at this basic level, the system functions well.

Local authority accountability

The powers of local authorities – as I have noted – have been reduced by recent governments of all political parties. In my view this has been a serious mistake. Replacing local democratic accountability by accountability to central government or, in the case of academies and free schools, by accountability to sponsors and the minister, seems to be a backwards step. It is in the opposite direction to many other countries (such as Finland) that are seeking to decrease central powers and increase regionalisation.

The existence of a middle tier of local authorities, with local knowledge and the capacity to monitor the work of schools and (if necessary) the power to step in and support a troubled school, is essential for a well-functioning system. I regard democratically elected local authorities (even in their reduced state) composed of members who have stood for, and been voted into, public office as a strength of our system.

Governing bodies

School governors for individual or groups of secondary schools were introduced by the 1944 Education Act. The Act also introduced 'managers' for primary schools. Over the years their role has frequently been amended and widened by regulation or by statutory Acts of Parliament. The 1974 'William Tyndale affair' – when the head and a group of teachers in an Islington primary school fell out with a significant section of the parents over its teaching methods – led to the role and the powers of governors being questioned.

As a result, the 1977 Taylor Committee[13] recommended an extended role for governors: monitoring the performance of schools and reporting to the local authority. It also recommended dropping the practice of joint governing bodies taking responsibility for several – or, in some cases, many – schools, and converting the managers of primary schools into full governing bodies. Further education Acts increased the number of parents on governing bodies so that it equalled the number of governors from the local authority.

Since the 1986 Education Act, governing bodies have held responsibility for the strategic management of their schools, supervising the budget and appointing the head teacher. Governors elect their own chair and are seen as 'critical friends' of the school. They also have a formal duty to review the exclusions of pupils and have powers to reinstate them. They are supported by various governor associations, some local authority staff and a DfE helpline.[14]

In my view, school governors are a good thing. Over the years I have both served as a governor and been involved in their training. I have been impressed by the commitment and enthusiasm brought to governing bodies by people who are volunteers – one of the largest bodies of volunteers in the country. I certainly count them as one of the positive features of our education system.

Quality of teacher education

As I noted in Chapter Five, how our teachers are trained has changed considerably over recent years. In my view, the combination of practical training with university study of subject knowledge, pedagogy and research is excellent and, although unpopular with recent governments that have constantly sought to increase school-based training, much better than in many other countries. An exception is Finland. where all teachers study in university up to the level of a master's degree as well as receiving practical training before beginning their careers. The partnership model of teacher preparation, including Teach First (described in Chapter Five) is, in my judgement, also good.

What is extremely worrying is the removal by the minister of the requirement for all teachers in free schools to be fully trained. Paradoxically, this relaxation has been accompanied by the introduction of 'tougher tests' for anyone planning to become a qualified teacher.[15]

Quality of school leadership

In England there is general agreement – not always found in other countries – that school leadership is necessary. The last Chief Inspector's verdict was 'good or outstanding leadership' in 65% of schools.[16] But perhaps we have too many heads displaying an unsustainable 'heroic' style, with too little delegation of power and insufficient opportunities for classroom teachers to develop leadership skills (by, for example, chairing task groups).

The system has a well-structured route to leadership via positions of special responsibility, allowing teachers to learn to be leaders of their colleagues. This is not always an easy role, combining as it does a certain amount of power and responsibility with an on-going collegial relationship. It is, however, an extremely important one. In my experience, it is often the quality of the heads of departments or of Key Stages that determines the effectiveness of a school.

One of the key skills of a good leader, in my opinion, is to allow a novice deputy to make mistakes as they learn their role – but to be so aware of what is happening as to be in a position to ensure these mistakes can be rectified without the school's being put at risk.

The National College for School Leadership was established in the late 1990s. It became an executive agency of the DfE on 1 April 2012. One year later it was merged with the Teaching Agency. It is now called the National College for Teaching and Leadership. Its role is to improve leadership through professional development and strategic initiatives. It offers the National Professional Qualification for Headship (NPQH), pitched at the level of a university master's degree (sadly, no longer essential for headship).

Since 1988 and the delegation of so many administrative and business functions to individual schools, the English system has seen professionals other than teachers assume leadership roles. School secretaries and bursars have been supplemented by a range of managerial and technical posts to do with finance and marketing, computing and the care of premises. In my view, this has been a mostly positive change and has increased the expertise of many leadership teams.

I do not, however, support the view that heads without any experience of working in education should be appointed to lead schools. I acknowledge that such candidates may have acquired valuable experience in a former career. The problem I have observed is that, no matter how good such people may be, their lack of knowledge of the details of schools' cultures means that they will always be in a weaker position than their teacher colleagues who have such knowledge.

There is, of course, a danger that the value of leadership is overstated and the status of classroom teachers is correspondingly reduced. In the Netherlands and Nordic countries, increasing the power of heads and heads of department has been resisted for fear that the professionalism of teachers will be adversely affected. In some countries, each subject department elects a chairman or woman – recognising that, although some leadership functions exist, the chair's major role is in coordinating rather than overseeing colleagues' work.

But, despite these risks, I consider that the way school leadership operates in England – with good classroom teachers progressing through the various stages to headship – is a positive element of our system.

Local Management of Schools

The 1988 Education Act delegated to individual schools many management tasks formerly undertaken by their local authorities. No longer exclusively educational, heads now had responsibility for their school's budget, appointing and dismissing staff, fixing pay, dealing with complaints, maintaining and extending the buildings and overseeing the school's catering arrangements. Their educational knowledge had to be supplemented by financial know-how, health and safety regulations and building management expertise – including the benefits and snares of letting premises.

These were significant changes to the role of the head and it took a number of years for some to adapt. For the heads of secondary schools and the larger primaries, it has been a good change. It has increased both their professional role and their status. Heads are more fully in charge of their institutions than before. They are no longer subject to the irritations of waiting for the local authority to fix minor repairs; they can appoint their own choice of maintenance companies. They can also use their facilities to generate extra income through letting them out in the evenings, at the weekends and during school holidays.

Of course, there are also disadvantages. Heads working in efficient local authorities had access to expertise in legal, personnel and building matters. Today, inexperienced heads have to rely on their governing bodies for advice and, depending on these bodies' composition, skills and availability of members, may or may not be lucky. This means that poor decisions can be taken, particularly over personnel issues, building contracts and the purchase of equipment. There have also been instances of criminal investigations of financial irregularities.[17]

The *Times Educational Supplement*, in 2012, reported how some primary schools, tempted by cash-back offers, had signed 'toxic deals' leasing office equipment 'worth a fraction of the £800,000-plus they can end up owing'.[18] In the past, heads were bailed out by the local authority. But now they are on their own. Furthermore, at least in the early years, some heads became so preoccupied with their management tasks that they neglected their educational leadership roles.

For small primary schools, the advantages of LMS are more doubtful. Heads – who may be teaching classes as well as managing the school – do not have the resources to employ specialist financial or premises-related staff. They have to deal with all personnel issues and oversee any building work. For them, having the local authority provide such 'back-office' functions made a lot of sense.

But, even with these disadvantages, I think self-managing schools are a positive feature of our system.

Quality of teachers

I have found a professional culture among teachers in England that embodies many of the positive features I noted in earlier chapters: a dedication to the safety and well-being of pupils, an ambition for pupils' success, a general sense of fairness and a loyalty and commitment to their school.

One of the undoubted strengths of English schools is the pedagogic skill of their staff. This is not a universal characteristic – as many pupils, to their cost, will know. But, from my observations in many countries, I consider that the predominant standard of preparation and classroom performance is pretty good. The last report from the Chief Inspector gave an overall figure of 59% for 'good or outstanding teaching'.[19] Obviously, we would rather the figure was 100%, but in what profession would you expect to find every single person outstanding? A national figure nigh on 60% – with others working towards it – is encouraging.

Many teachers undertake further study on a part-time basis while teaching (as I did at Birkbeck College in the early 1970s). I have frequently taught excellent students on master's or doctoral programmes who have been juggling evening and weekend slots in addition to their teaching jobs and family responsibilities. These teachers cope with the pressure, bring years of practical experience to their studies and are ideally equipped to grasp the reciprocal relationship between theory and practice.

In recent years, teachers have begun to monitor their pupils' progress in a much more systematic way than in the past. The use of individual data can be helpful in tracking patterns of learning and intervening when the evidence suggests there is a problem. In one school I worked with, for instance, the teacher responsible for a year group discovered that the same pupils were achieving contrasting grades in history and in geography. Both heads of departments investigated the quality of teaching, with the result that the geography teaching was radically improved. Such action – monitoring and, on the basis of data analysis, intervening in professional practice – would have been unlikely in the past but is now relatively common.

Furthermore, teachers are generally enthusiastic people. There are exceptions – as I noted in Chapter Five, with the teacher who believed the best part of his day started only at 4 pm – but, in the main, teachers tend to be encouraging and supportive of pupil ambition.

Teachers have been much berated by politicians over recent years. It is interesting, therefore, to learn that they are trusted by the public, second only to doctors. The regular polls carried out by Ipsos/MORI provide the evidence. Since 1983 the percentage of people reporting that they *trust teachers* has been around 80%. A similar question about politicians, over the same period, produced an answer of 14%.[20]

Caring relationships

As I noted in Chapter Six, one of the reasons why schools – with all their inherent problems – survive and flourish is because of the positive relationships between teachers and pupils, although this can sometimes be concealed in joshing banter. Banter can be part of the enjoyable theatricality of school life. Of course, it can also become an excuse for both teachers and pupils to insult each other. I have seen inexperienced teachers adopt this humorous style, only to be outsmarted by their pupils and revert to more traditional teacher–pupil relationships. On the whole, however, I have found the positive nature of teacher–pupil relationships in English schools deeply impressive and definitely one of the strengths of the system.

Promotion of active learning

Despite the fact that a high proportion of pupils' time is spent sitting at desks or tables, active learning is a feature of many English schools. I have seen how positively pupils respond to participating in experiments in design and technology and science classes. (What a pity that these are to be reduced by the Coalition government.)

Measuring sports pitches; undertaking traffic surveys; exploring streams on biology field trips; estimating the solar system's planetary interrelationships using different-sized balls; using a solar-powered model car to illustrate sustainability; or trying to design a cantilevered chair to rival that of Finnish designer Alvar Aalto are all activities that provide both challenge and fun and promote active learning. Again, this is a strength of our system that is not always found in other countries.

Zest for improvement

I have found teachers in England remarkably positive and willing to give time and attention to improvement projects. One of the most exciting innovations that I was involved with was the development of Records of Achievement (which I mentioned in Chapter Seven).

This work came about because teachers realised that pupils would benefit from a more structured approach to the monitoring of their progress. Some notable examples are the 'Personal Achievement Record' developed by teachers at Evesham School and Pupil Profiles developed by the Sutton Centre and the Scottish Council for Research in Education.[21] Large-scale initiatives were also undertaken by Tim Brighouse in Oxfordshire and by the team which produced the London Record of Achievement.

Although distinct, these schemes shared common features such as encouraging pupils regularly to record their reflections on their progress in different subjects. Commitment to the various schemes was so great that they survived the teachers' industrial action of the mid-1980s. Ironically, the initiatives lost their impetus only when they were finally adopted by the government of the day – a result perhaps of 'the dead hand of officialdom'.

Surprisingly, however, I have found teachers reluctant to boast of their success. When, with colleagues, I tried to establish a database of successful in-school projects I encountered teachers resistant to the publication of their schemes. This could have been because boasting always carries a risk of later humiliation if the project dips, or it could also have been a desire to keep a successful idea within the school. Probably it was a little of both.

Sense of fun

Though by no means universal, the existence in English schools of what an ILEA research team called the 'fun factor' is also a considerable strength. I believe that a great deal of learning can be fun. Not all aspects of it – there are some boring tasks that have to be mastered en route to more interesting work. But skilful teachers are adept at making the most unpromising material fun. And remember Mihaly Csikszentmihalyi (in Chapter Two), and how the experience of 'flow' in a challenging task is often more pleasurable than relaxation.

Schools often allow 'mufti days' for charity. And this idea has been used for National Book Day, when pupils and teachers dress up as well-known fictional characters. Doubtless many readers will have seen dozens of Harrys, Hermiones and Rons being greeted at school gates by assorted Professors Dumbledore and McGonagall. What a gift for a day devoted to fiction.

My grandsons' primary school has the motto 'Learning, love and laughter'. This cleverly links the school's main task – promoting learning – with affection and fun. What better combination could there be?

The secondary schools in which teachers participate in events such as an annual pantomime – letting their hair down and encouraging their pupils to laugh at their antics – provide positive memories that pupils often retain for life. I have a strong recollection, after nearly sixty years, of my funny old French teacher leading sixth formers in a lusty rendition of 'Les beaux gendarmes' in the annual French concert.

Citizenship studies

Citizenship studies provide an introduction to many of the concepts and values underpinning our democratic system of government.[22] Concepts such as justice, rights, duties and responsibilities are studied in relation to governmental and legal processes and international relations. The skills of critical thinking and enquiry are used to investigate such issues as diversity, the media and human rights.

A 2005 inquiry by the House of Commons Education and Skills Select Committee into the impact of citizenship studies concluded that it was too early to judge whether citizenship education was having a positive impact. The Coalition government has not, so far, included the subject as part of the primary curriculum (as had been planned by the previous administration), but it still needs to be taught at secondary level.

Citizenship, in my view, is a positive element of our education system, particularly at a time of such public disillusion with politicians.

School assemblies

Strengths of the English system also, in my view, include the tradition of whole-school assemblies. The community aspect of these regular meetings promotes a sense of shared culture and allows pupils to learn about the activities of older and younger peers. They also provide a good opportunity for the head teacher and staff to promote the values of the school.

Outstanding music

There are many schools in England with good choirs, orchestras, wind groups, jazz and steel bands. The annual Schools Proms in London's Royal Albert Hall illustrate the range of this excellent work. The National Youth Orchestra and regional youth groups (such as the Leicestershire Schools Symphony Orchestra, founded in 1948) have been associated with some of the most famous British conductors. The London Schools Symphony Orchestra (founded in 1951), which regularly performs at the Barbican, provides young people with stimulating and memorable experiences. (I was lucky enough to see, in the 1970s, a young Simon Rattle working with London school pupils. Electrifying.)

Classical music does not have to be restricted to pupils from advantaged families – although wealthy families can more easily afford private lessons and the cost of instruments. Nevertheless, thanks to the ILEA, which provided peripatetic instrumental teachers and free loan of instruments, I knew one Brixton comprehensive school that performed classical works, such as Bach's *St John Passion*, as well as four-part choral arrangements of Beatles' songs. The school benefited from an extremely talented teacher who was able to compose and arrange music for the available forces. For nearly 40 years he gave his all to teaching, composing, directing – and inspiring young people. What a legacy.

In Chapter Two I noted the remarkable work of the Simón Bólivar orchestra in Venezuela and reported that a sister scheme was being developed both in Scotland and in several English cities.[23] For many pupils, participation in concerts, drama productions or dance performances is the key to success in their schooling. In Chapter Four I noted the theory proposed by the Russian psychologist Vygotsky about what he termed the 'zone of proximal development'. Pupils working alongside skilled musicians and being stimulated to perform way beyond what is normally considered possible well illustrate the theory.

Visually stimulating environment

An outstanding positive feature of many English schools is the quality of the work by, and photographs of, pupils displayed in classrooms and corridors. The necessary mounting and framing requires extra work by teachers and support staff, but the results create a stimulating environment and provide models to inspire learning. Some schools look like art galleries. Of course, sensitive judgements are needed so that all pupils can, at some time, see themselves and their work valued.

Sport

A traditional strength of English schools has been the way that sport has been integrated into daily life. As a young teacher in inner London, in addition to playground sports, I used to accompany my class on a coach to a games centre in the outer suburbs. It was too long a drive relative to the time available for sport – but it was regular and (mostly) enjoyable exercise.

OECD figures from the mid-2000s for English 11-year-olds show that only 28% of boys and 19% of girls reported doing daily moderate-to-vigorous physical activity. In contrast, Finnish 11-year-old boys and girls reported figures of 48% and 37% respectively.[24] The Coalition government has removed the two hours per week commitment to sport that the previous Labour government had introduced.

But for many pupils sport is life, and all credit is due to the teachers who devote time to it.

School trips

Many teachers give up part of their holidays to take pupils on school trips. Whether these are ambitious foreign trips or weeks in local authority centres, for many pupils they are among the high spots of their schooling. This is the time when pupils really get to know each other and their teachers.

Seeing children without sight abseiling down a mountain side, at an outdoor centre in North Wales in the 1980s was for me a demonstration of what outdoor education is able to achieve with spirited pupils and dedicated teachers. More up-to-date examples can be found in the outdoor study of the Forest School Project. Influenced by Nordic ideas about the importance of teaching children to appreciate nature, this movement has spread so that there are now approximately 100 such schools in England.[25]

Lack of retention

A rarely noticed positive feature of our system is its lack of 'retention'. This is the practice whereby children failing to make sufficient progress are kept down for one or more years to be taught amid younger cohorts. The practice is common in, for example, France, Belgium, Portugal and Spain, despite evidence from the OECD that it produces overwhelmingly negative results.[26]

It is to the credit of ministers of all parties that, so far, they have resisted demands to introduce such a system here. Despite the seeming common-sense view that a pupil should not progress until he or she has passed the current year's course, anyone who has seen foreign classes containing 'retainees' will know what a bad idea it is and how counterproductive it can be both for the older and the younger pupils. The older ones, shamed by their situation, play up and the younger ones observe and emulate their patterns of negative behaviour.

Early years

As I have noted, my personal opinion is that formal schooling begins too early for many pupils. I think it would be sensible for children to start school at age six, as happens in many countries. That said, I recognise the progress that has been made in making appropriate provision for children below the age of five.

In 1998 the Labour government introduced the Sure Start programme.[27] This was designed to give all children, but particularly those from disadvantaged backgrounds, a good start in life. It was based on the American Head Start programme and influenced by similar initiatives in Canada and Australia. Many Children's Centres were established in the most disadvantaged areas and provided integrated care, education and parental support.

So far, evaluations of Sure Start have shown mixed results. A study of the impact on parents was positive,[28] but an evaluation by researchers at Durham University of the impact on children's learning was less so.[29] A research team appointed by the DCSF to evaluate the initiative, after an initially negative report, found evidence of positive gains in 2008.[30] Nevertheless, over 250 of the 3,600 centres were forced to close in 2011 as the result of cuts by the Coalition government.

I return to early childhood in Chapter Nine, when I deal with the less satisfactory aspects of the system.

Teachers' awards ceremonies

I should applaud the annual Teacher Awards Ceremonies. In theory I do. Recognising and celebrating exceptional teaching skill and dedication to pupils must be worthwhile. The practice, however, plays down the essential teamwork of a school. The winners are classroom 'stars' and deserve their well-earned glory. But many excellent teachers are involved in a pupil's career and are rarely nominated for awards because their skills are less obvious – the sort of teachers that pupils only come to appreciate years after they have left school. So I include this as a strength – but with reservations.

Conclusion

The strengths of the system that I have identified range from overall aims to minor, yet significant, details. These are, of course, my personal views and not everyone will agree with them. Some of the features I have cited also have associated weaknesses. But, all in all, it is an impressive list of the many strengths of the English system.

Let me now look at the more ambiguous 'grey' areas, where particular aspects of the system may have either positive or negative effects.

NINE

Ambiguities

Some parts of England's education system cannot be categorised simply as a 'strength' or a 'weakness': they can be either or both – depending on how they are used.

Education spending

According to policy analyst Chris Chantrill, public spending (mainly on education, health and other social services) increased from about 15% of the country's gross domestic product at the start of the 20th century to 47% in 2011.[1] Treasury calculations show that the amount required by the DfE for the financial year ending in March 2014 was just under £57 billion,[2] with over £13 billion earmarked for the Academies programme.

In comparison to similar countries, UK spending on education tends to be at, or just below, the OECD average. The latest figures reported by the OECD are for 2010 (converted from dollars into pounds). The figures show that annual public expenditure in the UK for all educational institutions, other than universities and colleges, was on average £5,124 per pupil. The figure for Denmark was £6,825, for Finland £5,006, for Norway £7,763 and for Sweden £5,983. The OECD average was just below the UK figure, at £4,998.

The Institute for Fiscal Studies' analysis of the 2010 Spending Review shows that 'All areas of public education spending are expected to see real-terms cuts between 2010–11 and 2014–15'.[3] In England, schools are likely to experience the least cuts, universities (which are expected to gain extra funds from their tripled fees) the most. One of the reasons for the protection of the schools' budget is that the Coalition government has created a 'pupil premium' to provide additional resources for schools dealing with the most disadvantaged pupils.

I have always argued that sufficient resources are an essential part of a good education service. I have also argued that high levels do not necessarily guarantee quality. In some countries, such as Norway (where there are mountainous regions and a sparse population) geography increases the cost of all public services. It is notable that Finland's high-performing education system is not particularly well funded in comparison to other Nordic countries (though teacher education – including continuous professional education – is prioritised).

I see spending on education in England as one of the ambiguous features of the education system. In my view, the education maintenance allowance (introduced in 2004 by the Labour government to encourage young people from poor families to remain in education[4]) was an example of good use of public resources. I regret that it has been so drastically reduced by the Coalition government.[5] I am less convinced of the value for money of the Private Finance Initiatives (PFIs) – used by Conservative, Labour and Coalition governments. PFIs can result in expensive repayments of public money over many years. The DfE 2012 *Guidelines on New Buildings* are reported as being much more modest than the Labour government's Building Schools for the Future. It is clearly important that public money should not be wasted – the reported cost of £80 million for the rebuilt Holland Park School[6] is astounding – but squeezing corridors and erecting poor-quality buildings will be a mistake, likely to haunt the education system for years to come.

National Curriculum

Until 1988 the only national curriculum in England was for religious education, and that was subject to local agreement. The knowledge to be studied in schools was regarded as something best decided by teachers. In reality, there was a general agreement over the subjects to be covered in primary schools, although there was considerable variation as to which specific topics were chosen to represent the subjects.

Some primary schools timetabled separate sessions for each subject, often dealing with reading and mathematics in the mornings – when the children were deemed to be fresher and more receptive – and the rest in the afternoons. Some teachers preferred to teach the subjects in a more integrated way, working them into projects. Interestingly, in 1978 an HMI Primary Survey drew attention to the traditional dominance of reading and mathematics and the consequent neglect of other subjects.[7]

Despite these HMI findings, the media then made much of the excessive use of progressive methods – influenced, journalists claimed, by the 1967 Plowden Report.[8] This exaggeration has led to an abiding myth. In the research in London primary schools, with which I was involved during the 1980s, the predominant practice was far more traditional than progressive. In secondary schools, teachers tended to use the syllabuses of the public examinations to determine the curriculum.

Not everyone was happy with the autonomy of primary teachers, or with the secondary teachers' choices of examination boards. When James Callaghan, Labour Prime Minister during the late 1970s, inaugurated what he termed a 'Great Debate' about the state of English education, he drew on a term coined by a Conservative minister – 'a secret garden'[9] – to describe the curriculum arrangements of the nation's schools, in which politicians were not expected to involve themselves.

HMI had already drawn attention to the difficulties faced by families with school-aged children moving from one part of the country to another.[10] Academics such as Paul Hirst (a philosopher),[11] and Denis Lawton (a curriculum specialist),[12] were also raising questions about how the curriculum should be organised in schools. A former education officer, Duncan Graham, caught the general mood of dissatisfaction when he cited the ridiculousness of pupils being forced to study the Vikings 'for the fourth time'.[13] Kenneth Baker, architect of the 1988 Education Reform Act, changed this situation by incorporating a National Curriculum into his new legislation.

The arguments for a National Curriculum were, and still are, strong: raising expectations of what pupils can achieve; creating an entitlement to 'a broad and balanced curriculum' for all young people, wherever they live; promoting more science and technology (especially necessary in some poorly equipped girls' schools); assisting teachers in planning; and imparting a sense of progress for pupils as they move through their schooldays.

The evolving National Curriculum created a number of problems. The pile of papers detailing changes often reached well above a metre in staff rooms. And teachers quickly realised that the curriculum was being driven by the assessment attached to it. An aphorism based on the idea that what could be measured was valued – rather than the opposite – featured in many staffroom conversations.

The nation's teachers, nevertheless, knuckled down and adapted to teaching the National Curriculum (including its frequent changes). But by the early 1990s it became apparent that it took up too much time and some slack had to be found. Ron Dearing, a former civil servant, was appointed to review it. His 1993 report reduced the curriculum by 20% and reduced the number of attainment levels from ten to eight.[14]

One of the main criticisms made by assessment expert Tim Oates is that the National Curriculum has been too inward looking and its officials have failed to notice the way other countries – particularly those whose young people perform better in international tests – organise their own curricula. Following his critique, Oates was invited in 2011 to chair an 'Expert Panel' as part of a Review to overhaul the National Curriculum once again.[15]

In a first progress report Oates and his colleagues published a set of principles. These noted that the National Curriculum should seek to raise standards for all children and that teachers should have greater freedom over what they teach, with only the 'essential knowledge' laid down by government. They also argued that the curriculum must be made more coherent, although they recommended preserving the subject-basis framework of the curriculum. They suggested downgrading citizenship, design technology and information and communication technology to what they termed the 'basic curriculum'.[16] It was expected that the Ministerial Review – into which this report was fed – would be completed in time for ministers to make a decision about changes in the National Curriculum by spring 2013. But the matter has been complicated by some members of the expert panel publicly disassociating themselves from the interim conclusions of the minister. One, Andrew Pollard, an experienced researcher, stated:

> The constraining effects on the primary curriculum as a whole are likely to be profound and the preservation of breadth, balance and quality of experience will test even the most committed of teachers.[17]

He also noted:

> The Government is keen to have high expectations, but they have to be pitched at a level which is realistic. If they are pitched too high, they will generate widespread failure.[18]

On 7 February 2013, the minister presented a new version of the National Curriculum with a consultation period lasting until April. This new version 'represents a shift in what we expect pupils and teachers to achieve, particularly in the core subjects of English, mathematics and science at primary level'.[19] Following consultation, a new National Curriculum has been published.[20]

So why do I see the National Curriculum as an ambiguous area? The principle of a National Curriculum, encompassing essential knowledge that this generation wishes to pass on to future generations, is sound. But, so far, it has failed to live up to expectations. Rather than leading teachers and pupils on a journey towards worthwhile knowledge and important skills, it seems to have forced learning into testable packages and pushed teachers into an over-passive role. Time will tell if a new version can overcome this legacy of problems. Furthermore, since academies (fast becoming the most common state secondary school) and free schools no longer have to teach the National Curriculum in its entirety, its revision seems rather pointless. It remains to be seen, of course, how many academies choose to follow it voluntarily.

Quality of assessment

Testing can be motivating. As I argued in Chapter Seven, it is an essential part of the learning process.

How beneficial are SATs?

There is a major problem with the crude league tables of SATs results. These take no account of pupils' starting-points and cannot, therefore, indicate the quality of schools. According to Warwick Mansell, a journalist specialising in the effects of testing on teaching, the pressure on schools to reach the highest positions in the league tables leads to 'teaching to the test'.[21] This has been defined by the House of Commons Education Select Committee:

> In extreme cases, a high proportion of teaching time will be given over to test preparation … with teachers coaching their pupils in examination technique, question spotting, going over sample questions similar to those likely to be set in the test.[22]

Practising tests is a boring activity for pupils and teachers – albeit one which may push them up the league table. But, ironically, the obsession with league table results may actually be based on spurious data. Three professors concerned with the analyses of test scores submitted evidence to the Select Committee showing that up to one-third of individual scores were likely to be inaccurate and result in pupils being given inaccurate assessments.[23] They also stated that many changes in the league tables lacked statistical significance and could have occurred simply by chance. League table pressure has also led, in some instances, to blatant cheating. Both the Mathematics Association and the Royal Society, in their evidence submitted to the same Select Committee, criticised the dominant role of testing in our education system.[24]

How worthwhile is the GCSE?

I noted the history and development of the GCSE examination in Chapter Seven. Here I want to focus on whether it is a strength or weakness of the system. In 1990, the proportion of pupils gaining five or more A–C grades (and A* from 1994) was 35%; in 2013, it was over 80%.

candidates have to take an oral examination in at least one of the five subjects they study in upper secondary school. Pupils are given a text to be studied and then have to make a presentation based on their analysis of it. The examiner and the candidate's teacher then engage in dialogue with the candidate. Such an examination is expensive – which is why it only happens in one subject – but it is better than our current A levels.

Each of our principal methods of assessment – SATs, GCSEs and A levels – is unsatisfactory in one way or another. Yet assessment remains a vital part of teaching and learning. An elitist approach to assessment is to limit success to those who are particularly able or whose advantaged status enables them to compete successfully with their peers. The more rigorous the assessment, the fewer the successful candidates and the higher the status of the winners.

A contrasting, egalitarian approach to assessment is to use it as a way of encouraging as many people as possible to reach a defined standard. Some people will do so easily, some will need extra help, others will require several attempts. This does not matter if the important consideration is the proportion of the age group who ultimately reach the standard.

The GCSE and A level examinations have developed from an elitist model (based on the bell curve that I described in Chapter Seven), although, over the years, examination boards have veered, if not towards the egalitarian model, at least towards a hybrid one. The SATs model – with its expected levels – was constructed more in the egalitarian mould. The reforms that the minister has inaugurated appear muddled and promise to turn assessment back towards an elitist approach.[38] It is for this reason that I have included assessment as an ambiguous feature of the system.

How desirable are faith schools?

As I noted in Chapter Six, our poorly funded, weakly developing, 19th-century education system depended on religious schools.[39] Today, faith schools often do well in the league tables, although whether this is because they are intrinsically better schools, because their pupil intake is significantly different in terms of economic status or because the families, schools and communities are better integrated is difficult to judge.

There is, however, a wealth of evidence pointing to the more economically advantaged pupil composition of faith schools. Simon Rogers, the editor of *Facts Are Sacred*, has analysed DfE data for free school meals by postcode area. He shows that three-quarters of Catholic schools have a more affluent mix of pupils than other schools in the same local areas.[40] The figures also reveal that most Church of England primary schools also have a more advantaged intake than their non-faith school neighbours and that the intakes have become more affluent in recent years, fuelling the suspicion that selection may be operating under the guise of faith.

Two academics from the London School of Economics and Political Science found that the more-advantaged parents were more likely to apply to faith schools and were more successful at navigating complex admissions arrangements.[41] Jessica Shepherd, a *Guardian* journalist, reported case studies of individual faith schools. In one school in Croydon just 7.1% of pupils were eligible for free school meals, in comparison with an average for the same postcode area of 28.7%. In Richmond one school had only 1% eligible for free school meals, compared with 9.7% in the postcode area. In one school in Leeds the figures were 8.5% for the school, compared to 40.2% in the postcode area.[42]

I have included faith schools as an ambiguous item because they are popular with parents and many do well. But, by having exclusive intakes, they run the risk of being divisive. I recently came across a cartoon in which a little girl is asking her mother, "Why do we have to go to church when we don't believe in God?", to which her mother replies "Because God has some very nice schools darling". I discuss my proposal for faith schools in Chapter Thirteen.

How sound is the national reading strategy?

An emphasis on developing reading skills should be a positive aspect of any education system. Ministers have made clear that literacy must be a priority for all schools. Government support for Every Child a

Reader – a project to help those who have not readily grasped the necessary decoding skills and who, if left unsupported, are likely to develop serious reading problems – has been welcome. It is bad news that a number of schools have since been forced by budget cuts to withdraw from it.[43]

How reading is initially taught has become a contentious matter. The traditional freedom of teachers to select whichever method they considered best for their pupils was overturned by the last Labour government. This had the effect of greatly reducing the influence of literacy specialists such as Margaret Meek or the late Harold and Connie Rosen. Michael Rosen (the children's author, and their son) comments:

> Policies on literacy were [formerly] thrashed out by people such as my parents alongside teachers in their professional organisations and local authority advisers and inspectors. This was supported by a massive body of theory based on close observation of how children learn and teachers teach.[44]

In contrast, the 'literacy hour'[45] was designed by a small group chosen by the minister (of the time). Teaching reading has been transformed from a pedagogical into a political act, with right- and left-wingers espousing different approaches.

The details of the debates – for all but committed experts – appear somewhat Byzantine. They feature fierce arguments, not only about the relative value of phonics (a system of decoding words using the sounds of single – and combinations of – letters) versus authentic story books, but even about the particular type of phonics to be used. Those interested in the difference between analytic and synthetic phonics and the strength of the research evidence underpinning the government's espousal of the latter should consult the many references available.[46]

As a researcher interested in the way children learn to read but not expert in the field, I worry that the evidence in favour of the government's chosen approach, synthetic phonics, appears mainly to be based on a small-scale project undertaken in Clackmannanshire,

Scotland[47] – evidence not supported by detailed work in either the United States or Australia.[48]

Since 1998 teachers have been instructed that there is 'only one way' to teach reading. This is a very different view to that taken by the Bullock Committee of language specialists in 1975:

> One of our main arguments is that there is no one method, medium, approach, device, or philosophy that holds the key to the process of learning to read.[49]

The use of a single 'approved' method means that young children have been drilled to pronounce words (even specially made up nonsense words) by building up the sound of each syllable. Proponents claim that phonics get the mechanics out of the way and free children to enjoy reading. Critics argue that children learn to read (even the nonsense words) in a mechanistic way without necessarily comprehending any meaning. Furthermore, it is suggested that these methods (termed by critics 'drill and kill'[50]) do not lead to a love of reading.[51] Stephen Krashen, an American linguistics expert, argues:

> Studies over the past 25 years show heavy phonics study … only helps children do better in tests where they pronounce lists of words out loud: it has no significant effect on tests where children have to understand what they read.[52]

Evidence from the latest results of the Progress in International Reading Literacy Study (PIRLS),[53] which tests skills and attitudes connected with reading for 10-year-olds from over 40 countries, shows that only 26% of English pupils liked reading. It seems clear that our centrally devised, 'top-down' methods are not the complete answer. But once ministers have stipulated a particular teaching method, it is increasingly difficult to change it – especially when Ofsted has a duty to police such orders. The political interest in reading – an undoubted good – has become an ambiguous, if not potentially negative, factor, illustrating that even those actions conceived with the best intentions can have unintended negative consequences.

How helpful is inspection?

No one wants a bad school where the head has low aspirations, teachers shirk their duties and pupils are neglected. Inspectors are experts whose presence should root out incompetence and ensure helpful feedback. The theory of inspections is sound, but, as I noted in Chapter Seven, the short history of Ofsted is less convincing.

Inspections have become a 'high stakes' activity, leading to heads being sacked and schools being placed in special measures. As a result, both teachers and pupils find it difficult to behave 'normally' during inspections. Preparations absorb substantial amounts of energy. Consultants are hired to undertake rehearsal inspections. (I know of a school where flowers were planted and potted plants installed to coincide with the impending inspection.) Yet inspectors are rarely able to spend sufficient time in a class to be able to blend into the background and capture the often subtle meaning of an action by a pupil or a teacher.

So is the impact of inspections generally positive or negative? Adrian Elliott, reviewing the 20-year history of Ofsted, notes that prior to the introduction of universal inspection, a teacher could survive 40 years without being inspected. However, he questions whether Ofsted judges schools with high proportions of disadvantaged pupils fairly. He also cites Dylan Wiliam – an assessment expert – challenging the lack of data on the reliability of inspection grades: whether different inspectors visiting the same school a week apart would award the same grade. His conclusion is that Ofsted's role in the English education system 'remains both significant and highly controversial'.[54]

I believe the former HMI inspection system, coupled with the work of local advisers, though far from perfect, worked reasonably well. The inspectors were of a high calibre and informal advice could be given in confidence. The disadvantage was that local advisory services varied in quality and some 'coasting' schools undoubtedly escaped scrutiny for too long.

The more intense approach of Ofsted[55] has ensured that all schools are inspected regularly, but has created other problems. In the first place, it appears to rely heavily on test data. As someone who has used data widely in my research, I appreciate its importance, but it can be open to misinterpretation and even manipulation. I believe that you need both sensitive data analysis and expert judgement in order to evaluate a school fairly. I can recall a time when inspectors relied completely on their judgements and ignored the data; now I fear they may be doing the opposite.

Another problem is that Ofsted has taken it upon itself periodically to 'raise the bar' of school practice previously deemed to be 'satisfactory' and to reclassify schools, once thought reasonable, as failing. It did this in 2010, and again in September 2012, when the 'satisfactory' judgement was discontinued and replaced by 'requires improvement'. This means that 26% of schools formerly deemed 'satisfactory' face three years of further inspections.

The current Chief Inspector, Michael Wilshaw, has courted controversy with some outspoken comments. While still a head teacher he was reported as having said: 'If anyone says to you that staff morale is at an all-time low, you know you are doing something right.'[56] Such a remark demonstrates an approach to leadership that I find disturbing and that may turn out to be counterproductive. I also fear that a collective dependence on inspectorial approval is preventing teachers from developing their own judgement skills.

There are also questions about whether Ofsted is free to comment on all aspects of schooling or whether – however subtly – it is under pressure to praise government initiatives (such as academies). Finally, Ofsted is expensive: its budget for 2014 is £171 million.[57]

Those in favour of inspections argue that they keep teachers on their toes, ensure that high standards are maintained and that the reports provide parents and prospective parents with the expert judgements of what school is like. I discuss in Chapter Eleven what I think to be the stronger arguments, as well as whether it is possible to keep the positive aspects of inspection while ditching the negative.

How useful is homework?

The major rationale for homework is that it provides more time for learning than is ordinarily available in the school day. It may also be easier for some pupils to work creatively at home rather than in a busy school setting. Furthermore, the habit of working independently encourages self-discipline. Teachers also tend to be keen on the idea of homework, though some complain that the efforts needed to set it, collect it on time, mark it carefully and provide detailed feedback outweigh any potential benefits.

The downside of homework is that takes up time that might be spent more enjoyably in other ways. Given that pupils attend school for about 30 hours each week over nine months of each year between the ages of 5 and (increasingly) 18, it could be argued that sufficient time is already allotted to formal learning. Moreover, young pupils may be tired after a day at school and need to enjoy unpressured time with their parents. Older pupils might prefer to spend time on sports, pursuing interests or 'chillaxing'.

Many parents, however, are positive about homework and pleased that it provides a justification for keeping their children at home at evenings and weekends. Others – working considerably longer hours than many of their continental equivalents – resent having to dedicate precious family time to forcing tired children to complete their work.

So is homework a generally good or bad feature of our education system? I give my answer in Chapter Thirteen.

How essential is school uniform?

This is another topic on which there is little consensus. School uniform is loved by some and hated by others. It is a British tradition, adhered to by many former Commonwealth countries. Blue coats and military caps were popular in German schools in the 19th century and Japan introduced sailor-suit school uniforms in the 19th century. Russia, having banned school uniforms after its revolution, insisted on them from 1948 up to 1992.

The US and Canada – except for some private schools – have generally resisted the idea of uniforms. In a number of European countries, while there is no requirement for a uniform, many younger pupils wear smocks or *grembiules* – based on traditional overalls.

In England each school decides on its own colours and style of uniform, and some use it to signal the school's status. Many state schools – particularly at primary level – have opted for durability and allow pupils to wear sweatshirts and trousers, albeit of all the same colour and style. If they stipulate hats or caps, these tend to be mainly for sun protection. In contrast, many private schools still require traditional blazers with badges, ties, formal trousers or skirts and caps and panamas. Some still insist on ostentatiously archaic clothes: Eton requires formal tail suits and special ('Eton') shirt collars; Christ's Hospital requires 18th-century blue tunic coats, breeches and yellow socks.

So is school uniform positive or negative? I provide my view in Chapter Thirteen.

How freely available are out-of-school activities?

Many parents will remember a time when the majority of out-of-school activities were provided by the school free of charge. Of course, payments were required for extended trips away (skiing trips have always been an expensive extra), but after-school sports, drama, choir, orchestra or special-interest groups were organised, for free, by dedicated teachers.

Physical education teachers (many more unsung heroes than the bullying 'Mr Sugden' from Ken Loach's 1963 film *Kes*) and many other teachers voluntarily devoted their Saturday mornings to taking school teams to matches. This was part of the informal covenant between the teaching profession and the government. Sadly, this broke down, due to the dispute between government and teachers in the 1980s. Once abandoned, such arrangements are impossible to re-create.

Today noble teachers in some schools continue to offer a range of extra activities at no extra cost, but, in others, activities are provided only by external companies – at a price. For children from low-income families such costs are prohibitive.

So an aspect of our education system that should be inclusive has – for some pupils – become exclusive. This exclusivity was highlighted by the 2012 London Olympics and the claim that there was a preponderance of athletes from private schools. Peter Wilby, a newspaper journalist and former editor, argued that, as sport has become more professional, private schools have increased their dominance. Citing a book by the former England cricketer Ed Smith, Wilby notes that in the 1984 Olympics six out of nine gold medallists were state-school educated, as were two-thirds of the England rugby team and over 90% of the England cricket team.[56] Today the composition of teams is markedly different.

Wilby rejects the frequently claimed reason that state schools discourage competition. He believes that the explanation of the change is much more likely to be due to the selling of state schools' playing fields. At the same time, there has been an increase in facilities offered by private schools. (He notes, for example, that the facilities in Tonbridge School – by no means the most lavish – include a 50-metre Olympic pool, 12 rugby pitches, 18 tennis courts and 20 cricket nets). Wilby also points out that wealthy private schools can afford to hire top-class professional coaches.[57]

It is, of course, impossible to turn back the clock. Playing fields turned into housing estates cannot be redeemed and the families of physical education teachers would no doubt resist attempts to reinstitute Saturday morning games. But many after-school events could be reinstated through 'full-service extended schools' that encompass health and social service support and youth programmes.[58] The term has been imported from the US,[59] but the idea comes from the 'village colleges' founded by Henry Morris[60] (Chief Education Officer for Cambridgeshire for 30 years) and the community schools pioneered in England in the 1970s – an example of how some ideas come round again in different guises.

I have included after-school activities in this chapter because, while I think they are excellent, if they are available only to reasonably well-off families they can have a divisive impact.

Conclusion

The topics discussed in this chapter – education spending; the National Curriculum, with its scope still unfulfilled; our assessment system, which has grown into an accountability monster rather than providing constructive feedback to learners; the teaching of reading, which ought to imbue a love of the written word but too often resembles a killjoy phonic exercise; school inspections, which have become over-bearing; the positive and negative aspects of homework; the tradition of school uniform, seen by some as helpful but by others as enforced conformity; and finally, the provision and funding of out-of-school activities – can all enhance or diminish our system.

In the next chapter I turn to the definite downside – what I consider to be clear weaknesses in our current system.

TEN

Weaknesses

Chapters Eight and Nine have detailed a number of positive features of the English system as well as some that – with changes – could be made positive. Here I discuss what I consider to be the major weaknesses of the system.

Over-dominance of Westminster

Politicians play a central role in a democratic society. We elect them to represent us, take account of our wishes and make wise decisions on behalf of society. However, to someone who has voted for over 50 years, too often it feels as if, once in government, ministers tend to pursue their own agendas.

Government's intense interest in education in the 19th to 21st centuries has been sporadic. Whereas Arthur Balfour retained his responsibility for the 1902 Education Act when he became prime minister, his 20th-century successors, up to James Callaghan, tended to neglect the subject. Since then, prime ministers seem to have woken up to the global importance of education and Tony Blair made famous the slogan 'Education, education, education'.

Since the 1988 Act education ministers have awarded themselves numerous new powers (there has been a six-fold increase in legislation) and appear to feel entitled to introduce whatever changes they want. Where the government has a substantial majority, and the matter does not trigger a House of Lords revolt, ministers get their way – no matter how foolish their ideas. Readers will have their own examples of absurdity, but mine include Kenneth Clarke's abolition of HMI and the creation of Ofsted, John Patten's introduction of 'specialist schools' in a system already harmed by over-specialisation, David Blunkett's volte-face on selection, Estelle Morris's promotion of faith schools and Michael Gove's expenditure on free schools in a time of austerity.

Why do ministers pursue ideas that frequently are untested, help only a section of the population or are often plain daft? Is it that they employ ill-chosen advisers, pay too much attention to lobbyists or feel that they have the right to ride their own hobby-horses? Probably all of these factors have played a part in the worst policy decisions. But there is a third consideration that applies specifically to education: a seemingly common view that teachers – and what is termed the educational establishment – are not quite up to the task and cannot be trusted to know what is best for the nation's children.

It is as if the status of teaching is still uncertain. In Chapter Five I discussed the evolution of teachers into a mainly graduate profession in the 21st century. Yet old prejudices linger. I suspect that a there is still a perception among politicians that teachers are just not good enough, and so advice from almost anyone else is usually preferred.

In the past, ministers were aided by a Central Advisory Council, authorised by the 1944 Education Act[1] to advise on education issues. In addition, a number of ad hoc committees were set up by the governments of the day to tackle difficult issues and produce independent proposals for their consideration. Some of the most notable committees were: Robbins (1963), recommending the expansion of universities;[2] Bullock (1975), advocating a broader approach to the teaching of reading;[3] and Warnock (1978), creating the concept of special educational needs instead of the existing focus on handicap.[4]

In recent years, governments have appeared nervous of creating anything so powerful. In the 1990s a group led by Claus Moser (a professor of social statistics and distinguished head of an Oxford college), with support from the British Association for the Advancement of Science, the Royal Society, the British Academy and the Royal Academy of Engineering, obtained funding from the Paul Hamlyn Foundation for a National Commission on the state of education in the UK.

The Commission worked for two years. Like the former independent committees, it was made up of experienced people from within and beyond the field of education. It produced a report of great wisdom, supported by a number of research articles and surveys.[5] The report was instantly rejected by the then Conservative minister.

There was an almost identical occurrence during Labour's time in government. A large-scale independent inquiry, funded by the Esmée Fairbairn Foundation, was undertaken by a team of researchers and policy analysts from Cambridge University.[6] Its report is the most comprehensive investigation of primary education since the 1967 Plowden Report. Yet the Labour Minister for Schools claimed that he found it 'at best woolly'.[7] Thus was three years of intensive work jettisoned. In Chapter Twelve I will consider what could be done to limit such autocratic tendencies.

Market model of schooling

Since 1988 our education system has systematically been transformed into a market economy – as if schooling is similar to shopping or using an estate agent. The ideological inspiration for marketisation stems from the work of Milton Friedman. His book *Capitalism and Freedom* provoked a new strategy for governing: new public management.[8] The key elements of this strategy are individualism, competition, choice, privatisation, decentralisation, deregulation and the use of the market in all public services.

Underlying these ideas is the principle that only financial reward can motivate – leading to a mercenary view of people and a rejection of the notion of public service. These ideas have encouraged the disparagement of teachers. For example, 'knaves not knights' is the theme of a book by the English academic and former government adviser Julian Le Grand. He suggests that teachers will generally act in their own interest rather than through any commitment to their pupils or to public service.[9]

Of course, it is true that some limited educational markets have long existed: fee-paying parents generally judge private schools by setting each institution's reputation against its costs. But this applies to only a small proportion of the nation's schools. I note that few prestigious private schools have chosen to create replicas. Eton, founded in 1440, has so far preferred exclusivity to following market principles by opening a second branch (or 'franchising the brand'). However, it seems to have bowed to pressure and is providing a teacher of English for the Newham sixth-form free school that is being opened by a group of private schools.[10]

A major problem with the market approach is that in all developed countries schooling is compulsory. Unlike customers in a shop, parents do not have the freedom to decline to buy anything: they have to send their child to one school or another.

A second problem is that, unlike most commercial organisations that can flourish or go out of business without too many national consequences, schooling is intimately bound up with the future success of society. A good society needs a good system of schooling – and a good system of schooling makes a good society more likely.

It has become increasingly obvious that any market will favour the interests of those likely to be its best customers – the rich and powerful. Such people are adept at discerning the best options for themselves and their families and ensuring, by any means, that they achieve them. Yet, in a country which has an increasingly large gap between the richest and poorest citizens (graphically portrayed by Wilkinson and Pickett in *The Spirit Level*[11]), strategies that further divide the rich and the poor will exacerbate the problem. As a group of researchers note:

> Research increasingly shows that contemporary education policies promoting parental choice, competitive school enrolment, performance league tables and school specialisms generate an ethical framework that encourages and legitimates self-interest in the pursuit of competitive familial advantage.[12]

A third problem for educational markets is that few children welcome changing schools. In my experience, when parents decide to transfer a child from a school that they consider unsatisfactory, they are generally very reluctant to repeat the experience – even if, to their horror, the chosen new school turns out to be worse than the first one. Instead, often prompted by their child, they tend to stay and make the best of the situation.

Furthermore, as I noted in Chapter One, marketisation has created enormous stress for parents and children. My neighbours have a young son. They are already worried – almost to the point of obsession – about his schooling. They are moving home and their choice of where to go has largely been determined by the availability of what they see as a 'good state school'. But, because the school market is so difficult to read, they are planning various back-up strategies, including coaching for the 11-plus, and have already registered their son for a private prep school (where he is 29th on the waiting list). As I write, their child is 22 months old.

My neighbours are not unusual. Talk to any group of parents at primary school gates and their main topic of conversation will be the availability – or not – of places at reasonable secondary schools, curiously drawn catchment zones, designated 'partner school arrangements', to say nothing of faith requirements. The choice of schools has become a nightmare of gamesmanship. The scope for recriminations – and abject guilt if parents make the wrong call – is immense. Imagine how great must be the sum of the parental anxiety caused by this education market. Add the insecurity felt by their children and you get a substantial package of national misery.

Yet this is the system that successive ministers have imposed on our country – without any debate or referendum. In all areas, except where the population is too sparse, they have forced an end to the long-standing tradition of children attending their local school. Choice has become the mantra of successive governments – even though, in reality, parents can only nominate preferences. True choice of pupils is operated only by over-subscribed schools.

Competitive behaviour, by school heads and governing bodies, has been incentivised so that they vie with each other for both pupils and resources. Ministers appear to believe that only the stiffest competition is likely to bring about school improvement. Yet, paradoxically, they have been happy to allocate extra powers and to feed extra funds into their favoured types of schools. In the days of New Labour these were beacon schools, city academies and faith schools.[13] In the Coalition era, the favourites are academies and free schools (regardless of the local need or desire for such provision).[14]

Most reprehensibly, in terms of our democratic entitlement, until 2011 ministers exempted academies from the need for compliance with Freedom of Information legislation. Curiously, it does not seem to have occurred to them that, if markets were indeed the best way to organise education, such obvious attempts to 'fix them' – with secrecy, privileged status and greater resources – would be unnecessary.

The Coalition government seems to want to go further – possibly changing regulations to allow private companies to make a profit by taking over schools from local authorities. Like New Labour before it, the government seems to believe that only private management can be efficient. Stephen Ball, who has written extensively about business interests in education, draws attention to a DfES comment that:

> The era of state-only funding is over ... we must remember that no public service model has ever delivered high quality services for every child.[15]

This is a quite unrealistic criterion of success. 'Every child'! Will the Department apply the same judgement to private sector ventures – no payment unless there is 100% success? Ball also quotes Allyson Pollack (a doughty questioner of the value of PFIs) describing a meeting with Gordon Brown (clearly prior to the banking debacle) in which he repeatedly declared that the public service is bad at management and that only the private sector is efficient and well managed.[16]

There appears to be a wilful blindness to the often excellent management undertaken by local authorities. It is true that the role of chief education officer has been diminished by the corporatisation of local government and affected by the combination of education and childcare responsibilities. The government also seems to have an unrealistic faith in the capability of private management to handle education, despite the fact that takeovers of local authorities have had mixed success.[17] It also seems to be the case that many of the most successful of the new education managers are people who spent years – and honed their skills – working in local authorities. I worked with one particularly outstanding manager in the ILEA. When the authority was abolished, he was hired by a private education company to take over the running of a troubled local authority. He recruited several of his former colleagues and set to work. Ironically, his success was hailed as a victory for private management. Whether or not the government gives the go-ahead for private companies to make a profit, I fear that the marketisation of schooling will turn out to be a grievous mistake.

A 1970 book by Caroline Benn and Brian Simon, reviewing the national moves towards a fully comprehensive system, reported the remarkable progress that had been made.[18] Examination data illustrate the substantial increase in numbers of candidates and in their success: pupils who would not even have taken public examinations in the old secondary modern schools have been achieving success in comprehensives. According to Fiona Millar, writing in 2012:

> Around six times as many pupils get five good GCSEs as did in 1968. Five times as many go on to university and, contrary to one of the best publicised myths, the proportion of students admitted to Oxbridge from state schools has almost doubled since 1961.[19]

Of course, the late-20th-century education system was underfunded and buildings needed to be refurbished. But it was moving in a coherent direction and was contributing to an improving society.

Inexplicably, New Labour, when it came to power, colluded in the myth that comprehensive schooling, managed by local authorities, had failed. Melissa Benn details how New Labour politicians used the same methods as their Conservative predecessors to fund schools differentially, maintain the high-stakes testing programme, promote faith schools, privatise management and further weaken local authorities.[20]

New Labour ministers used their time in office to create schools of different status, continued to publish league tables and relied on targets to raise standards. They were clearly unaware of 'Goodhart's law', formulated by a one-time chief adviser to the Bank of England, who argued that 'when a measure becomes a target it ceases to be a good measure'.[21]

There are many anecdotes about the distorting effects of targets on services: late-running trains, where rigorous punctuality targets sometimes caused drivers to miss out some scheduled stops; hospitals where several simple operations are scheduled, rather than fewer, more complex ones and where waiting lists are manipulated by rebooking appointments.[22]

For Labour, too, the mainstay of accountability has become a 'high stakes' system, with the naming and shaming of those at the bottom a regular occurrence. As I argued earlier, the fly in the ointment of a high-stakes system is that no testing methods are – or can be – robust enough to cope. Tests used to judge pupils or schools will only ever produce a crude estimate. Using results to judge the skills of teachers will be even less accurate, given the potential impact of different home circumstances and numerous other factors – such as the number of teachers involved over a pupil's school career.

Impact of private schooling

R.A. Butler, principal architect of the 1944 Education Act, failed to develop any degree of integration of private schools into the new state system. This possibility had been debated by the 1944 Fleming Committee,[23] but it was unable to agree a satisfactory solution. The inclusion of private schools – with their influences and resources – within a national state system would have been a challenge. But ignoring the problem was bound to create a two-track society.

The private/state distinction is even stronger today. Many aspiring parents – encouraged no doubt by marketing agents – have been persuaded that private schools are always superior to state schools and that they ought to send their children to the former, even if this involves considerable sacrifice. Even Estelle Morris, a former Labour education minister, has been quoted as saying 'State schools have a lot to learn from fee-paying schools'.[24]

The claim of inherent superiority is impossible to prove or disprove. Private schools vary greatly, from the world-famous Eton, Winchester and Harrow to poorly resourced private schools catering mainly for families living abroad. Some might be better than most state schools, but others will be far worse. David Bell, a former Chief Inspector, noted in a 2003 speech to the head teachers of private schools that:

> While the independent sector contains very many schools that are very good, it also includes a number of schools that are among the worst in the country.[25]

Few teachers switch between private and state schools, and those that have done so generally admit that teaching in private schools is much easier.

As I argued in Chapter Six, in order to judge the quality of a school with any validity, it is necessary to know what sort of pupil intake it receives. Self-evidently, private schools are unlikely to take in many pupils from poor families. Even when the assisted places scheme existed (1980–97) to encourage families of modest means to send their children to private schools, few came from working-class families and a number came from middle-class families that had fallen on hard times.[26]

One obvious attraction for parents is the small classes boasted by many private schools (as noted in Chapter Five). In any prospectus this will be a major feature, designed to catch the eyes of anxious parents. Writing in the *Guardian* in defence of her decision to send her daughter to a private school, one parent cites small classes as the key factor: 'What really matters is size – and this is where the state sector is still getting it wrong.'[27] She seems to disregard the difference in the funding of the two sectors, as if most state school teachers would not love to have such small classes.

Most private schools do their best to recruit the most able pupils by holding entrance examinations and conducting interviews. (A small number cater for pupils with learning or behavioural difficulties or with specialised medical problems, but these are the exception.) Furthermore, private schools are much more able than state schools to expel 'undesirable' pupils. These factors do not guarantee success – which is why private schools have their share of failures – but they do help.

The second claim – about parental 'duty' to use private education – is more difficult to deal with. Of course, parents want the best for their children. The problem is how to decide what is the best. Is it a private school, where children will mix with others from, on the whole, only advantaged backgrounds? Or is it a state school with a population from all classes and cultures – perhaps providing a better preparation for life?

The majority of families cannot afford the option of private schooling (nationally, only 7% of pupils actually attend private schools). Some parents may have the resources and yet may not wish to buy privilege. They may have reservations about the pressure on their children of being coached for, and taking, entrance examinations, or they may want to help create a fairer society in which people compete on their own merits rather than being aided by a privileged start.

It seems to me that private schools – no matter how good some of them undoubtedly are and however much they help individual pupils – are divisive. They prevent pupils of different backgrounds from mixing. This perpetuates the social divisions in our society. The 2011 British Social Attitudes Survey, after taking other factors into account, concluded that:

> Private education does, indeed, perpetuate a form of separate development in Britain, or 'social apartheid'.[28]

Moreover, private schools lessen the possibility of pupils with advantaged backgrounds participating in the state system. This means that in some cities state schools will not be likely to receive a balanced intake of pupils. This will accentuate the dilemma facing parents of able pupils.[29] Should they entrust their children to the school despite the lack of balance – and by doing so help the balance to improve – or might this prove too difficult for them? Some do so; others find the risk too much and withdraw regretfully from state education. In some parts of the country, state schools rise and fall in prestige according to their share of middle-class pupils. Such a shortage, perhaps coupled with the appointment of a dynamic new head in a neighbouring school, or even a slight shift in the area's demographics – can send a perfectly good school into a downward spiral.

Furthermore, private schools inevitably encourage snobbery. Even if the teachers refrain from telling their pupils directly that they are better than those in the state sector, this is an attitude that young people can easily pick up and which fosters a sense of entitlement.

Parents – paying high fees – may encourage this in order to reassure themselves that they are getting value for their money. This can lead to what the Social Attitudes Survey research team call 'a sense of superiority bonus'.[30]

Finally, private schools have, over many years, established effective networks of influence. Although 'closed scholarships' to Oxbridge colleges (open only to pupils of a particular school) no longer exist, many private schools use their networks to foster access to our most prestigious universities and, from there, to elite professions. The figures tell the story: from 7% in private schools to 50% of those accepted at Oxbridge colleges. Data from the Social Attitudes Survey also show that the business of government is particularly prone to private schooling, with two-thirds of the current ministers, half of the civil service and two-thirds of senior judges being privately educated.[31]

Undoubtedly, many private schools are excellent and employ highly gifted teachers. They also own impressive buildings and have superb cultural and sporting facilities. To destroy them would be madness. In Chapter Thirteen, I will propose how private schools might be preserved in ways that complement – rather than undermine – state schooling.

Selection

As I noted in Chapter Six, the 1944 Education Act provided universal free secondary education for the first time. But the subsequent Labour government established the tripartite system of grammar, secondary modern and technical schools. The grammar schools had the pick of pupils, yet, despite recruiting the seemingly most able ones, some grammar schools still performed poorly. Many streamed their intakes and, while lavishing the best teachers and the highest expectations on the top stream, wrote off those at the bottom. Melissa Benn cites the 1959 Crowther Report, which states that only 38% of grammar school pupils achieved more than three passes in the GCE examination.[32] Melissa Benn and Fiona Millar also argue that:

> A closer look at the so-called golden age of the grammar schools also shows that the majority of university students came from professional and managerial backgrounds and comparatively few working-class children gained a good education and route out of poverty and low aspirations.[33]

Adrian Elliott, in his research into 1950s schools, presents evidence drawn from documents, pupil accounts and HMI reports that show how uninspiring much of the grammar school teaching actually was. He argues that the minority of pupils from working-class families often encountered low expectations, snobbery and bullying.[34] Brian Jackson and Denis Marsden undertook a detailed study of 88 Huddersfield working-class families with a child at a grammar school. They portrayed children caught between two cultures, with many ultimately rejecting the working-class culture of their parents.[35]

So it appears that grammar schools were not all they were cracked up to be. A myth endures that they were engines of great social mobility, carrying bright children from working-class backgrounds into higher education and prestigious occupations. This was certainly true for some people and they – naturally – are profoundly grateful for the opportunities given to them by their schools. But the reality is that they represent only a small minority. Bernard Barker, a former head teacher, comments:

> Grammar schools may have enabled some exceptional students to achieve success, but there is no evidence of a general improvement in access and opportunity before their eclipse.[36]

The more prosaic reality is that the 11-plus selection process – like any competitive test that draws on accumulated 'cultural capital' (see Chapter Six) that middle-class families can accrue – was heavily biased towards children from middle-class homes. Put simply – the middle classes successfully colonised grammar schools for their own benefit.

Despite the reluctance of politicians to grasp this nettle, local voters made clear their view that a high-stakes test that divided their children into 'academic sheep and goats' at the age of 11 was not acceptable.

Between the 1950s and the 1980s there was, in most local authorities, a steady move away from the grammar/secondary modern divide and a gradual introduction of all-ability comprehensive schools.

The local authority in which I was living in the 1970s was a good example of what happened. A Conservative council was influenced, and finally overwhelmed, by parental pressure so that, in order to remain in office, it introduced a fully comprehensive system.

The popular move towards a comprehensive system, however, was fiercely contested by many traditionalists. The education Black Papers, published by right-wing thinkers between 1969 and 1977, criticised such progressive tendencies and inaugurated a long campaign for the restoration of grammar schools. Publications from the right-wing Hillgate Group[37] influenced the Conservative Party and contributed to the thinking behind the 1988 Education Reform Act. These pressures seem also to have affected Labour governments. As Melissa Benn and Fiona Millar have commented, successive ministers have gone out of their way to preserve existing grammar schools and even to allow comprehensive schools to select a proportion of their pupils.[38]

The decisions by two senior Labour figures to send their sons to grammar schools derailed party education policy just before Labour's 1997 election victory. Moreover, the system under which parents had the opportunity to vote for the abolition of selection in their local areas was skewed in favour of retention. Melissa Benn and Fiona Millar note that:

> In one county it would require more signatures than voted in the last European elections in order to trigger a vote on whether to abolish grammar schools.[39]

Selection remains a major issue for our current education system. It underpins a hierarchy of status, promotes snobbery and prevents many schools from gaining a sufficient share of able pupils. Parents pay for years of tailored coaching for their children's entrance tests, in the hope that it can make a crucial difference. It can. Evidence from studies in Northern Ireland, where the 11-plus was abolished in 2011, show that coaching can increase test scores by 30–40 points[40] and 'the effect of sustained coaching over a period of nine months is substantial'.[41]

A 2009 investigation in Buckinghamshire stated:

> Current research evidence would suggest that unless you can ensure equal effectiveness or access to coaching, then you cannot make assumptions about ability based on the verbal reasoning tests.[42]

Over the years selection has been criticised by, among others, the British Psychological Society[43] and the NFER.[44] The latter showed – in marked contrast to the false claims of Cyril Burt – that IQ tests could seldom be reliable indicators of educability, as they were too prone to significant levels of error. Recent research also shows that children develop at different speeds and at different ages.[45]

Researchers involved with the OECD's international assessment (PISA) have also drawn attention to the detrimental effect of early selection:

> Data suggest that the more and the earlier students are divided into separate groups according to their academic performance, the more the students' socio-economic background matters.[46]

There is an underlying issue at work here that needs to be spelled out: the relationship between ability and socio-economic background.

I know of no evidence showing that children from more advantaged backgrounds are intrinsically more intellectually able than those from disadvantaged ones. But there is substantial evidence that advantaged pupils perform better in most competitive academic situations. The explanation for this – as I noted in Chapter Six – is that pupils from advantaged families able to afford many enrichment activities are likely to excel in competitive tests.

The economist Will Hutton reports that middle-class families in America spend '11 times more than those at the bottom'[47] on just such enrichments. There would likely be the same pattern in many

Children's stress

Children in England are also subject to stresses that stem from society rather from than the education system. At its most basic level, they are more likely to suffer poverty than are adults. Poor adults (in households with income less than 60% of the national median income, once housing costs have been deducted) make up 22% of the population; the proportion of children living in poverty is 30%,[61] up from 14% in 1979.

Child poverty is one of the main reasons why the UK – unlike the Nordic nations – ranks so badly in the Social Justice scale produced by the Berlin-based Bertelsmann Foundation.[62] According to social researchers Richard Wilkinson and Kate Pickett, the UK has a poor record of child well-being, proportion of teenage births, imprisonment, drug abuse, obesity, social mobility and mental illness.[63]

The last Labour government endeavoured to improve children's lives with the provisions of the 2004 Children Act, based on the Green Paper *Every Child Matters*. Children's services were combined at both government and local levels with education, and a Children's Commissioner was appointed to champion the interests of children and young people.[64]

UNICEF Survey

In 2012 the United Nations Children's Fund (UNICEF) examined the proportion of children living in 'relative poverty' in 35 'developed' countries. The definition of relative poverty used was:

> Those children, between birth and 17, living in a household in which disposable income, when adjusted for family size and composition, is less than 50% of the national median income.

The results show that Finland had 5.3%, Norway 6.1%, Denmark 6.5%, Sweden 7.3% and the UK 12.1% of its children living in relative poverty. Most shocking, and almost the highest figure of the 35 countries, was the United States with 23.3%.[65]

The survey shows that the UK has hardly improved the situation for children since the 2007 UNICEF survey of well-being. This showed that the most supportive environments were found in the Netherlands and the Nordic countries. The UK's profile could scarcely be worse. It fell in the bottom third on five of the six dimensions and, when all ranks were aggregated, it sank to the lowest position. Only in 'health and safety' did the UK perform marginally better than most other countries. Possibly the most distressing outcome was that less than 45% of the sample felt that their peers were 'kind and helpful'. The equivalent figure for the Netherlands and for Scandinavian countries was over 70%.[66]

In 2011 Ipsos MORI carried out a follow-up of 3 of the 21 countries in the original (2007) survey: UK, Spain and Sweden. This study found that all families faced greater pressures than in 2007. But UK parents felt that they faced much greater pressure on their time – working long hours and trying to support their children's learning. In comparison to families in the other two countries, they considered that there was greater inequality in our society. They were also more conscious of snobbery – referring to the frequent mockery of 'chavs' and of a materialist culture in which 'brands' were seen as important, with those not having the 'right' ones being mocked.[67]

In 2013, UNICEF reported its 2007 survey in a slightly modified form. The UK had risen to a midway position though it was still well behind the Netherlands and the Nordic countries.[68]

York University happiness index

Further evidence on children's happiness – or lack of it – comes from the work of Jonathan Bradshaw and his colleagues at York University. His team constructed league tables of 'happiness' for 29 of the richest countries in the world. The tables are based on measures of health, education, housing and the environment, the quality of relationships, level of resources given to education, and children's behaviour and risk taking. Again, the Netherlands had the best environment for children, followed by the five Nordic countries. The UK came 21st – almost at the bottom of the table.[69]

ELEVEN

How good is the system?

In Chapter Seven, I posed some questions by which to judge the quality of the English education system. Drawing on the material of the last three chapters – supplemented where necessary – I now present my answers.

How worthwhile are the aims of the system?

Perhaps because of its evolutionary nature, specific aims have never featured much in our education system. Rather, they seem to have been adopted along the way. Aims have often been overly limited and – as philosopher John White has noted – have seldom been accompanied by any justification.[1] The most detailed version was set out in a 2007 revision to the National Curriculum of 1988. The revision stressed the importance of: 'successful learners', 'confident individuals' and 'responsible citizens' but still – unlike the Nordic countries – neglected any aims for strengthening democracy or fostering equality. My answer, therefore, is that the somewhat limited aims of the English system are worthwhile, but underdeveloped.

How appropriate are the structure and governance?

The structure of today's schooling in England, again because so much of it has evolved over many years, is confusing. Primary education is sometimes divided between infant and junior schools and sometimes combined. Transfer to secondary school generally takes place at 11, but, in areas where there are still middle schools, it can vary between 9 and 14 years.

Secondary education now takes place in schools differing in status, governance, funding and power as well as according to whether they are private, selective, single sex or associated with a particular faith. The loss of a common, comprehensive model and the hierarchical nature of the different types of schools that Parliament has created have fragmented what was once a reasonable system.

For 16-year-olds, there are additional confusing options involving a plethora of courses in school sixth forms, further education colleges and a variety of sixth-form colleges and tertiary colleges. Universities and adult education, both outside the scope of this book, are also facing serious problems with cuts to funding and an increasing dependence on high student fees. Adult education, in particular, is a shadow of its former glory.

England pioneered the role of school and college governors and, in my experience it works well.[2] I cannot understand why ministers do not seem to value it more.

The governance of the system as a whole has changed radically with the abolition of many advisory, curriculum or coordinating bodies. Particular losses have been the Central Advisory Council for Education and the Schools Council. The Central Advisory Council produced many influential publications, as I noted earlier. The Schools Council was, for 20 years, an important forum for ministry officials, local authority representatives and the teachers' unions. It managed a series of innovative science, social science and humanities projects. But, since 1988, we have seen an increasing centralisation of powers, with ministers (from all parties) taking more and more decisions over curriculum and pedagogical matters.

My answer, therefore, is that both the current fragmented, marketised structure and the way the system is governed are now unsatisfactory.

How adequate is the funding?

Right from its faltering beginnings as a national system, England's education has been underfunded. The investment of more resources by the last Labour government was necessary and, indeed, led to improvements in facilities and resources, even if not directly in the standards achieved.[3] Under the Coalition government the education budget is being cut, although, as I noted, schools are likely to suffer far less than other parts of the education service.

The ways in which recent governments have channelled extra funding to their favourite kinds of schools are shockingly unfair. Peter Downs, a former head teacher and an expert on educational finance, has calculated that in 2011 the 'bonus' for a school leaving the local authority system in order to become an academy amounted to £445,000,[4] far more than the true cost of remaining within the authority. The bonus probably explains the popularity of many academies, although the first to convert gained the most.

I have already noted my concerns about the lack of accountability of the sponsors of academies and free schools. I was interested to see, from Treasury minutes, that some of the sponsors that promised cash contributions have failed to honour their commitment.

> The Committee was also concerned that some existing sponsors had failed to fulfil the financial contributions they originally pledged to their academies. The status of some of these debts is unclear and, especially as sponsors of new academies are no longer required to make a financial contribution, there is a risk that they will never be paid.[5]

This looks like another unwise financial decision on the part of government.

My conclusion, therefore, is that the funding of the system is barely adequate and is currently distributed on an unfair basis.

How satisfactory are the buildings and equipment?

Because of the inadequacy of funding over previous decades, many educational buildings are no longer appropriate for use today. The previous Labour government's Building Schools for the Future programme set out to improve the nation's stock of educational buildings. The programme was undoubtedly wasteful – especially when it was combined with the PFI. This sometimes involved knocking down schools which could have been refurbished at less cost and then committing schools or local authorities to damaging long-term payments. It is also questionable whether the employment of 'signature architects' to design 'wow-factor' buildings made sense. Norman Foster's Thomas Deacon Academy in Peterborough is reputed to have cost £60 million. Aedas Architects' Holland Park Academy cost £80 million – or, according to the *Times Educational Supplement*, the equivalent of six 1,200-pupil secondary schools built under new ministry guidelines.[6]

Despite these caveats, the Building Schools for the Future programme undoubtedly improved life for many pupils and teachers. Rather than reform the programme, the Coalition government dispensed with it and issued new 'Baseline design guidelines for school buildings'.[7] These guidelines stipulate smaller and cheaper buildings. Premises will be 15% smaller, with reduced space in corridors, assembly halls and dining areas. While public savings are to be welcomed at a time of austerity, these plans appear short sighted. Bad buildings are always poor value for money. They will contrast even more sharply with the superb buildings of many private schools.

In terms of equipment, considerable amounts of money have been spent on computers and technological teaching aids. Judging by my own visits to English state schools, I consider them to be better equipped than those in many other countries – albeit far less well equipped than many private schools.

My conclusion, therefore, is that most buildings are adequate – though future schools may not be – and are reasonably well equipped.

How wise have been the major policies affecting education since 1988?

Among the wise decisions, the following stand out.

- Contentious though it continues to be, the principle of having a National Curriculum is surely right. It does, however, need simultaneously to be both limited in its scope and obligatory for all schools – including independent ones.
- Emphasising the importance of reading (but not the methods chosen).
- Including the study of citizenship in the National Curriculum in order to prepare young people for participation in a democracy.

- Professionalising the training for headship – accepting that a good school leader needs an additional qualification (the qualification was made voluntary in 2011[8]).
- Increasing funding for education and – until the last couple of years – increasing the number both of students and of universities. A 2010 report from the Higher Education Funding Council for England noted a 50% rise in the likelihood of England's poorest young people going to university.[9] (Sadly, this is likely to decline as higher fees and 'more rigorous' A levels do their work.)

But I also need to highlight the following, drawn from what I see as some of the 'least wise' decisions.

- Reducing funds for Sure Start, causing hundreds of centres to close and children and working parents to suffer.
- Increasing the powers of central government and correspondingly reducing those of local authorities.
- Establishing a plethora of different types of schools and turning the system into a market economy.
- Changing the role of academies. Much of the original theory behind academies was praiseworthy: providing the most generous resources for the neediest pupils, allowing freedom for innovations and installing the pupils in 'wow-factor' buildings. But, unfortunately, the way academies were created – through secret negotiations, enhanced funding and exclusion from Freedom of Information legislation – aroused suspicion as to whether they were intended to be a novel way of addressing the challenge of inner-city schooling or an incremental stage in the eventual privatisation of schooling. The Coalition government switched the task of academies – and the accompanying extra resources – from improving struggling inner-city schools to enhancing those already performing well and often enjoying great advantages. Furthermore, even in the face of widespread local opposition, ministers forced some schools to become academies.
- Subverting pupil assessment into a misleading form of school accountability through the use of league tables.

- Promoting the establishment of free schools in areas well served by existing provision at a time of rising pupil numbers elsewhere and cuts in public funding (the first 24 are reputed to have cost around £130 million[10]).
- Selling off playing fields at a time when sport is popular and vital for young people as the nation faces an epidemic of obesity.
- Permitting Kent to plan a satellite grammar school, and so establishing a precedent for other local authorities to extend selection.
- Striving to make all examinations harder – with the expressed intention of raising standards – but blind to the reality that this will simply increase the number of failing pupils and of schools falling below a rising 'floor standard'.[11]
- Approving Ofsted's strategy of making what was previously seen as a 'satisfactory' rating into 'unsatisfactory', with all the subsequent implications for pupils and teachers.
- Permitting the employment of untrained teachers in free schools.

All these decisions appear to me to be ill conceived and potentially highly damaging.

How good are the administrators?

Because much of the work of the people administering the education system is not generally visible, this is a difficult question to answer. I have generally found the ministry civil servants dealing with education information and statistics most helpful. But, in terms of policy work, the civil service appears to me to be stuck in a time warp. It remains over-hierarchical and somewhat elitist. It also seems to me that senior civil servants have lost confidence in their right – and indeed duty – to argue with ministers if they think a policy will do harm. The relationship of ministers to the civil service is a difficult issue – well outside the scope of this book. But is an issue that clearly needs attention.

There have been a number of financial scandals overseen by the ministry. One of the worst concerns the Individual Learning Accounts scheme, designed to enable learners to gain information technology skills. Launched in 2000, this scheme was abandoned in October 2001 when 279 of the 8,500 providers were being investigated for fraud. The House of Commons Select Committee on Public Accounts subsequently reported that fraud and abuse accounted for £97 million.[12]

Another financial scandal involving private higher education colleges seems likely to be uncovered by an investigation by the National Audit Office. These colleges – stemming from the planned expansion of privately run higher education colleges inaugurated by the higher education minister in 2011 – are allegedly benefiting from government subsidies for poorly qualified or otherwise unsuitable students who fail to turn up for classes.[13]

The inspectors working for Ofsted undoubtedly work hard but – in my view – are serving a flawed system and risk undermining the professional confidence and goodwill of teachers.

My impression is that, even though local authorities still vary considerably, their overall competence is reasonably good. This view is supported by a 2012 report from one of the teacher unions.[14]

As noted, the dealings that I have had over the years with school and college governing bodies have given me a positive picture of their contribution.

My conclusion, therefore, is that the major problems stem from misguided political directions rather than from lack of competence.

How inspiring and competent are head teachers?

In general, English head teachers are among the most inspiring and competent of any I have met in the world. As noted earlier, the specific training introduced in 1998 has paid off and heads are increasingly able to cope with the wide-ranging demands on their skills. As I argued in Chapter Six, however, the rising trend of one head running two – or even a string of – schools does not impress me. In my experience, inspiring and galvanising colleagues, pupils and the local neighbourhood is more likely to happen if the head is a full-time member of the school.

How skilled are teachers?

I consider England's teachers to be a prime education asset. They certainly compare well with the many I have seen over the years in other countries. Their weakness, perhaps, is over-compliance. I suspect that this is because of the way they have been treated by successive ministers, aided and abetted by an over-aggressive inspection regime and a frequently critical media. The contrast with how teachers are treated in Finland is stark. The decision to allow non-qualified people to teach in academies and free schools illustrates that ministers still do not value the professional skills of properly trained teachers.

How well does the system work for pupils of different ages?

In my view, the system does not work well for young children of those working parents struggling to find affordable day care. It does not work well for three- to five-year-olds in the less-good nursery provision or for pupils in primary and secondary schools that do not receive balanced intakes.

The system works well for those children lucky enough to experience good nursery provision from age three upwards. It also works well for many children in primary schools, particularly for those in schools with balanced intakes of pupils and likely to do well in the SATs testing. Such schools are in a position to focus energy on the broader aspects of good primary education.

One of the primary schools that I visit regularly is a delight. The school's atmosphere is caring and friendly and it is properly attentive to educational standards. The inspirational head and talented teachers are conscientious and systematic in their approach. They are also committed to the broader aims of education. Behaviour is excellent. The creative arts flourish – last year the whole school, from nursery to Year 6 classes, was involved in a week-long art project. The only problem is that, having enjoyed this haven of stimulating childhood, the 11-year-old pupils are then dispersed among a score of secondary schools of differing types, statuses and reputations.

The system also works well for those secondary pupils lucky enough to attend schools with balanced intakes. These schools can provide a good, all-round education. From a narrow point of view, the system works well for pupils in selective grammar schools. Surrounded by able – and often 'advantaged' – peers, pupils are likely to succeed both academically and in other ways. The same is true for the 7% attending private schools. Although recent research, undertaken for the Department for Education, has found that – on average – university students from less effective state schools can have higher potential and greater staying power than those from private or selective schools.[15] My concerns about both of the latter types of schools relate to the impact they have on the remainder of the system.

The system does not work well for 11-year-olds whose socially or economically disadvantaged parents struggle to gain a place in a secondary school 'uncreamed' by private, selective, faith-based or better-located schools. Finally, it does not work well for children who are unusual – too mature or too immature, or 'looked after children' in the care of local authorities or some of those with special needs (issues to do with special needs have not been addressed in this book) as well as those who suffer socio-economic disadvantage. Many of these children and young people see their initial disadvantages accentuated by their experience in the education system.

Does the system generate well-qualified intellectually curious young people?

In Chapter Eight I described the ways in which pupils are assessed in our system. Here I will focus on what the results reveal.

National tests and examinations

Phonics

Screening of phonics was introduced in 2012.[16] It is compulsory and all six-year-old pupils, other than those in private schools, are tested.

In its second year 69% of those tested reached 'the expected level' of 32 or more marks out of a total of 40 (Table 11.1). Girls outperformed boys. The ethnic group with the best results was from an Indian background. The percentage of pupils eligible for free school meals reaching the expected level was 17% lower than for those who were

Table 11.1: Phonics screening by gender

Gender	% scoring 32 or more
Girls	73
Boys	65
Both	69

not eligible. The two groups with the highest scores were those used to speaking more than one language. It is too early yet to evaluate how the pupils performed subsequently, but it will be interesting to see if this screening helps teachers more effectively to target reading tuition and resources.

Key Stage 1

At the end of Key Stage 1, seven-year-old pupils are assessed by their teachers – taking into account the child's work over the year – in five areas: reading, writing, speaking and listening, mathematics and science. Pupils are considered to have made appropriate progress if they are judged to have reached the 'expected level 2' on the National Curriculum scale of 1–8. There has been virtually no change in the average scores for any subject since 2008.

The percentages reaching the expected level 2 in 2013 are shown in Table 11.2.

Table 11.2: Percentage of pupils achieving the expected level 2 in Key Stage 1 in 2013, by gender (2012 figures in parentheses)

Gender	Reading	Writing	Speaking and listening	Mathematics	Science
Girls	92	90	92	93	92
Boys	86	80	86	90	89
Both	89 (87)	85 (83)	89 (88)	91 (91)	90 (89)

Girls outperformed boys in all five subjects, with the biggest gap being in writing (10%). Pupils with Indian backgrounds had the best results in reading and writing. Those with Chinese backgrounds did best in mathematics. Pupils with Irish backgrounds had the highest proportion doing well in science.

Table 11.3 shows the proportions of pupils performing at higher than the 'expected level'.

Table 11.3: Percentage of pupils achieving at least one stage higher than the expected level in Key Stage 1 in 2013, by gender (2012 figures in parentheses)

Gender	Reading	Writing	Speaking and listening	Mathematics	Science
Girls	33	20	27	21	21
Boys	25	10	19	25	23
Both	29 (27)	15 (14)	23 (22)	23 (22)	22 (20)

Girls outperformed boys in reading, writing, and speaking and listening but scored below boys in mathematics and science. All scores were marginally higher than the previous year.

How good are these Key Stage 1 results? This is a difficult question to answer, given that few National Curriculum statistics have been subjected to independent evaluation. However, 80% or 90% achieving the expected level looks pretty good – especially as around 20% of pupils exceeded this and achieved higher levels. But much depends on how reliable the assessments are (remember the views of the three professors cited in Chapter Seven) and on how accurately the 'expected levels' were calculated in the first place.

Key Stage 2

Tests provided by the Standards and Testing Agency in English and mathematics are mandatory for all 10- to 11-year-old pupils at the end of Key Stage 2. These externally set and marked individual tests are complemented by teacher assessment (of the whole year's work) in English, reading, writing, mathematics and science. The expected level to be achieved is level 4. The proportions of pupils reaching level 4 or higher in 2013 are shown in Table 11.4.

Girls outperformed boys in reading. The percentages for boys were the same as for girls in mathematics. Reading scores were marginally lower and mathematics slightly higher than the previous year's.

Scores in 2013 for both reading and mathematics were slightly higher when assessed by teachers than in the tests.

Table 11.4: Percentage of pupils achieving the expected level 4 or higher in Key Stage 2 tests in 2013, by gender (2012 figures in parentheses)

Gender	Reading	Mathematics
Girls	88 (90)	85 (84)
Boys	83 (84)	85 (84)
Both	86 (87)	85 (84)

The proportions of pupils performing higher than the expected level are shown in Table 11.5.

Table 11.5: Percentage of pupils achieving at least one grade higher than the expected level in Key Stage 2 tests in 2013, by gender (2012 figures in parentheses)

Gender	Reading	Mathematics
Girls	48 (54)	39 (36)
Boys	41 (43)	43 (42)
Both	45 (48)	41 (39)

This shows that almost half of the girls and over 40% of the boys exceeded the 'expected level' by at least one level in reading and that 43% of boys and 39% of girls did the same in mathematics. Table 11.6 shows the proportions of pupils reaching level 4 in the Teacher Assessment of the five subjects.

Table 11.6: Percentage of pupils achieving level 4 or higher in Key Stage 2 teacher assessments in 2013, by subject and gender (2012 figures in parentheses)

Gender	English	Reading	Writing	Mathematics	Science
Girls	90 (89)	91 (90)	88 (87)	87 (86)	89 (88)
Boys	83 (81)	84 (83)	78 (76)	86 (85)	86 (85)
Both	87 (85)	87 (86)	83 (81)	87 (85)	88 (86)

Girls performed better than boys in all subjects; mathematics had the smallest gap (1%) and writing the largest (10%). There were marginal gains over the 2012 results.

How good are these Key Stage 2 results? Again, this is a difficult question to answer. When the assessments were first introduced, 'expected levels' had to be calculated on the basis of the statistical analysis of pilot tests using samples of pupils.[17] These pilots would have produced various statistical measures. The measures would have included the mean and median, the standard deviation and the standard error.[18] From these data a test provider would have to judge what level could reasonably be expected from the majority of the age group – hence creating an 'expected level'. Obviously this has to be lower than the average, which would always occur in the middle of the range and be above 50% of the pupils.

There should certainly have been a general improvement since the 1988 Education Act as the idea of regular assessment became more common and teachers learned how to operate the system (influenced no doubt by the dire penalties of being in a 'failing school' slipping below the 'floor standard') and improved both their teaching and pupils' learning. Readers may well wonder, therefore, why there have been so many accusations of grade inflation at the GCSE – as discussed in Chapter Nine.

The percentages look pretty good and, where the assessments can be compared to previous years, there have been slight increases. The Standards and Testing Agency[19] clearly makes considerable efforts to ensure that the standards of the test remain as constant as possible. But with so many changes in assessment procedures this is a difficult task, drawing on statistical evidence and the judgement of expert markers – a mix of science and art. The Agency stresses that 'the level setting process is observed by representatives for the teacher associations and unions'.[20]

Key Stage 4 (GCSE)

The GCSE was described in Chapter Seven and commented upon in Chapter Nine. In Table 11.7, I report the latest results for maintained schools.

Table 11.7: Percentage of pupils in all state-funded mainstream schools achieving five or more A*–C GCSE grades or equivalents and those achieving the English baccalaureate in 2013, by gender (2012 figures in parentheses)[21]

Gender	5+ A*–Cs or equivalent	5+ A*–Cs or equivalent (including English and maths)	English baccalaureate
Girls	86.5 (86.3)	65.7 (63.7)	27.5 (19.2)
Boys	79.6 (79.8)	55.6 (54.2)	18.3 (13.5)
Both	84.0 (84.0)	60.7 (59.3)	22.9 (16.3)

Girls achieved considerably better results than boys on each of the measures. And results generally improved over 2012. These results include what are termed 'equivalents'. These are qualifications/grades gained on vocational courses – including those that are worth four GCSE A*–C grades, as discussed in Chapter Nine. I asked the ministry, during the last Labour government, for a breakdown of the impact of 'equivalents' on the results but was informed that this information was not analysed. It obviously is now, and I have been able to view its effect in 2012. In schools termed 'comprehensive' the addition of 'equivalents' lifted the percentage from 54.9 to 81.2, and in academies it rose from 38.4 to 82.6.[22]

How good are these Key Stage 4 results? This question is also difficult to answer. They appear to be good. As I have noted, about six times as many pupils achieve five good GCSEs as did so in the GCE in 1968. A research paper describing the situation in 1976 illustrates the scale of all that has changed:

> Students took O level, aimed at the top 20% of the ability range, or CSE, aimed at the next 40% of the ability range, leaving 40% of 16 year olds for whom there was no specific national school leaving qualification. Less than 20% of the cohort stayed at school beyond 16, about 15% took A levels, and less than 10% went to university – there were only 46 universities in the UK.[23]

In comparison, today's results look good, but questions about the value of 'equivalents' and about grade inflation need to be resolved by well-conducted, independent research. As I have commented, if the steadily increasing SATs scores have been well calibrated with the GCSE, corresponding increases should be expected. As a writer in the *Times Educational Supplement* puts it, 'It is simply insane that teachers and schools are expected to show ongoing improvements in a system engineered to ensure results stay the same'.[24] Whether the examinations are a good use of resources and whether they are appropriate for life in our society today are different questions that I will address in Chapter Twelve.

A level and equivalent studies

A levels and their equivalents were described in Chapter Seven and commented upon in Chapter Nine. Here I will simply report the results for all schools for 2013 (Table 11.8).

Table 11.8: Percentages of all school pupils achieving A levels or equivalents in 2013, by gender (2012 figures in parentheses)

	Passes equivalent to at least 2 GCE/ Applied A levels	AAB grades or better	3 or more A* or A grades	Average point score per student
Female	98.4 (98.0)	22.9 (22.5)	13.9 (13.6)	814.2 (809.2)
Male	97.6 (97.2)	22.4 (21.9)	14.7 (14.4)	786.2 (780.6)
Both	98.0 (97.6)	22.7 (22.2)	14.3 (13.9)	801.0 (795.7)

Well over 90% of both female and male entrants achieved the equivalent of two A levels – up marginally from the figure for the previous year. Nearly 23 per cent achieved two As and a B grade or better in a selection of subjects nominated by the DfE. Just over 14% of entrants achieved three or more A* or A grades, a slightly higher figure as compared to 2012. Males achieved a marginally higher proportion of high grades, even though females notched up a considerably higher overall point score (814.2 as opposed to 786.2).

How good are these A level and equivalents results? They certainly look good. Passes in two A levels was the requirement for a university place for the 10% of the age group that gained admission in the 1970s. Today this is achieved by over 98% of students who enter these examinations. The average point score per student in 2013 is slightly higher than in 2012. The results of these national examinations are impressive, but an important question, as with the GCSE, is whether the examination is appropriate for our modern world – in terms not just of how demanding it is, but also of whether it is eliciting the right kinds of skills, knowledge and understanding. I will return to this topic in Chapter Thirteen.

Until a few years ago these would have been the total data available to answer the question of whether the education system produced academically able, well-qualified young people. Now, however, there is also a set of international tests to help complete the answer.

International tests

As international tests have become more reliable, it has become possible to ask questions of how well the education systems of different countries work. Previously, each country tended to consider that its system was good – often 'the best'. No other country possessed sufficient evidence to dispute such a claim. The situation changed with the growing sophistication of educational testing and the creation of different sets of international data. Today, the publication of assessment programmes is anxiously awaited by politicians and educators.

The three best-known programmes are:

- Progress in International Reading Literacy Study (PIRLS)
- Trends in Mathematics and Science Study (TIMSS)
- Programme for International Student Assessment (PISA).

All international assessments are open to criticism. The challenge of having to treat pupils from up to 50 nationalities in a common manner is daunting. Pupils from a range of cultural backgrounds may react in different ways to common questions, and even to a common formal testing situation. Clearly, it should not be the intention of test designers to iron out such cultural differences (which may be crucially important to the identities of different peoples). It is vital, however, that the existence of such differences be borne in mind when interpreting test outcomes.

Some questions may vary in difficulty in different translations and some languages will be more difficult than others – those with the most regular grammatical constructions, for instance, may be less likely to generate spelling problems.

With any sample survey of an age group (as opposed to a census that includes everyone) there will always be questions about the representativeness of the selected group. For instance, have those with learning difficulties been included in the correct proportion?[25] There are also dangers that some countries will seek to over-represent their most able students in the sample. There is an account of the chosen sample in one country being accompanied into the be-flagged test room by the national youth band[26] (no pressure there, then).

All international tests, however, suffer from methodological and statistical limitations. For instance, the tests assess a very limited amount of what is taught in schools. Furthermore, the manner in which their results are presented encourages a superficial 'league table' reading of what is inevitably a complex picture.[27]

In May 2014 a group of prominent international academics wrote to Andreas Schleicher, the director of PISA, listing reservations about the tests and requesting that the next round of assessments be postponed.[28]

Progress in International Reading Literacy Study (PIRLS)

PIRLS is a programme of reading assessment.[29] It was first used in 2001 to compare attainment in, and attitudes towards, the reading attainment of 9- to 10-year-olds in 35 countries. It was repeated in 2006 with more countries participating. The latest tests were taken in 2011 by 4,000 pupils from 150 primary schools in England. The results were reported in December 2012 and are shown in Table 11.9.

The 2011 results show that most English 10-year-olds scored significantly above the mean score (500) for all those taking part. England's score was significantly higher than its score for the equivalent age group in 2006. But there was a large gap between those who did well and those who did badly on the test (109 points).

Table 11.9: Mean reading scores and the achievement gap between those gaining the highest and the lowest scores for England and the Nordic countries in PIRLS 2011 (2006 scores in parentheses)

Country	Mean score	Achievement gap
England	552 (539)	109
Denmark	554 (546)	85
Finland	568 (n/a)	83
Norway	507 (498)	83
Sweden	542 (549)	83
Mean score for all participating countries	500 (500)	

Note: The achievement gap in each country is the difference between the average score of its top 25% and the average score of its bottom 25%.

Finnish 10-year-olds had a significantly higher mean score and a much smaller achievement gap (83). The scores of both Finland and England were significantly higher than those of Norway and Sweden. The only country (of those shown) where the 2011 score was significantly lower than in 2006 was Sweden. Girls outperformed boys in England, as they did in all participating countries.

The test has two components – one concerned with literary, and the other with informational, purposes. English pupils gained similar scores in each. However, they reported less positive attitudes to reading than did pupils in many other countries. Only 26% of English pupils claim to like reading, while 20% report not doing so. These attitudes, however, were similar to those of the Nordic pupils. Even in Finland only 26% report that they like reading and over 20% report that they do not. Such figures contrast markedly with pupils in Portugal (46% report liking reading and only 3% claim not to do so), Canada (35% and 14%) and Germany (34% and 16%).

Trends in Mathematics and Science Study

TIMSS is a study of the mathematics and science achievements of 9- to 10-year-old and 13- to 14-year-old pupils. It was first conducted in 1995 and has been repeated every four years.[30] The scores for England and the Nordic countries in 2011 can be seen in Tables 11.10 and 11.11.[31]

The mathematics results (Table 11.10) for the younger pupils show that England scored highly – well above each of the Nordic countries (Finland's 9- to 10-year-olds did not participate with this age group) and the overall average. They were significantly outscored only by Singapore, Korea, Hong Kong, Chinese Taipei, Japan and Northern Ireland (which was judged separately). In comparison to the results in 2006, the 9- to 10-year-old English pupils maintained the scores they had achieved then (an extra 10 points on the 2001 scores). English boys' scores were three points above those of English girls. The only criticism is that the achievement gap between those at the top and at the bottom had increased since 2006 and was markedly greater for the English sample (122) than for any of the Nordics (87–92).

Table 11.10: Mean grade in mathematics scores for 9- to 10- and for 13- to 14-year-olds and achievement gap between top and bottom of the distribution in TIMSS 2011 for England and the Nordic countries (2006 scores in parentheses)

Country	Mean score for 9- to 10-year-olds	Achievement gap	Mean score for 13- to 14-year-olds	Achievement gap
England	542 (541)	122 (113)	507 (513)	119 (115)
Denmark	537 (523)	92 (93)	(n/a)	(n/a)
Finland	545 (n/a)	91 (n/a)	514 (n/a)	89 (n/a)
Norway	495 (473)	91 (102)	475 (469)	89 (92)
Sweden	504 (503)	87 (89)	484 (491)	92 (93)
TIMSS average	500 (500)		500 (500)	

Note: The achievement gap is the difference in each country between the average score of its top 25% and the average score of its bottom 25%.

The English 13- to 14-year-olds gained a score of 507 (well below the score of 513 in 2006). Ostensibly, this was considerably less impressive than the score of their younger peers. But only Korea, Singapore, Chinese Taipei, Hong Kong, Japan and the Russian Federation significantly out-scored them. The scores of the Nordic countries were much lower, except for that of Finland (514), but, as in the scores for the younger pupils, they showed a smaller achievement gap (89–92) than England (119, four points higher than 2006). The average score for English girls was three points higher than that for English boys.

In science, English 9- to 10-year-olds performed well – although significantly worse than in 2006 (down 13 points). Korea, Singapore, Finland, Japan, the Russian Federation, Chinese Taipei, the United States and the Czech Republic gained statistically significantly higher scores. In the Nordic countries Finland had a very high score, Sweden was a little better and Denmark was similar to England. Norway, despite showing a considerable improvement on its 2006 score, performed significantly worse than all the other Nordic countries. The English achievement gap was considerably greater than that of any of the Nordic countries (110 compared to 85–100). English 9- to 10-year-old girls and boys performed at almost exactly the same level.

The English 13- to 14-year-olds' score was 533 – again one of the highest, with only Singapore, Chinese Taipei, Korea, Japan and Finland significantly outperforming them. (Slovenia, the Russian Federation and Hong Kong had higher scores but the difference was not statistically significant.) The scores, however, were considerably lower (but not statistically significantly so) than those for 2006 (down nine points). The Nordics – except for Finland – did much less well. But the English achievement gap was again much larger (117) than Finland's (88). The difference between the genders was small, with English girls gaining just three points more than English boys.

Table 11.11: Mean science scores for 9- to 10- and for 13- to 14-year-olds and achievement gap between top and bottom of the distribution in TIMSS 2011 for England and the Nordic countries (2006 scores in parentheses)

Country	Mean score for 9- to 10-year-olds	Achievement gap	Mean score for 13- to 14-year-olds	Achievement gap
England	529 (542)	110 (105)	533 (542)	117 (116)
Denmark	528 (517)	95 (102)	(na)	(na)
Finland	570 (na)	86 (na)	552 (na)	88 (na)
Norway	494 (477)	85 (101)	494 (487)	97 (101)
Sweden	533 (525)	100 (97)	509 (511)	108 (104)

Note: The achievement gap is the difference in each country between the average score of its top 25% and the average score of its bottom 25%.

Despite the drop in scores, the TIMSS results remain very good. In both mathematics and science, English pupils outperformed almost all the other European countries and were overshadowed mainly by Pacific Rim nations. Furthermore, England was one of the countries in which there were no significant gender differences in the results for either age group. But, worryingly, the tests also revealed that the achievement gaps between the highest- and the lowest-performing groups of English pupils were usually much higher than those of their Nordic peers. While the quality of the TIMSS performances in mathematics and science is good, the equity is not. Yet it is possible to combine the two – as Finland is able to demonstrate. Furthermore, larger proportions of English pupils reported not enjoying either mathematics or science than did many of their international peers, although Finnish pupils generally reported enjoying them even less.

Programme for International Student Assessment

PISA was launched in 1997. It involves triennial cycles of tests in reading literacy, mathematical and scientific competence of national samples of 15-year-old students. Unlike the other test programmes, the basic purpose of PISA is not to test school subjects but to consider how well pupils in different countries 'are prepared to meet the challenges of today's knowledge society'.[32] The programme, therefore, should not be affected by the presence or absence of particular curriculum subjects. It is building up a pattern of how the various achievements of different countries have changed over time.[33] In 2000 the initial survey focused on reading literacy; three years later its focus was on mathematical competence. In 2006 the emphasis was on scientific competence and in 2009 it returned to reading literacy. In 2012 it focused again on mathematical competence.

As noted earlier, PISA has been much criticised. My considered view is that this criticism has been somewhat overstated. I have already commented on the limitations of international data sets. Nevertheless, I believe them to be extremely useful tools which any country can use to explore its own system of education. PISA will seldom provide clear answers but it will certainly frame useful questions.

The UK results are difficult to interpret because of the low participation rate in 2000 and the even lower rate in 2003.[34] The score in literacy ostensibly dropped from 523 in 2000 to 499 in 2012. In mathematics, the fall was from 529 in 2000 to 494 in 2012. In science the slippage was less marked – from 532 in 2000 to 514 in 2012. While observing due caution with these results, I believe it is fair to note the downward direction of the scores.

The 2000 results of PISA had been welcomed as a sign of how well the Labour government was doing in improving the education system. (In fairness, the pupils being tested then would have spent all but a couple of years in a system run by a Conservative government.)

The 2003 results were hardly discussed because, due to the refusal of some schools to take part, the UK sample was too small for the OECD to be certain that it was truly representative. The results were omitted from the published report. Subsequent statistical analysis commissioned by the ministry in the UK revealed that the sample was slightly better than 'representative'. The results – which showed a decline in literacy, mathematics and science from those of 2000 – would probably have been worse had the sample been a normal one. The 2006 results confirmed the decline from 2000 – yet they received remarkably little press coverage.

The results from 2012 can be seen in Table 11.12.

Table 11.12: Mean reading, mathematics and science scores in PISA 2012 for the UK and the Nordic countries (2000 scores in parentheses)

Country	Reading	Achievement gap	Maths	Achievement gap	Science	Achievement gap
UK	499 (523)	129 (137)	494 (529)	131 (122)	514 (532)	136 (136)
Denmark	496 (497)	113 (132)	500 (514)	112 (117)	498 (481)	125 (144)
Finland	524 (546)	127 (116)	519 (536)	114 (108)	545 (538)	123 (117)
Norway	504 (505)	131 (139)	489 (499)	124 (126)	495 (500)	135 (132)
Sweden	483 (516)	142 (125)	478 (510)	128 (124)	485 (512)	135 (132)
OECD mean	496 (500)	128 (136)	494 (500)	128 (136)	501 (500)	127 (141)

In the measure of reading achievement, Finland had the highest scores, of the countries shown, in both 2000 and 2012. Between these dates, Sweden, the UK and Finland dropped over 20 points. But, because of their different starting point, Sweden ended up some 13 points below the mean for the OECD countries, the UK just above, while Finland remained 28 points above. In contrast, both Denmark and Norway remained stable respectively just below and just above the mean.

The country with the most serious achievement gap in reading in 2000 was Norway (139); the one with the least was Finland (116). But, by 2012, both Sweden (+17) and Finland (+11) had increased this gap, while Denmark had reduced its gap by 19 points.

In mathematics, Finland had the highest scores for both years though the second figure was 17 points lower. The UK and Sweden dropped over 30 points and Denmark and Norway had dropped by 14 and 10 points. By 2012, Sweden's mean score was 16 points below the OECD mean but Finland's was still 25 points above it.

The country with the biggest achievement gap in mathematics was Norway, and that with the smallest was Denmark. By 2012, Finland and Sweden had increased this gap though the country with the largest gap and largest increase was the UK (131). Denmark and Norway had both reduced the gap but only by small amounts.

In science, Finland had the highest mean scores in both years (144 and 125), and Denmark, from a low starting point, had increased its mean score by 17 points. Sweden and Denmark had dropped (by 27 and 18 points) with the result that Sweden ended up some 16 points below the OECD mean.

Denmark had the most serious achievement gap in 2000 (144) followed closely by the UK (136) and Finland had the smallest (117). By 2012, the UK had the largest gap, and even Finland had increased its gap by 6 points. Only Denmark was able to boast a sizeable reduction.

The small UK sample in 2000[35] and the especially small one in 2003 prevent any certainty. Nevertheless, the data suggest at best a flat-lining and at worst a downward trend in the skills of UK pupils over the decade. This view has been disputed by, for instance, John Jerrim of the Institute of Education.[36] He has sought to explain the decline in scores by the entry into PISA of new countries (although these are mostly not high performing), the bringing forward of the test schedule in 2009 to avoid the GCSE examination season, and the impact of schools opting out of the 2000 test sessions.

My view is that these factors, important though they may be, are not sufficient to overcome the trend in UK scores. However, PISA scores tell a different story to the more positive TIMSS results. The discrepancy might be because, as I noted, TIMSS is more closely related to the school curriculum, while PISA attempts to estimate how well young people cope in the 'knowledge society'. Perhaps English pupils have learned how to perform well in tests when they are fairly similar to SATs but do less well with the different approach of PISA?

Finland – the European country that has excelled in most of the PISA results – participated in only the 2011 TIMSS. However, these results, together with Finnish PISA results, demonstrate that excellence and equity can work together. Finland's high average scores are generally combined with the smallest achievement gaps.

In Denmark and Norway young people do not perform particularly well in TIMSS or in PISA. But they go on to increase their skills, either in the Danish voluntary year 10 (which I described in Chapter Six) or in the upper secondary phase of schooling, with the result that these two countries end up with well-educated adult populations. Their slow, patient approaches to education – avoiding early and unnecessary failure – seem to pay off. Sweden's results suggest a steady decline.

So what is my conclusion about the UK from the results of the international test programmes? A 'mixed bag' is the answer. There are varied results for reading (PIRLS); generally good ones overall for mathematics and science curriculum-based tests – although it is disturbing that there are such achievement gaps (TIMSS); and rather disturbing results for the different approach of PISA. In the 2012 global study of 50 countries undertaken by the Economist Intelligence Unit and published by Pearson, the UK is ranked sixth behind Finland, South Korea, Hong Kong, Japan and Singapore. The rankings draw on published international data supplemented by literacy rates, school attendance and university graduation rates. Unfortunately, the inclusion of higher education data makes interpretation of the quality of schooling impossible.

It is also difficult to make sense of the relationship of the international data to SATs, GCSEs and A levels. But, as Andreas Schleicher, an OECD education expert, argues:

> in this rapidly changing world the benchmark is the best-performing education systems internationally, not improvement by national standards.[37]

It seems to me that under all recent governments English pupils have been well trained in taking tests.[38] I have already noted the 'teaching to the test' commented upon by the House of Commons Select Committee[39] and the lengthy practising of tests reported by Warwick Mansell.[40] I have also drawn attention to how schools are frequently inspected and teachers are ruthlessly judged. Yet these measures do not appear to have created an outstanding system, according to Schleicher – 'the PISA results have remained flat'.[41]

The PISA scores have been (perhaps over-hastily) grasped by Coalition ministers and used to condemn the policies of the previous Labour government.[42] Ironically, however, rather than reversing the policies espoused by Labour (universal testing, frequent inspection and the use of an education market), ministers have further emphasised them.

So, to return to my question of whether the English system generates well-qualified, intellectually curious young people, my answer is that it produces lots of young people good at passing tests and examinations. But I am less convinced that the system generates the intellectually curious. I fear that our system may depress rather than stimulate such a characteristic. In the next chapter I will sketch out my suggestions as to how the system could be adapted to give them a better education through which to develop and deploy their undoubted talents and energy.

Does the system bring about happy and well-adjusted young people?

The evidence from international surveys of well-being, described in Chapter Ten, suggests that our system also fails to produce a preponderance of happy and well-adjusted young people. Of course, many pupils are happy and well-adjusted but too many appear to be anxious and unhappy. This is bad news for our society.

Conclusion

The English education system possesses many strengths of which the country can justly be proud. It has a number of characteristics – which I have termed 'ambiguous features' – that could become positive. But it also has a number of problems that need to be addressed.

In my view, many of the problems have been predominantly caused by the direct actions of politicians across the political spectrum. They have fragmented – almost to destruction – what was once a national system, albeit one haphazardly developed and poorly funded. This system could have been built on and improved. Instead, it has steadily been undermined. The TALIS Survey of 2013 reported that 79% of heads (far more than the international average) gave the view that government regulation and policies prevented them from being more effective.[43]

We are left with a muddled system in which pre-schooling is inconvenient and expensive and pupils are divided into those attending a small, but hugely influential, private sector or a bewildering mix of competing schools, differentially funded and differently empowered. Pupils are allocated into streams or sets and subject to different levels of expectations. Scope for innovation and development is sorely limited. Stress is common and for many the experience of childhood is unnecessarily negative.

My considered verdict is that – rather than an effective education system capable of meeting the needs of society – England's system is failing. Yet let me repeat, I have seen some of the best classroom teaching of any country I have visited and I have been impressed by many inspirational English head teachers. My observations, over almost 50 years, convince me that it is not teachers that are the problem. It is the system in which they have to work. I remain hopeful that this system can yet be repaired. How this can happen is what I discuss in Chapter Thirteen.

TWELVE

A better system?

If we were able to tear up our current system and create a better one overcoming all the problems I have discussed, what would we want it to be like?

Real or virtual?

Do we want – or need – a physical system of schools and colleges? Or are the advances in technology so good that we might prefer a virtual system?

The arguments for a virtual system are persuasive. Many homes are already wired and, with the advent of 4G signals, not even wiring will be necessary: information will be available on the internet. Teaching packages – often involving star academic performers from the world's most prestigious universities – are being developed. Furthermore, children and young people seem to have a natural ability to handle technology. So why go to the expense of maintaining an actual education system, with all the problems I have discussed, if a virtual one will do the job?

This is the challenge thrown down by those who point to the availability on the internet not only of information but of whole courses of study and methods of assessment. They question why anyone would wish to send their child to a school with less up-to-date equipment than they might routinely possess in their home.

But there is another side to this argument. Consider the realities facing children who remain in their homes for their education. They could not be left at home on their own every day and, if they had a parent who worked from home, both might find it stultifying.

The family is a great institution, but, in even the best ones, both children and adults might chafe at constantly being in each other's company with no room to let off steam or mix with people of their own age. Furthermore, while families with large gardens – in which pupils can play, be creative or conduct botanical research – might find the situation acceptable, those in city tower blocks would be more likely to experience claustrophobia. The strains on family life caused by such confinement could rapidly become intolerable.

E.M. Forster's 1909 novella, *The machine stops*, tells of how increasing dependence on a machine leads to almost total isolation of humans and the worship – until it breaks down – of the machine.[1] This remarkably prescient story eloquently makes the case for human contact. And human contact, for children, means having somewhere safe, administered by trusted adults, in which to play, learn and communicate as part of their development.

In my view, for the foreseeable future, we are likely to need a real education system based in schools. So what, then, should the system be like?

Democratically led

A national education system will need a minister to oversee it, provide support and, if necessary, take action to defend its quality. A central government ministry is required in order to coordinate education with other policy areas, ensure adequate funding and define national priorities. The question of whether the ministry should do more than this is debatable. Our country is relatively small and nowhere is more than a day's journey from the capital. In theory, the system could be managed by central government. But, while the land mass might be small, the population (56.1 million in 2014) is not. For this reason, local government appears to be the appropriate democratic middle tier to take responsibility for educational provision and quality.

Unfortunately, recent trends in England have been moving in a contrary direction: increasing, rather than decreasing, the powers of the minister. Many new educational powers have been garnered by central government since 1988.[2] All academy chains have to sign specific funding agreements with the minister. This raises the question: how can a ministry, based in London, deal satisfactorily with all the issues formerly dealt with by officials in over 300 local authorities who were fully aware of the context and history of their schools?

I consider that there still needs to be a local body elected by – and answerable to – voters to oversee all the schools in its area.

This view is in sharp contrast that of James O'Shaughnessy, a former government policy adviser, who claims that local authorities have no legitimate role to play. He and I are in agreement that the ministry will never have the capability to deal with the problems of schools and that schools are more likely to improve if they collaborate. But, whereas I see the obvious solution to be a democratically elected authority, he opts for a profit-making private company. Finally, and perhaps with a certain irony, O'Shaughnessy suggests that any criticism of his views must be ideological.[3]

In my view, the school supervisory authority could be either a dedicated school board, as is common in the US, or a committee of the local authority, as was the case in England for nearly 100 years before ministers began to usurp their powers. England has a good tradition of central–local government partnerships. This cooperation was well described by a former minister, George Tomlinson, and his permanent secretary in a 1950 Government report:

> This is the story of a progressive partnership between the central department, the local education authorities and the teachers in schools. To build a single, but not uniform, system out of many diverse elements; to widen educational opportunity and, at the same time, to raise standards; to knit the educational system more closely into the life of an increasingly democratic and industrialised community.[4]

Although now more than 60 years old, this view still seems admirable. I recommend, therefore, that we reassert local democracy and plan a new system to be overseen by elected local representatives.

Whether these should be the same elected councillors that form the local authority, or a special board directly elected on the basis of their interest and expertise in educational matters, is an interesting question that would need to be resolved. The first model is more likely to ensure that education is integrated with other local services. The second, the school board model, is more likely to attract knowledgeable members of the community. Either model seems to me to be acceptable. The important thing is that responsibility should be held locally and those taking decisions should be democratically answerable to the local electorate. In 2014, the Labour Party published a new policy paper about the middle tier.[5] Known as the Blunkett Report, the paper proposed the establishment of a set of independent local directors of school standards (DSS). These posts would be based regionally and would relate to local authorities and all providing bodies in the region. My initial reaction is that the proposal is interesting in its novelty but the document provides insufficient information about potential costs, staffing, powers and structure for an adequate consideration of its advantages over established local authority structures.

Functional and well-designed buildings

We like institutions to look pleasing, and good, functional architecture tends to lift the spirits. Whether architecture influences what goes on inside the building is less certain. We will all be aware of impoverished buildings in which excellent work nevertheless occurs, and of their converse. But if we were starting from scratch, we would certainly want the most attractive, best designed, schools that could be afforded. These are what some private schools possess and what the previous Labour, and to some extent the present Coalition, governments have tried to provide. But, unfairly, 'wow-factor' buildings have mainly been provided for each government's favourite types of schools.

In an ideal system we would surely want all educational buildings to be of high quality. We would also want them used efficiently – not just during school hours. There is a good argument to be made for a school's accommodation to be shared with community organisations providing childcare or after-school and weekend services and adult classes. There will be issues over ownership, and joint use will inevitably produce problems, but – with enough goodwill – these should not be unsolvable. The value for money and the benefits to the community are obvious.

We would also want all institutions to have the best equipment and facilities: libraries (still useful), computer suites, science laboratories, music and art rooms and, of course, provision for many different sports. The contrast between what most state schools have and what many private schools offer is startling. Greater parity would be welcome.

Inspiring teachers

It goes without saying that society will still need well-qualified, expertly prepared teachers and support staff, able to inspire pupils to learn and able to foster the many positive attributes that we expect young people to develop during their education.

It is of paramount importance that teachers and support staff strive to instil in their pupils a love of learning. And this – as teachers well know – is challenging. It might be easy in a one-off presentation, or in the Royal Institution annual lectures, but giving challenging and stimulating classes daily, year upon year, is extremely demanding. Bored or exhausted teachers will seldom inspire. An effective education system will need, therefore, to find new ways to keep staff fresh and enthusiastic. We know, from the longitudinal research of civil servants already cited,[6] that the more control people have over their work, the better they feel. This is why I have doubts about initiatives designed to be 'teacher-proof' (such as the literacy hour introduced by the last Labour government).

Reduce the teacher to a learning technician, and that is how the teacher will act. Top-down programmes inhibit innovative acts inspired by flashes of insight and foster dull compliance and increasing boredom. We need to give teachers more control, involving them more in the overall planning of syllabuses, working as a team, sharing ideas and monitoring each other's work.

One of the most effective ways of improving teaching skills that I have seen is through reciprocal observation. This involves pairs of teachers observing each other in turn, once a week over a term or so. After each observation session the observer gives feedback to his or her partner on the quality of the teaching and on the impact it has seemed to have on pupils. The next time the roles are reversed. The system is confidential to the pair – so that the participants can be frank – and it is reciprocal. Each participant has the chance to criticise and be criticised. Each pair will come to realise that flattery is a waste of time and that destructive criticism exacerbates, rather than helps to solve, problems.

Some teachers will nevertheless fail to take steps to keep up to date and action will be needed to ensure that pupils do not suffer. This is the task of the head of department or, in primary schools, the head of the key stage. As in any other job, how people are advised, reprimanded or disciplined is crucial. Done well, it can achieve wonders; done clumsily, it can engender deep resentment.

When the country sorts out its finances, it would be good to build in the possibility – first proposed in the 1973 James Report[7] – of a term's sabbatical every seven years in which the teacher or support staff worker can attend a course, undertake a project or catch up on developments in his or her field. Such sabbaticals will be especially important as the age of retirement is extended.

An efficient system

An effective education system must also be efficient (though not the 'either efficient or cheap' of Lowe's time, quoted in Chapter One). Heads and teachers must make good use of resources. They must constantly seek to improve. They must prevent the waste of pupils' talents. But schools must be good places for staff too. Anyone who thinks that something that is bad for teachers will be good for pupils – playing one interest directly against another – is surely mistaken. As I noted in Chapter Seven, the quotation attributed to Michael Wilshaw about staff morale is deeply worrying: unhappy teachers too often make for unhappy schools full of unhappy pupils.

Mutually respectful relations

In the best schools there is mutual respect between teachers and pupils: each being prepared to listen to the point of view of the other. This is one of the strengths of the Nordic systems, with the collective voice of the pupils supported by their student union. It is also one of the ways in which the next generation of citizens is introduced to democracy.

Schools tend to be conservative institutions: practices grow entrenched and newcomers are expected to accept existing norms. Norms can be positive, bolster stability and impart a sense of tradition. But they can also be negative and stifle innovation. In my experience, most administrative systems need to be updated regularly in order to improve ways of working. The key to improvement is to encourage those working in the system to take charge of designing the changes. They are the experts in teaching and are likely to know what might work better. There is also a need to listen to the pupils – the experts in learning or in failing to learn. Their concerns – whether about the quality of teaching or information technology support or the state of the toilets – need to be taken seriously.

The OECD review of the Danish school system coined the phrase 'the culture of evaluation'. This can be defined as: 'A society or organisation in which there is a normal expectation that all its members will engage in honest inquiry in order to reflect on and improve performance.'[8] The critically important words in this definition are: *normal* – it has to be part of everyday work; *honest* – there is no point in pretence; *reflect on* – staff members need to think deeply about the issue rather than casually considering it; and *improve performance* – signifying that the process is serious and that the goals are improved teaching, better pupil care and more efficient administration. Schools with this positive culture tend to succeed.

Inclusive

Unless our society becomes more inclusive, it will waste further energy on internal conflicts and will fail to offer many a safe and happy country in which to thrive. One of the most pressing problems in England is inequality. This subject was addressed in a speech in 2012 by Angel Gurria, the secretary general of the OECD:

> The average income of the richest 10 per cent of the population is about nine times that of the poorest 10 per cent, up from seven times 25 years ago … What's more: the top 1 per cent of the population has recorded particularly large income gains over the past two decades

> ... In countries with high inequality – such as Italy, the United Kingdom and the United States – the income of the younger generation is highly dependent on the income of the previous generation. Put simply, this means that countries with high inequality essentially reinforce the vicious cycle of poverty ... There is nothing inevitable about high and growing inequality. The OECD's recent landmark report on Inequality '*Divided We Stand*' provides powerful evidence of the need to put 'better policies for better lives' at the centre of our reform efforts and to provide people with equal opportunities and confidence in their future.[9]

The best way to help our society to become less exclusive is to create an inclusive, effective education system. But, given our national history, this is bound to be a challenge.

Since its faltering beginning, our education system has been riven with divisions between rich and poor, private and state, religious and secular and even within different religious denominations. There have also been divisions between those who find learning easy and those who do not. One South London secondary school is reported as dividing its incoming pupils into three mini-schools on the basis of their ability. Pupils in these mini-schools wear different uniform and have different lunchtimes.[10]

In our education system even the teachers divide themselves into six separate trade unions. This reduces their influence in national negotiations and makes them vulnerable to government manipulation.

Conclusion

An appropriate system for the 21st century would be democratically led, under the auspices of local authorities working collaboratively under the national direction of the minister. In it, schools would function in well-designed and well-equipped buildings with inspiring and efficient teachers and support staff. The more inclusive the system, the better it would be for our children and for our society.

Is this too utopian? Perhaps. But isn't it what our children and our society deserve?

In Chapter Thirteen, I make a series of suggestions as to how the current system could be improved

THIRTEEN

Steps towards a better system

The proposals that I present here have been designed to build on the strengths of the education system and address its weaknesses. This is a task that might have been done by our government, but many have relinquished hope that it will do so. Michael Bassey, a retired professor of education, argues:

> Over the last quarter of a century, education has been pushed and pulled, twisted and turned in the maelstrom of party politics … It must now be recognised that this has not worked: politics has polluted the schools and is failing our children.[1]

Like Bassey, I think the system has suffered from what appears to be little more than ministers' personal whims. I believe that it is now time for others to speak up for a better system. As I have stressed throughout this book, an education system is closely aligned with its host society. The more civilised the society – in terms of the fairness with which it treats its citizens – the more likely it is to have an education system based on positive values (displaying the sorts of characteristics that I described in the previous chapter). Similarly, the values underpinning a country's education system influence its next generation of citizens.

This book cannot provide an instant panacea for all the problems of our education system. We are not starting with a blank slate. There is much history and many well-established patterns of expectations and behaviour that first need to be altered. My principal intentions are to demonstrate that there is an alternative to the current harsh system, and to provide the basis of a long-term, non-party political plan for change.

I begin with my proposals for high-quality pre-school care and education.

Expanding pre-school provision

As I have noted, education begins at birth, and the care of young children is crucially important. In different times, most pre-school children were looked after at home by their mothers. Today, even single parents are expected or wish to work outside the home, at least on a part-time basis. Even if there are two parents, the cost of living – and especially of housing – frequently requires them both to be wage earning. This necessitates childcare. But, in England, childcare is extremely expensive – often exceeding one parent's take-home pay. According to the *Daily Express*: 'Parents are handing over a quarter of their salaries to pay for childcare.'[2]

Many families manage, with the help of maternity pay, for one parent to stay home for the first few months of a baby's life. But after this some parents have to balance childcare and work. High-earning parents hire nannies or pay for expensive day care, but most people have to muddle through, working part time, using a child minder or relying on the help of grandparents and friends.

In contrast, Nordic countries finance one of the parents to remain at home for the first year or – in Sweden – year and a half of a child's life so that she or he can nurture the baby. After this they provide high-quality day care at reasonable cost. According to a 2012 report from the Institute for Public Policy Research (IPPR), the cost to a Danish family of childcare is not only far lower than that in England but is capped so that those with three or more children can still afford it.[3]

In Finland, day care is completely free for children from eight months to five years.

> We see it as the right of the child to have day care and preschool … It's a place for your child to play and learn and make friends.[4]

According to Polly Toynbee, high-quality day care not only relieves the stress on children and parents but also makes good economic sense, since it leads to what our country, with its ageing population, needs – a higher birth rate.[5]

Child care for 0- to 3-year-olds

A universal childcare service for 0- to 3-year-olds, managed by the local authority, subject to the same supervision as the rest of the education service and run by fully trained staff would be of great value to children and their parents. It could draw on the statutory framework that already exists.[6]

The cost of the service would have to be met from general taxes, and parents' contributions could be related to their income and collected via income tax. The benefits to our economy and to the health and welfare of families would make it an extremely cost-effective service. A similar scheme proposed by the IPPR concludes that

> universal childcare pays a return to the government of £20,050 (over four years) in terms of tax revenue minus the cost of childcare for every woman who returns to full-time employment after one year of maternity leave.[7]

We also need more comprehensive nursery provision for 3- to 5-year-olds. Government-funded longitudinal research has demonstrated the lasting value of positive early experience – especially for those who have disadvantaged home lives.[8]

Like early childcare, this needs to be part of the local authorities' statutory provision – paid for out of general taxation, with parental contributions assessed according to income and collected through their taxes.

Early years provision for 3- to 6-year-olds

Like Robin Alexander, the director of the Cambridge Primary Study,[9] I suggest that, ideally, early years provision should last from age three until six. This would involve putting back the start of formal schooling for one year. It would mean that children below their fifth birthday would not have to struggle with the formality of Key Stage 1 schooling. Of course, five-year-old children would still be engaged with learning, but – like their Nordic counterparts – mainly through the experience of play. They would be less likely to be traumatised by the experience, at such a young age, of learning to fail.

As well as improving the children's experience, due consideration needs to be given to families' other needs. Given that such a high proportion of parents are in full-time employment, school hours would have to be flexible so to facilitate early arrival. Breakfast and, where needed, after-school activities to fill the gap between the school day and parental pick-up time, should be provided.

Allied to this provision would be the freedom of a parent (of either gender) to take one day off work if their child is sick, as is the case with some English local government schemes. In Denmark, such an arrangement enables the parents to judge for themselves the severity of the sickness and to make arrangements for the child's subsequent care. This makes unnecessary the situation – not uncommon in England – whereby parents pretend that it is they who are sick and require the time off work.

The question of how best to deal with school holidays would also need to be resolved. This is an issue that affects not just the early years but all young children. One solution would be the establishment of holiday activity centres – managed and supervised to the same standard as the early years service – funded in the same way as the provision for 0- to 3-year-olds.

Decommissioning the education market

I have commented in earlier chapters on how the English school system has been turned into an education market by recent governments. The impact of the market has been to fragment the national system, emphasise the hierarchy of different types of schools and give parents the nightmare of making the 'correct' decisions over where to live and in which school to try to obtain a place.

As Ron Glatter, an OU expert on schooling, has argued:

> International experience indicates that emphasising choice and competition to drive improvement is not effective and that changing structures does not yield better results for students. A whole system approach is

> required based on a strong and democratic multi-level infrastructure of support and a common administrative and legal framework underpinned by the principles of public not contract law.[10]

I suggest that the time has come for parents to call for an alternative to this inappropriate market.

Reviving local authorities' statutory duties

Since 1988 many of the education functions of local authorities have been pared down to insignificant levels. Governments have given themselves many new powers and delegated others to head teachers and sponsors. The democratic middle tier has been reduced to impotence.

The outcome – as I have sought to demonstrate – is a muddle. Ministers, despite lacking professional and local knowledge, constantly interfere in professional concerns. And many head teachers lack the professional guidance that they previously obtained and – if they do not have wise governing bodies – can find themselves in difficulties.

Following publication of the 2012 Chief Inspector's Report, *Guardian* columnist Simon Jenkins drew attention to the report's criticism of 'a postcode lottery' indicated in its league tables of local authorities. Jenkins declared:

> Accountability for England's schools is now a total mess. How can anyone tell if the postcode lottery … is the result of too little central control or too much?[11]

Jenkins went on to claim that agencies of central government, such as Ofsted, 'demand all the credit but delegate the blame. Centralise success, localise failure.'[12]

Rather than adopt the new – and possibly expensive – posts of 'School Commissioners' created by the Coalition government[13] or the 'Local Directors of School Standards' as advocated by the Blunkett Report (noted in Chapter Twelve), the obvious solution is to use the wide-ranging powers created by the Coalition government to reinstate the full role of the local authority. This would provide a legitimate – democratically accountable – middle tier between government and individual schools.[14] In this way each local authority's existing responsibility for special education and school transport and its nominal role in school improvement could be integrated with authority-wide planning and supervision.

Local authorities are gaining new powers for public health under 2012 Health and Social Care Act. This will give them 'a new set of duties to protect and improve public health'[15] and will entail a reorganisation of many of their functions. Combined with an enhanced set of duties to protect and improve public education, this could make effective localism a reality.

Such changes would require some adjustment of roles but would provide an effective middle tier with corresponding powers and duties.

Restoring academies and free schools to local authorities would also provide heads with a source of professional advice and a place for discussion, which they currently lack. The proximity of most local authorities' schools – unlike the somewhat random collections of schools within nationwide chains of academies – would make meetings of heads and teachers geographically feasible.

In order to monitor the progress of all schools in their jurisdiction, local authorities would need to develop an effective way of dealing with their schools.

Getting this relationship right may be difficult. While in the past local authorities may sometimes have retained too much control over their head teachers, currently they manifestly have too little – as the number of scandals involving misappropriation of funds demonstrates. Ideally, heads would have scope for independence but would work under the watchful eye of the authority. The authority would need to recruit a small, high-quality team of former heads with experience of school improvement and a number of designated part-time associates drawn from the authority's own schools. These practising heads and teachers could be hired for a set number of days each year in agreement with their schools. Teams could be hand-picked from this pool to work with any school experiencing difficulties. If it were judged that an external team would be more appropriate, then a reciprocal arrangement could be made with a neighbouring authority.

The most crucial need, however, is to create schools with balanced intakes of pupils.

Creating balanced schools

A balanced school is one in which there is an intake of pupils from different family backgrounds: advantaged and disadvantaged; those who find learning easy and those who do not. As I have noted, however, while in rural areas schools often attract balanced intakes of pupils, this tends to happen less frequently in urban areas. There are two reasons for this: parallel private and selective schools cream off those who find learning easy, or who come from advantaged home backgrounds; and many housing areas are sharply divided along social class lines.

This is why a 'local school policy', attractive idea though it is, cannot provide a solution. Children living in 'poor' areas would attend their local school and those from more advantaged areas would attend theirs in an educational apartheid. (I will come to the private and selective school issues later.)

In a fair system, each school should have broadly the same proportions of different kinds of pupils. But, to achieve this situation, parents would need to give up the 'notional choice' of a school for their child. I stress 'notional' because, in our current market system, the reality is that many parents have very little choice – merely the right to express a series of preferences. Popular schools are the ones exerting the choice over their applicants, rather than the other way round.

Even so, the notion of 'choice' is attractive and many people will baulk at a system of allocation without the opportunity for expressing a preference. The pay-off, however, would be the end of the current neurosis-inducing process of finding a suitable secondary school for one's child.

Allocating pupils

It should not matter where you live, what you earn or how able your child seems to be, your children should be free to attend a school with a group of learners similar to all other schools. In other words, it should not matter to which school your child goes. The challenge is how to achieve such balanced schools. Both primary and secondary schools would benefit from a balanced intake, but it is the secondary schools where the imbalances currently create the greatest problems. So it is these that need a new system of pupil allocation.

There are only three ways of ensuring balanced intakes:

- bussing pupils between areas;
- using some kind of banding system to distribute pupils;
- random allocation to schools within a defined area.

Bussing

Bussing pupils was used extensively in the US following the Supreme Court's insistence in 1954 on desegregation.[16] Its benefits and costs are still being argued over.[17] But there is agreement that it caused problems for children who resented the need to travel long distances and wished to attend after-school activities, as well as for parents visiting the schools. Were it to be introduced in England today it would undoubtedly cause similar problems.

Banding

Banding systems usually requires pupils to be assigned to one of a number of bands on the basis of their academic performance, and schools to admit set proportions from each band. This allows a measure of choice of schools, but only of those with unfilled vacancies in the appropriate band. This was the system used by the ILEA for many years. Its major defect – in my opinion – is that it depends on a formal estimation of ability and, as I have argued, the labelling of children according to perceived ability is too unreliable to use. The irony is that, even though it is unreliable, it nevertheless has a powerful impact on young learners. Being assigned to a low band leads to lower expectations by pupils, their teachers and their parents.

Random allocation

Random allocation to all secondary schools appears to me to be the best way to achieve schools with balanced intakes. The problem is that it sounds inhuman – being selected by a machine instead of by a caring person. Yet it is this very impersonal element that permits it to be free of bias.

Under such a system each school would receive a mixture of those who learned easily and those who did not; and of those whose families were economically well off and those who were not. Each secondary school would represent a microcosm of the society existing within the local authority. There is a downside: primary friendship groups would not necessarily be maintained.

Allocations would obviously need to be applied carefully. Exceptions would have to be made for siblings – especially twins – so that families would not have to cope with different school times or holidays. Furthermore, most education authorities – except for London boroughs and a few others – would be too big a geographical area and would need to be subdivided (carefully ensuring that they included a range of different housing patterns). Ideally, each sub-area would represent a 'normal' population from which schools could be allocated balanced entries.

Brighton and Hove proposed using random allocation in 2007 as a tie-breaker for over-subscribed places, but was immediately challenged in the courts by a group of parents. The court, however, dismissed the parental objections and the scheme was started in 2008. The authority considered the scheme as successful, as the proportion of parents gaining their first choice increased, but a 2010 research study by academics at Bristol University and the Institute of Education found that the new system had failed to reduce segregation between rich and poor pupils.[18]

The researchers pointed out that the way the new catchment areas had been established and the fact that pupils were only randomly distributed within them meant that poor families from outlying areas were very unlikely to gain places in the most popular city-centre schools.

This does not seem to me to be a fair criticism of random allocation as such, but of its limited use as a tie-breaker rather than for the whole allocation, and of the way that the catchment areas were established. It would obviously be difficult to get all areas right, and they might need to be revised periodically. But the principle of random allocation still makes it – to my mind – the fairest way of managing the primary–secondary transfer.

If such a system were to be implemented, schools would receive a balanced intake of pupils. The other component of fair allocation, however, concerns teachers.

I also want to propose allocating teachers (and support staff) to schools.

Assigning teachers

The potential benefit of having a movable teaching force is that it would maximise the chance for all schools to improve. Under our current system, better schools improve as they attract better teachers and the weaker schools deteriorate as they lose their better ones, who are afraid of being trapped in a failing environment.

I expect that teachers and allied staff will raise a host of objections to the idea of being assigned to a school. At first sight, it might seem overly authoritarian and out of keeping with the rest of my suggestions. But its potential benefits are significant.

Under this plan teachers and support staff would be employed by the local authority rather than by an individual school. (In large authorities they could apply to a subdivision – as described in the section on pupil allocation – so as not to involve them in unreasonable travel.) Their contracts, as now, would be secure. What would be different would be the ability of the local authority to move them between schools in order to obtain the optimum match of staff and schools.

There are historical precedents for this arrangement. Local education authorities used to be the employing body for the majority of teachers and some, rather than allocate them all to particular schools, would retain a proportion and deploy them where they were needed. This system provided flexibility and enabled schools to cope with the rise and fall of pupil numbers without having to engage extra or dismiss surplus staff. It became unpopular because there was a tendency to view such staff as of lower status than those assigned to a particular school. Two-tier systems are always viewed with suspicion. This would not apply here, however, as all staff would be employed on a common basis.

Regular movement between schools is what happens to teachers in South Korea – a country that does particularly well in international tests.[19] Of course, this is only one factor in a country with a different history and culture to England's. But there, teachers are moved every five years in order to prevent staleness and to enable as many schools as possible to function at the highest level.[20] Alberta in Canada is another place with an impressive education record.[21] There, teachers and heads are moved around the system in order to ensure that each school has a capable staff and that no school slips into a vicious spiral of decline.

This lack of freedom to choose one's school might appear to teachers to be an imposition. But it can also be viewed as an opportunity for career development. It would provide a teacher with experience of a range of schools which, crucially and unlike our current situation, would have similar, balanced intakes of pupils. There would be no question of one teacher being assigned to a failing school and another to a highly successful one: all schools would have an equal chance of success.

What about head teachers – could they also be moved around? In my view this would be crucial. Like other staff, they would have secure contracts with the local authority but their assignments would be coordinated with the needs of the schools. For new heads, the benefits would be obvious: an initial placement in a smaller or better-established school, followed by transfers to more challenging environments. There would also be advantages for experienced heads. Instead of their possibly growing into a rut, a transfer could provide novelty and fresh challenge.

Under the system I have proposed, local authorities would play a key role in establishing and maintaining high-quality schools. They would ensure that schools received balanced intakes, appropriate staff and suitable head teachers. Local authorities would also be responsible for rigorously monitoring the progress of schools and for changing the heads or individual staff in order to maximise each school's effectiveness.

It would, of course, be necessary for the authorities to take on appropriate staff for these vital senior management roles. They would need people – though not huge bureaucracies – with the skills and experience to undertake the oversight of schools. These could be outstanding former heads, and the role could provide the tranche of suitable 'post-headship' positions that have been missing in recent years.

Balanced schools would be a first step. But other challenges remain if a high-quality system of schooling is to be established.

Democratising private education

If private education did not exist, it would be much easier to design a good state system. Children from high-earning families would be scattered among state schools, helping to create good social mixes.

But private schools do exist and have a long history in England – which I touched upon in Chapter Ten. Some (though not all) are fine schools with gifted teachers. Many have superb buildings and grounds and facilities. It would be a tragic waste to close them – even were it possible.

So how can we use this resource positively for many more of the nation's children and not just for the 7%? And, equally importantly, how can we heal the state/private fault line in our society, with the latter's inbuilt sense of entitlement, snobbery and domination of so many professions?

As I noted earlier, this question foxed the Fleming Committee in 1944. Since then many people have inveighed against the privilege and excessive influence of private schools. The Sutton Trust – a charity which works to find ways to make the education system less divisive – has suggested that the solution might be for the state to pay for the brightest pupils passing an entrance examination to attend private schools.[22] The Trust goes to great lengths to argue that this proposal, piloted in an independent girls' school (since transformed into an academy), is markedly different to the Assisted Places scheme introduced by the Conservative government in 1980. However, it seems to me to be very similar in that it seeks to cream off the most able pupils at the end of their primary schooling.

Peter Wilby's solution to the problem is quite different. He sees the major advantage of private schools to be their access to Oxbridge. He proposes that Oxford and Cambridge colleges should ask state schools to nominate their most able 15-year-old pupils and then coach them for A levels. In this way, he envisages that 'the stranglehold of the public school gang' would be broken.[23] The scheme deserves praise for it originality, but I fear that, while it might increase the proportion of state school pupils going to Oxbridge, it would strengthen elitism and cause grave problems within state schools having to cope with a 'chosen few' alongside everybody else.

My suggestion is to encourage private schools to become state schools or academies – as the *Times Educational Supplement* reports some private schools (for financial reasons) are already doing.[24] A more popular option might be for private schools to convert into sixth-form colleges specialising in A level teaching. This would be a good way to draw on the teaching expertise of private schools and it might help a greater proportion of state school pupils to gain access to the most prestigious universities. And gifted teachers could use their talents for the benefit of many more of the age group.

The limited numbers of 16- to 19-year-olds would also mean that the schools' boarding provision and grounds could be used by many more than the current elite group.

Since these schools are private, changing their status would not be straightforward and would require a sustained effort. But, given that, before being colonised by the rich, many private schools were committed to working for the poor (Andrew Adonis points out: 'Henry VI set up Eton for poor scholars'), such a change would redirect the schools to their original missions.

There will be many dedicated teachers in the private sector who – although they might wish to keep its benefits – would be happy to work in a less elitist setting. They have much to offer and should be welcomed into the state system. Their more generous contracts might prove to be a sticking point, and it might be that some accommodation would have to be made whereby these were maintained for a set period. Of course, there would be a cost for the state. The expense of having to educate the current 7% who attend private schools would have to be met from the public purse. But the benefit of removing such a fault-line from our society would be priceless.

Removing selection

I discussed ability in Chapter Three and considered much of the evidence about selection by ability in Chapter Ten. My conclusions were that the tests used were unreliable and that selection takes place at far too young an age, when brains are still developing. Moreover, the whole process is biased towards the advantaged, who can afford coaching.

Over the years, I have met many successful people who very quickly informed me that they had failed the 11-plus examination. Many of them were proud of what they had since achieved but some suspected that it was a bit of a fluke, since the 11-plus had shown that they were really academic failures. This is the most invidious aspect of any high-stakes assessment: it can determine the way people view themselves throughout their lives.

The other, related criticism of selection is that it distorts the natural balance of pupils in schools. Removing a specially selected sample of those with seemingly the most ability from the general pool of pupils prevents many schools from receiving the balance that they need in order to function well.

I have no doubt that abolishing selection will be a hard battle to win. It is an issue that cuts across political parties (as I noted in Chapter Ten). Former grammar school pupils are powerful lobbyists. But there is surely little sense in dividing our 11-year-olds into sheep and goats when the evidence I cited in Chapter Three shows that selection tests are unreliable and that children continue to develop their capabilities for many more years.

It would, of course, be tragic to lose successful grammar schools from the system. No school should have to close. Instead, selective schools could convert into non-selective ones (some have already converted into academies, although these have been permitted to retain selection). In a system in which all schools receive a balanced intake, all pupils could benefit from experienced former selective school teachers. Furthermore, no teacher from a former selective school would have to teach in a school without such a balance.

Opening up faith schools

The English system has always depended on churches, as I noted in Chapter Nine, and, due to current government policies, their number is growing. In other countries there is a clear distinction between the state and religion. This does not seem to prevent people from following their particular faiths.

I propose that we should open all schools – faith or not –to all pupils. If, as is often claimed, faith schools are more effective than others, their benefits would available to a broader group. Faith-based religious practice would not be included, although the study of religions could be part of the curriculum. Schools that wished to do so could provide voluntary after-school classes in faith observance – funded by different faiths – for children whose parents requested this. Such an arrangement would prevent there being any misunderstandings over the difference between science – taught within the school curriculum – and aspects of beliefs – taught in after-school voluntary sessions.

These changes are likely to be strongly resisted by those happy with the current situation whereby religious authorities enjoy freedom to proselytise their faith while being funded by the public purse. But they may be supported by others, like the Accord Coalition – a body that believes that selecting pupils on religious grounds contributes to greater segregation in the school system:

> Rather than helping to segregate, all state funded faith schools should open their doors to the fresh air of intercultural mixing and understanding.[25]

A fair system would also pose questions about the practices of grouping pupils according to their perceived ability.

Rethinking pupil grouping

I discussed the way pupils are grouped in schools in Chapter Six – noting that it was one of the most difficult pedagogical issues facing schools in England. I noted that there is a substantial body of evidence showing that streaming – and its milder version, banding – does not work. Nevertheless, streaming and banding are widely used in English schools and are strongly supported by ministers.

I would like to propose that both streaming and banding be banned – but I hesitate to do so because of the absence of satisfactory alternative ways to group pupils. I know that Finland's highly successful system works without ability grouping and that this approach is possible. But the culture of Finnish schools and their society are different and Finnish teachers are comfortable with ensuring that classes make (excellent) progress together. In contrast, in England, teachers are expected to maximise the differences between pupils. It would take some time to alter this approach.

Currently, in England there appears only to be a stark choice between grouping by ability – which we know can lead pupils to lower their estimates of their own ability and hence their expectations – and mixed-ability teaching – which may put in the same class hard-working pupils with others who have given up trying to learn and seek consolation in disruption. What are the alternatives?

- We could group by effort. But where would we put the brilliant but lackadaisical pupil?
- We could group by seriousness of approach to study. But this would allow too subjective a judgement by teachers, and what would they do about the pupil who veers from one extreme to another?
- We could group by progress and override the age of pupils. But this could lead to particularly able (or well-coached) younger pupils learning in classes dominated by older, less able, and possibly less motivated classmates.

Innovative ways of grouping pupils need to be a research priority. The Finnish mixed-ability model may be what we should be working towards. But any different methods would require considerable professional development.

Taming assessment

Assessment is one of the most powerful elements of the education system. As has been made abundantly clear by experts such as Gordon Stobart,[26] it has, since 1988, been elevated above its technical capability and used for the wrong reasons. As Tamara Bibby found in her research on primary classrooms:

> Children start to think of themselves as levels. And it's wrapped up with morality and goodness. Good people work hard and listen in class. If it suddenly becomes clear your mate gets lower levels than you, are they a good person? It can put real pressure on a friendship.[27]

The thought of a generation of children growing up thinking of themselves as 'levels' is horribly reminiscent of Aldous Huxley's *Brave New World*,[28] with its finely graded people. Of course, teachers have always graded pupils, and children quickly realise that some of their friends get higher marks. But the formality and the regularity of the SATs add a legitimation to the process even though, as I noted earlier, the reliability of individual grades is highly questionable. The GCSE and A levels are both open to criticism, as noted in Chapter Seven. Furthermore, we have seen the problems caused by the action of the regulator and the morass of the world of vocational assessments has been revealed by the Wolf Report.[29]

We surely need – as Gordon Stobart argues – 'to define assessment's rightful – and humbler – role, and to show how it can contribute to learning'.[30]

How can we do this? Teacher assessment of progress is too good to lose. Teachers need to maintain the valuable skills they have acquired in judging pupils' work, but the steam needs to be taken out of the process. It should be stressed to pupils that grades are not infallible and represent only their current stage, rather than indicating what they may ultimately achieve (as I argued in Chapter Three).

I have considered whether SATs – the formal tests – should be retained as a check on how teachers judge their pupils, but decided against it. If SATs were to remain, it would be hard to convince pupils that levels could be unreliable. Also, it would encourage the unending practice and the teaching to the test that blight the system. However, it would be important to build in some national mechanism to enable teachers to check their grades so as to prevent them drifting in different directions. Teachers in the Nordic countries visit different schools in order to act as moderators in the grading of examinations. This seems to work well.

I am pleased that the minister has dropped his plans to turn the GCSE into the EBacc. I just wish he would have the courage to drop the GCSE altogether. With all young people being required by law to remain in education or training until age 18, there seems little point in holding a 'big bang' examination two years earlier.

Andreas Schleicher, a senior OECD education expert, argues that:

> In the 21st century, examinations need to reflect the knowledge and skills that matter for the future of students, not just those that parents remember from their own schooling or those that are easy to measure … and to use assessments that emphasise formative feedback and promote connections across activities and subjects, both in and out of school.[31]

A levels – and vocational examinations – need to fit in a sensible framework. The minister has some ideas of extending the scope of A levels, which sound mostly reasonable, but the starting point should be Mike Tomlinson's 2004 report[32] in which he suggested ways to link academic and vocational assessments. His recommendations, at the time, generated much support from teachers, employers and assessment experts. Obviously, the arguments would need to be re-examined in today's light, but they offer a helpful pointer.

Reforming inspections

England is unlikely to have a flourishing education system until it sorts out the issue of inspection. As noted in Chapter Nine, a punitive style of inspection has – in my opinion – become too dominant a force. Furthermore, there is a danger that inspection – a means to the end of better teaching – becomes over-interested in itself. Reading the 2012 Report of the Chief Inspector, I was struck by how much of it was devoted to Ofsted rather than to issues affecting pupils and schools.[33] I wonder, therefore, if we need inspections at all. If Finland – a country that does well in international tests (and has exceptionally small proportions of pupils with reading problems) – does not have any system of inspections, why should England?

The reasons usually put forward for inspections are that they:

- inform ministers and the general public about the state of our education system;
- guarantee national standards;
- keep heads and teachers on their toes – and weed out the bad ones.

Informing ministers and the general public

In fact this role has already mostly disappeared. It was a major part of the HMI remit, but by removing most HMIs and creating a free-standing Ofsted,[34] ministers cut off this source of confidential advice.

It is true that the publication of inspection reports informs the general public. But much of the intense interest is due to the stress of choosing which schools to prioritise for one's children.

Guaranteeing standards

A guarantee of standards is an attractive idea. It is, however, difficult to implement. Schools – as I have argued – are complex institutions affected by their histories, geography and intake of pupils as well as by what the head and staff actually do. Ofsted inspection reports can get it wrong, particularly in the shorter, little-notice, new inspections. The time pressure and lack of local knowledge make understanding such a complex institution as a school and diagnosing its strengths and weaknesses – to say nothing of what it needs to do to improve – a very difficult task. This makes the notion of a guarantee of standards unrealistic.

Keeping heads and teachers on their toes

This is probably the role that most of the public sees as the job of Ofsted. Does it actually work? My answer is that – at its best – it works only partially. Knowing that you are to be inspected – and that there might be serious consequences as a result of the inspection – will motivate most teachers to prepare thoroughly for the ordeal. But, with a successful inspection completed, might not many of us relax and let our preparation slip?

Some will argue that the answer is to institute random inspections so that the teacher has to start each day in the expectation of one. But this is to generate an atmosphere of mistrust as a motivation to work hard, which I do not believe would be fruitful. It might force teachers always to have a good lesson plan available – so that they would not be caught unawares – but it would be unlikely to encourage them to be innovative. In an atmosphere where teachers do not feel trusted, they are more likely to do the minimum sufficient to keep themselves out of trouble.

In my view, the best people to keep teachers on their toes are the teachers themselves. It is the knowledge that they are being trusted – as qualified and fully trained professionals – to do their best work that provides intrinsic motivation. But we all get tired and can need some prodding or coaching from the senior management.

What if senior management is not up to the job? Challenging it is probably the most important role for the governing body, but if it shirks the task, a new-look local authority must be prepared to intervene. As I argued earlier, the local authority is best placed to monitor, provide support to or challenge its schools. The authority's education officer should be the school's 'critical friend', able to use local knowledge, provide resources and, as argued earlier, move staff – heads, teachers and support staff – around the system. With the availability of so much data the task would be much more manageable now than in the past. There should be no need for special measures or threats of closure, with all their negative consequences for pupils and staff.

So is there any role for inspections? Yes – but not the current Ofsted model. Instead, I suggest a small body of knowledgeable and experienced HMIs whose role would be to monitor and support the local authorities' management of their schools. Among its duties would be to publish an annual report on the state of the education system, to be debated in Parliament.

In this way, the system would be monitored from the classroom to the minister and, where necessary, interventions would be triggered. However, such actions would be undertaken within a generally supportive (though not necessarily uncritical) atmosphere. Each party – teacher, head teacher, local authority officer, HMI and, ultimately, Parliament – would hold responsibility for its part in the education system.

Limiting homework

I discussed the pros and cons of homework in Chapter Nine. Frustratingly, most British and American reviews of research on homework fail to come to clear conclusions as to its value. International surveys find it a mixed blessing. Even a 1999 Ofsted study reported the 'there is no hard evidence that homework raises educational standards'.[35]

Research cannot be more helpful because it is impossible to separate the effect of homework from family, school and other background characteristics. Ideally, this is where a randomised controlled trial would provide a clear judgement of the efficacy of homework over and above the effects of everything else. But the practical, ethical and political difficulties of randomly assigning pupils to 'regular homework' or to 'homework free' conditions have – so far – proved too daunting.

Abolition of homework might reduce tensions between parents and their children and between teachers and pupils. But it would require schools to reorganise their timetables to provide longer periods of time for individual work: extended reading, research and writing.

Perhaps the best solution is to discourage primary schools from setting formal homework. This would allow working parents, in particular, to enjoy valuable evening and weekend time with their offspring with a good conscience, and children to continue learning in a less formal way by, for instance, reading. This is one of the goals the French government sought to promote in 2012.

For those of secondary age, however, I fear that dropping homework would reduce too drastically the time for formal learning. Better, perhaps, to ensure that this time is used well. This would entail setting worthwhile tasks, ensuring that assignments are marked promptly, that pupils always receive feedback (not only on shortcomings but on how the work could be improved) and – since few things are less conducive to the habit of lifelong study than inconsistent demands – ensuring that homework is set on a regular basis. Secondary schools – many of which currently end classes around 3 pm – could provide accommodation not only for those pupils who lack adequate space at home but also for those whose parents' working hours extend until late in the day.

Relaxing school uniform

I discussed school uniform in Chapter Nine, classifying it as an ambiguous issue. I understand how, when schools are competing for pupils, each may try to outdo competitors by adopting traditional and expensive uniforms. I can also understand parents who say that uniform prevents endless hassle over what should be worn. But surely. children have to learn which clothes to wear for different occasions. and uniforms too often serve as distractions from the true purpose of schooling.

Extending after-school activities to all

Today's full-service extended schools offer a model of how to organise a range of sports, cultural and leisure activities and provide suitable care for pupils during the 'twilight hours' before and after school – the times of the day when working parents are most stretched.[36] As I noted with regard to homework, the availability of safe, supervised accommodation would solve many problems faced by individual families and by communities affected by large groups of school pupils with nowhere to go.

Reducing children's stress

As I noted in Chapter Ten, children in England are subject to stress. Improving the education system by itself would not relieve children of all the pressures bearing down on them. That needs major changes in the way society is structured – principally, the alleviation of poverty – but education could be a good starting point. The dropping of SATs would alleviate much stress, as would the establishment of a simpler system of transfer from primary to secondary schools.

Creating an independent Education Commission

In the legal sphere, there is a permanent Law Commission charged with monitoring the legal system and suggesting improvements and revisions.[37] Surely this is what we need for education?

A permanent commission of experts should be non-party political. Of course, much thought would need to be given to its size and composition, but its principal purpose should be to improve the system for all. As John White – the education philosopher – argues in relation to the setting of aims: 'it should not be up to a government temporarily in power to impose its own idiosyncratic views about what these aims should be'.[38]

Any proposals made by the commission would need political authority from the government – this is what living in a democracy entails – but they would be formulated in a non-partisan culture, adequately researched and, where possible, fully piloted.

The commission would need to engage with all aspects of education: its financing and administration as well as issues of pedagogy, the curriculum and assessment. Its expert contribution would be particularly helpful in dealing with changes to the curriculum. As noted in the last section, the new National Curriculum is likely to prove highly contentious. The difficulty is that once politicians start to define the framework, they cannot stop themselves going further down the path of control.

But, if there is to be a National Curriculum, it has to apply to all schools. And here is a funny thing: the revised National Curriculum is only intended to apply to a minority. As Michael Rosen amusingly comments:

> This curriculum will only apply in England and only in schools working within local authorities. So central government is going to lay down a compulsory curriculum for the schools that it's trying to turn into schools where the curriculum won't apply.[39]

The commission would also need to oversee changes to national assessment. English pupils are over-tested and over-examined. Some sense urgently needs to be brought to bear on this important part of the system. Tests and examinations – as noted in Chapter Nine – are a part of the system, but must not be permitted to dominate it. They should be seen (in the Victorian words quoted in a pamphlet on assessment) as 'a helpful servant not a dominating master'.[40] There is scope to restore tests and examinations to their proper role as spurs to learning.

Challenging the current model of schooling

Changing the model of schooling may turn out to be the hardest task of all. Despite the best efforts of the futurologists (see Chapter Six) no one has yet come up with a feasible – affordable – alternative to our traditional model. Individual tuition is financially unrealistic and online tuition is fine for some aspects of learning but – as I have argued – cannot carry out the *in loco parentis* role of a school. So, if we are stuck with the basic structure of schooling as we know it, how can it be modified so that it becomes a better vehicle for the kind of education I have described?

Some improvements would flow from the other changes I have proposed. An inclusive culture and treating all learners with equal respect – as currently happens in the best systems – would help. The abolition of league tables would make cooperation between schools easier. The allocation of pupils and teachers to schools on a fair and equal basis would abolish 'sink' schools. If we could ensure that all had a balanced intake and a share of the best teachers, all schools could be good schools.

These changes would be likely to make a significant difference. But, in addition, we need to change the way that all schools deal with pupils. Young learners, of course, need to understand the boundaries that contain them. But as pupils grow older they benefit from greater independence in their learning. Teachers and administrators need to allow pupils more of a voice. In the Nordic countries, pupils belong to students' unions and are taken seriously – even by ministers. At both the individual and collective levels, pupils are more likely to learn if they are active rather than passive and if their lives incorporate an element of democracy.

Trying to make schools into more democratic places requires skilful handling: offering unguided choices to young pupils or encouraging them to take decisions at a stage when they are unaware of the implications of their choice is irresponsible. But so is treating 16-year-olds as if they are still 10.

Schools for profit

It has been suggested by lobbyists for private companies that schools should be permitted to make a profit. The problem is that profit – although claimed to be the means to a good end – has an insidious way of asserting itself as the principal aim.

Peter Wilby, to whom I have referred earlier, has argued that there is much evidence to show that privatising services and allowing them to make profit seldom produces the desired effects:

> Privatised water companies sell off reservoirs and neglect to repair pipes and sewers. Privatised energy companies confront us with rising charges and impenetrable tariff structures. Supermarkets drive farmers out of business, reducing Britain's capacity to feed itself. Banks sell

> 'payment protection plans' and 'structured' savings schemes that are little more than frauds on the customer.

He concludes.

> We should not expect profit-making companies to behave any more virtuously when they take charge in schools.[41]

However, according to educational journalist Warwick Mansell, ministers are now considering 'outsourcing some policy making to companies, consultants and think tanks'.[42] For companies like the giant publisher Pearson – with contracts for supplying tests and textbooks around the world and with its own think-tank in King's College, London – this would be yet another opportunity to extend their influence. Yet Pearson's influence has been criticised by the American education writer Diane Ravitch:

> The corporation is acting as a quasi-government agency in several instances but … is a business that sells products and services … at what point do conflicts of interest arise?[43]

I am not anti-business. I believe that large companies play an important role in our society. I also believe that education and the best commercial companies, especially well-established ones with philanthropic traditions, share many values and attitudes. Both strive to be ethical. Both recognise the value of teamwork. Both know that success will be most likely if they engage with the hearts and minds of the people working in them – the 'John Lewis model' of partnership – and both realise that they need their members to feel a loyalty to the institution rather than to a section or department.

Businesses provide employment and should be the driving force of the economy. They generate profits which, provided they pay taxes, they can reinvest or use to pay dividends to their backers. But this is very different from their making a profit out of publicly financed services. Governments should resist the high-pressure lobbying.

Conclusion

I believe that England must embrace changes to its education system. But such changes must be based on fairness and supported by evidence. They should be aimed at achieving the highest standards not just by an elite group but by as many as possible. They should certainly not be about giving the market freedom to make profits for big companies. Changes must encompass the all-round development of children, including academic success, and foster the future prosperity and happiness of our society. In the final chapter I discuss how we can take forward these ideas.

FOURTEEN

What next?

The proposals described in Chapter Thirteen have been formulated to challenge the claim, so frequently heard from ministers, that there is no alternative to their current approach to education policy. The crucial difference between the approach – no doubt promoted by lobbyists – of recent governments to education reforms and that of most education thinkers is that ministers have been seduced by the market model, while education thinkers have not. Education thinkers point to evidence that the market favours the advantaged and, since the education system has itself always favoured the same group, they believe that the market is more likely to exacerbate, rather than solve, education problems.

Advantaged families, in addition to material benefits, can provide numerous cultural experiences to help their children learn. And, if necessary, they can buy coaching. Even in terms of luck, where the chances of rich and poor should be equal, advantaged families are adept at seizing opportunities. More credit to them. But the result is an ever-widening gulf in a society in which education has become one of the major tools by which to transmit privilege from one generation to another.

Our politicians talk about the need for greater social mobility – and criticise schools for not enabling more disadvantaged youngsters to buck the trend – but they baulk at addressing the crucial question of how to create a fairer society.[1] This resistance might be because, if it were to work properly, social mobility would mean some children from advantaged families doing less well than their poorer peers. This would create an awkward situation for politicians committed to the status quo, in which advantaged families view continued privilege as an inalienable right. In countries such as Norway, Finland and Denmark social and economic divisions are not so pronounced and manual workers often earn as much as professionals and enjoy comparable social status.

We now have an education system in which there are almost unscalable barriers. Making GCSE and A levels harder to pass makes little sense in a modern world where everyone's achievement is necessary for the future well-being of society. The image of the *Titanic* comes to mind – secure in its sharply differentiated accommodation, from luxurious cabins to the hammocks of steerage – steaming towards an iceberg.

English parents today are expected to fight for places for their children in the so-called 'best' schools. But the operation of league tables means that only a lucky few will ever get their wish. How much better it would be if parents could feel confident that all schools were good schools. No school is likely to be perfect for all of its pupils all of the time – but every school would be acceptable if parents could be confident that their offspring would have a realistic chance of success.

I hope that this book will contribute to discussions about what education is for, about how it should be organised and – indeed – about the kind of society in which we wish to live. I hope that it will also convey the message that the country's education system is ours. It does not belong to any minister or political party. It is public property and, if enough people believe it is not serving the best interests of the nation's children and of our society as a whole, it should be changed.

Some readers will see my ideas as too radical, particularly if their children have fared well under the existing system. Others may see them as utopian – too far from the realities of 'human nature' – but human nature can be pro-social as well as selfish. Scottish philosopher Adam Smith recognised this:

> Sharing the sensations of our fellows, we seek to maximize their pleasures and minimize their pains so that we may share in their joys.[2]

Of course there are people who will seize every personal advantage without a thought for how their actions might damage anyone else. But I am constantly impressed at the good deeds that so many people perform, the voluntary and financial contributions they make to charities and the times they put the needs of others before their own.

Some readers will see the proposals as too timid. They want a social revolution and do not want to wait much longer.

I hope that this book will encourage people to demand a better, fairer education system – and a better, fairer society. As I have noted many times, England has excellent teachers; the problem is that they have to work in a poor system. That system is not all bad – it has good features – but it is based on too many false claims: that private is always good and public is generally bad; that 11-year-olds can be adequately judged; that frequent testing, by itself, ensures learning; that teachers cannot be trusted; and that people care about only their own children. We have to rid our policy formulators of these negative attitudes and encourage them to adopt a more positive view of people and of our society.

Changing the system means standing up to the politicians who, because of ideology or as a result of lobbying by interested parties, have created the problem. The historic reasons for failing to create a sound national system – an unwillingness to pay for public education; the inability to appreciate the economic advantages of an educated populace; and a desire to maintain the existing social order, which regarded education as appropriate only for gentlemen – are long outdated. Our society has come a long way, but we still have a system based on winners and losers, on sheep and goats.

The elitists' insistence that, in the words of Kingsley Amis, 'more will mean worse'[3] is still used to criticise the expansion of educational opportunities. This view epitomises the attitude that high-quality education should be restricted and that much of its value stems from its exclusivity.

Such a view has come about because from the earliest times education has, with few exceptions, been colonised by the well-off. This does not apply just to England. In every country in the world for which there are data, the well-off – as a group – outperform the disadvantaged in educational attainment. This is not because the well-off are always more able but, rather, because they use their advantages to such good effect. I do not blame them for using their talents or for wanting the best for their children. But this is where the state needs to help everyone else's children. Nordic countries do this; why cannot we? As OECD education expert Andreas Schleicher argues, a common factor in the best-performing countries is 'the belief in the possibilities for all children to achieve'.[4]

It will take years to deal with the confusions of our current system, but a good start could be made by ignoring labels such as 'academy' and 'free school' and treating all schools fairly: with funding on a common basis (with extra money only for pupils with special needs) and common governance and regulations.

As we learn more about the biochemistry and functioning of the brain and as the results of the 'school in the cloud' (noted in Chapter Four) become apparent, teachers will need scope to adjust their ways of working. It will be important, therefore, for all schools to be given freedom to innovate in both pedagogy and general organisation.

A new, fairer system would be easier to understand. It would be open and honest. No one would have to pretend to be a believer in order to gain admittance to a faith school. No one would need to furnish a false address in the hope of winning a place in a popular school. No one would be written off as a failure at 11 years of age.

If, as I have proposed, schools received balanced intakes of pupils and teachers of comparable quality, they could compete in academic, sporting or cultural activities on equal terms. Rather than some schools being outstanding and some unsatisfactory, such a system would promote the possibility of excellence for all. Parental anxiety about which school to apply for – and subsequent guilt if a wrong call were made – could fade away.

I have also discussed how unhappy many of our young people seem to be. This is not helped by our exceptionally early start to schooling and our obsession with testing and grading pupils. Finland and Norway start later and pursue a less pressured approach – and still outperform our young people. We must learn from them.

Let us create an education system suitable for a modern world in which all pupils can attend a school which mirrors society and which can foster their talents in accordance with their own commitment to hard work. Let us, finally, leave behind the class-ridden system which separates out and labels our children.

Of course, these proposals are mere outlines and need much fleshing out. Like the education reports of the past, I have deliberately not calculated the financial costs of any changes I am proposing. And I recognise that funding any transitional costs to the sort of system I have envisaged will be difficult in these days of austerity.

I hope the my ideas will feed into the education debates already begun by educational thinkers such as Melissa Benn,[5] Michael Fielding and Peter Moss,[6] John White,[7] Richard Pring,[8] Diana Reay, Gill Crozier and David James[9] and Stephen Ball,[10] and into wider debates about our society raised by Danny Dorling,[11] Pat Thane[12] and Richard Wilkinson and Kate Pickett.[13] Such debates need to be open to all rather than limited to politicians and the media, and, given our advanced communications, social networks and system of public polling, this ought to be possible.

I fear that the Coalition government may be too committed to its market-oriented policies to change course, though I hope I am wrong. Nor am I convinced that the Labour opposition will want to change course either, given that even party stalwarts, like education writer Fiona Millar, have expressed reservations about whether Labour can develop a coherent set of proposals to 'restore confidence and belief in a high-performing public education system as the route to a fairer society'.[14]

My doubts about Labour were not eased by the 2012 publication of Andrew Adonis's *Education, Education, Education*.[15] As a Downing Street apparatchik and subsequently ennobled education minister, Adonis was at the heart of New Labour's policy making. His book is vehemently anti-comprehensive – 'a cancer at the heart of society'.[16] He recommends taking power out of local democratic hands and giving it to big business. His book is aggressive, attacking those who questioned New Labour's policies. Ted Wragg's droll humour, which kept teachers smiling through successive waves of reform, was clearly not appreciated in Downing Street. Michael Marland, a great innovator whose 1975 book for new teachers is still read today,[17] is sadly mocked for his sartorial style. A blaming of the comprehensive principle for the lack of achievement by what were secondary modern schools, a partial version of educational history and a rose-tinted view of New Labour build up to a rather worrying manifesto of 'more of the same'.

Where Adonis and I are in agreement is on the need for ambitious standards, the recognition that individual schools can make a difference and the wish to lessen the gap between the achievement of the advantaged and the disadvantaged. I was pleased to note his firm rebuttal of whether schools should be run for profit ('I am opposed to this')[18] and his chosen Book of the Year: Pasi Sahlberg's description of Finland's highly successful education system.[19]

Despite Finland's radically different approach, Adonis's proposed methods by which to accomplish a better system depend on a continuation of the policies of New Labour. If politicians – even progressive people like Adonis – are stuck in a well-worn policy rut, change will occur only if ordinary people assert themselves. Citizens must take the lead and demand change.

I witnessed an impressive example of how democracy can work when, in spring 2012, I attended an assembly of London Citizens – a broad grouping of faiths, trade union members and citizens' groups[20] – meeting with four of the candidates for the post of London's mayor. Unlike any other political hustings I have ever attended, candidates were prevented from attacking their rivals' policies and barracking was banned. The citizens interrogated the candidates on their policies and sought their support for the organisation's campaigns on the London living wage, safer streets, preserving an Olympic legacy and better housing in the capital. These were citizens who knew what London needed and who grasped that they could take the initiative with politicians seeking public office.

So what should we do? If you agree with the main thrust of my argument – even if not all of the detail – speak out: at home, work, social events, your children's schools, political meetings, trade union conferences and church gatherings. Use social networks to build up pressure. Enlist leaders to take forward the ideas. Persuade politicians of all parties to support a campaign for the better system that our children and our society deserve. The key to Finland's success is the continuity provided by a 25-year agreement between its main political parties on the principles underpinning the education system it was developing. We must strive to create such an agreement in England.

Those seeking change will be up against strong opposition from all who see such ideas as dangerously liberal. Right-wing think-tanks – funded by anonymous donors – will do their best to rubbish the arguments. Madsen Pirie, the founder of the Adam Smith Institute in 1977, has documented the way lobbyists, newspaper reporters and think-tank researchers, over the last 30 years, have manipulated the political agenda of successive governments.[21] He boasts that his institute was behind the privatisation of public utilities and the railways and the contracting-out of public services to private companies. Who knows who has been behind the systematic fragmentation of the education service?

Well-organised opposition can be overcome only by a mass desire for a fair education system, serving the interests of *all* society, led by determined campaigners.

Readers, create the opportunity for an 'education spring' and do your part in building an education system – and a society – worth leaving to your children and your grandchildren.

Afterword for paperback edition

I am writing this Afterword some 19 months after submitting the manuscript for the book's first edition. In some ways England's education system appears to have changed little since then – the same Coalition government rules and the same Chief Inspector remains in post. The minister, however, has changed, and it will be interesting to see how much she is prepared to address the issues highlighted in this book. Already a number of cracks are appearing in the system and a number of subtle changes have been – or are likely to be – made. Whether the 2015 general election will cause more dramatic transformation remains to be seen.

English people seldom take to the streets to demand change. Even so, politicians tend not, completely, to ignore their voters. As a result, some of the issues highlighted here may possibly be moving towards resolution.

There seems to be general agreement that oversight of academies and free schools cannot remain solely with the minister. There are now simply too many such schools and some have produced high-profile scandals. Whether a new 'middle tier' (envisaged by the Coalition government as local commissioners and by the Blunkett Report[1] as independent directors of school standards) comes into existence or whether local authorities will return to favour remains to be seen. But some structural change appears inevitable. As Simon Jenkins argues, ministers 'have long been frantic to seize schools from local control, convinced that councils are incompetent or ideologically unsound. But they have persistently failed to find a substitute for local accountability.'[2]

The role and style of inspection is also changing – the Chief Inspector has announced an end to the use of private contractors undertaking inspections. But more changes may be required to stem the mounting criticism brought to public notice by the furore surrounding the so-called 'Trojan horse' episode affecting a number of schools in Birmingham in the summer of 2014.[3] The rapid reversal of Ofsted gradings from 'outstanding' to downright failure and the threat of government takeover raises questions both about the reliability of judgements and the independence of the inspectors.

The same episode has highlighted some of the unpredicted (at least by ministers) consequences of permitting the establishment of so many faith schools and even to allow non-faith ones to embrace religious behaviour. This has led to more fundamental questions about how prudent it is, so casually, to mix education and religion.

Insisting on the teaching of 'British values'[4] may appear to be a unifying idea but, without a commonly agreed set of values, it may be interpreted by some as simply another way to subdivide society or even as a way to encourage Islamophobia.

Ironically, many people's sense of fair play – frequently lauded as a traditional British value – is being offended by increasing inequality. Oxfam marked the beginning of the 2014 World Cup football competition with a report detailing the relative inequalities existing within the 32 competing countries. In the Oxfam investigation Belgium emerges as the sixth richest but the most equal country while England is ranked as ninth richest but only the fifteenth most equal. Oxfam comments: 'We live in a country where the richest 10% earn more than the bottom 40% and where five families between them own more than 12 million people (do).'[5]

A report from the Parliamentary Education Committee draws attention to the issue of the relatively poor achievement of white working-class children and notes the differences in achievement between those who attend effective schools and who do not.[6] One of its recommendations deals with the need for government 'to maintain its focus on getting the best teachers to the areas that need them most'. While this suggestion echoes one of the proposals I make in Chapter Thirteen, it is important that any response incorporates a full range of strategies. Certainly, the Chief Inspector's suggestion that head teachers should be given powers to fine unsupportive parents[7, 8] should be firmly resisted on the grounds that this is most likely to alienate such parents still further.

The shortage of good candidates applying for headship may also force changes to the role and responsibilities of head teachers. While many heads appear satisfied with their jobs[9] and have increased their powers – some think too greatly – a number are facing increasing insecurity. As one (successful) head commented to me, "working in an academy chain can mean that you are just one bad inspection report or one poor set of results away from dismissal".

Pressure on teachers has mounted to such an extent that some are seeking alternative careers. According to the TALIS survey of teachers' conditions in England, only 35% of them believe that their profession is valued by society.[10] Furthermore, shortages in subject specialisms are beginning to occur once more. If, as must be hoped, the economy improves and employment opportunities grow in other fields, we may well again suffer a serious teacher shortage with its implications for the overall quality of the profession.

Another potential driver of change may be a growing feeling among head teachers that – despite ministerial drives for endless competition – collaboration is an essential part of an effective education system. This feeling may stimulate the growth of voluntary associations to bring together individual schools of many different types. The representative of a regional body recently revealed to me how it was covertly supporting a number of projects fostering cooperation.

Over the last year I have enjoyed numerous opportunities to discuss – with a variety of audiences – the arguments set out in this book. The reactions I have received have been overwhelmingly positive. Many have not agreed with all my suggestions for change but most have welcomed the chance to discuss how our system might be improved. Like Alan Bennett (talking about the need to incorporate private schools into the education system), I believe that 'the nation is still generous, magnanimous and above all fair'[11] and that – sooner or later – the tide of public opinion will turn, and future ministers will be obliged to reverse the most objectionable of their current education policies.

Paradoxically, therefore, even at a time when the English state education system – through the actions of our politicians – is being more violently fragmented than at any time in its history, I feel cautiously optimistic about its future recovery.

Notes

Chapter 1

[1] Aristotle (c 350 BC) *Politics*, Book 8, Part 2 (trans B. Jowett), The Internet Classics Archive, http://classics.mit.edu/Aristotle/politics.8.eight.html.

[2] Wikipedia needs to be used with caution, as not every entry has been validated independently. But it offers an impressive open resource in tune with our times.

[3] Jean Piaget was a Swiss developmental psychologist and philosopher. For a sample of his work see Piaget, J. and Inhelder, B., trans. H. Weaver (1969) *The psychology of the child*, New York: Basic Books. For a description of his work see Smith, L. (ed) (1996) *Critical readings on Piaget*, London: Routledge.

[4] The Oxford Dictionaries, http://oxforddictionaries.com/definition/english/attitude.

[5] 'The knowledge', see Transport for London, http://www.tfl.gov.uk/businessandpartners/taxisandprivatehire/1412.aspx.

[6] Maguire, E., Gadian, D., Johnsrude, I., Good, C., Ashburner, J., Frackowiak, R. and Frith, C. (2000) 'Navigation-related structural change in the hippocampi of taxi drivers', *Proceedings of the National Academy of Sciences of the United States of America*, published online before print, 14 March 2000, doi: 10.1073/pnas.070039597, http://www.pnas.org/content/97/8/4398.short.

[7] Prange, K. (2004) 'Bildung: a paradigm regained?' *European Educational Research Journal*, vol 3, no 2, pp 501–9.

[8] John Amos Comenius, entry in *Encyclopaedia Britannica*, http://www.britannica.com/EBchecked/topic/127493/John-Amos-Comenius.

[9] Comenius, J. (1984) *The school of infancy*, ed Ernest McNeill Eller, Chapel Hill, NC: Carolina Press.

[10] John Amos Comenius, entry in *Encyclopaedia Britannica*, http://www.britannica.com/EBchecked/topic/127493/John-Amos-Comenius.

[11] Ryan, A. (1995) *John Dewey and the high tide of American liberalism*, New York: W.W. Norton and Company.

[12] Ryan, A. (1995) *John Dewey and the high tide of American liberalism*, New York: W.W. Norton and Company, p 134.

[13] Barnes, J. (2011) *Sense of an ending*, London: Jonathan Cape.

[14] An Englishman who had served as a politician in Australia, Lowe was Vice President of the Committee of Council responsible for education and, later,

Chancellor of the Exchequer in one of Gladstone's administrations. *Hansard* CLXXXVIII, cols 1548–9.

[15] Lowe, R. (1862) Statement to the House of Commons, quoted in Johnson, B. (1956) 'The development of English education 1856–1882', MEd thesis University of Durham.

[16] Green, A. (1997) *Education, globalisation and the nation state*, London: Macmillan, p 42.

[17] Chomsky, N. (1979) *Language and responsibility*, Sussex: Harvester Press.

[18] Fagin is a fictional criminal character in *Oliver Twist*, a novel by Charles Dickens.

[19] Barber, L. (2009) 'My harsh lesson in love and life', *Observer*, 7 June.

[20] Churchill, W. (1930) *A roving commission: My early life*, London: Charles Scribner, p 12.

[21] See the Open University 40th Anniversary Poem, http://www8.open.ac.uk/platform/events/arena/40th-anniversary/open-university-40th-anniversary-poem.

[22] *Educating Rita*, a 1983 film based on the play of the same title by Willy Russell.

Chapter 2

[1] Orwell, G. (1948) *Nineteen eighty four*, London: Penguin.

[2] See for instance *The quiet American* (1955), London: Heinemann; *The Comedians* (1966), London: Bodley Head.

[3] For an alternative, though overlapping view, readers should consult Pring, R. (2012) *The life and death of secondary education for all*, Oxford: Routledge.

[4] Jewish Virtual Library, http://www.jewishvirtuallibrary.org/jsource/judaica/ejud_0002_0015_0_14977.html.

[5] Apartheid legislation in South Africa, http://africanhistory.about.com/library/bl/blsalaws.htm.

[6] The Gettysburg address, http://myloc.gov/Exhibitions/gettysburgaddress/exhibitionitems/ExhibitObjects/NicolayCopy.aspx?sc_id=wikip.

[7] Key facts, history highlights, New Zealand democracy, http://www.elections.org.nz/study/education-centre/nz-electoral-facts-stats/key-facts-history-highlights-nzs-democracy.html.

[8] See, for instance, Seldon, A. (2011) 'Toby Young has a point', *Guardian*, 3 September.

[9] Flavell, J.H. (1976) 'Metacognitive aspects of problem solving', in L.B. Resnick (ed) *The nature of intelligence*, Hillsdale, NJ: Erlbaum Associates, pp 231–6.

[10] Einstein, A. (1931) *Cosmic religion: With other opinions and aphorisms*, New York: Dover Publications, p 97.

[11] Sigmund Freud (1856–1939), see Internet Encyclopaedia of Philosophy, www.iep.uutm.edu/freud/

[12] Collins Dictionary, http://www.collinsdictionary.com/dictionary/english/happiness.

[13] Maslow, A. (1943) 'A theory of human motivation', *Psychological Review*, vol 50, no 4, pp 370–96.

[14] Marmot, M., Rose, G., Shipley, M. and Hamilton, P. (1978) 'Employment grade and coronary heart disease in British civil servants', *Journal of Epidemiology and Community Health*, vol 32, no 4, pp 244–9.

[15] For a discussion of mindfulness, see for instance: Germer, C., Siegel, R. and Fulton, P. (eds) (2013) *Mindfulness and psychotherapy*, New York: Guilford Press.

[16] Layard, R. (2009) 'This is the greatest good', *Guardian*, 13 September, www.guardian.co.uk. See also Layard, R. (2011) *Happiness: Lessons from a new science* (revised edn), London: Penguin.

[17] Office for National Statistics (2011) 'Initial investigation into Subjective Wellbeing', *Opinions Survey*, 1 December.

[18] Stiglitz, J., Sen, A. and Fitoussi, J. (2009) *Report by the Commission on the Measurement of Economic Performance and Social Progress*, www.stiglitz-sen-fitoussi.fr.

[19] Csikszentmihalyi, M. (1990) *Flow: The psychology of optimal experience*, New York: Harper and Row.

[20] Jenkins, S. (2012) 'Gove's centralism is not so much socialist as Soviet', *Guardian*, 12 October.

[21] Those interested can find full details on: http://www.newfoundations.com/GALLERY/Hirsch.html.

[22] Those interested should read the entry on the dyslexia website, http://www.bdadyslexia.org.uk/about-dyslexia/schools-colleges-and-universities/dyscalculia.html.

[23] For an interesting discussion of this problem and possible ways to cure it see Buxton, L. (1981) *Do you panic about maths?* London: Heinemann.

[24] Young, C., Wu, S. and Menon, V. (2012) 'The neurodevelopment basis of maths anxiety', *Psychological Science*, vol 23, no 5, pp 492–501.

[25] European Organisation for Nuclear Research (2011) 'The Large Hadron Collider', press release, 21 September, http://press.web.cern.ch/public/en/LHC/LHC-en.html.

[26] Hawking, S. and Penrose, R. (1996) *The nature of space and time*, Princeton, NJ: Princeton University Press.

[27] Rees, M. (2011) 'Educating Einsteins', *Guardian*, 20 September.

[28] Higgins, C. (2011) 'Historians say Michael Gove risks turning history lessons into propaganda classes', *Guardian*, 17 August.

[29] See, for instance, Cobain, L. (2011) *Cruel Britannia: A secret history of torture*, London: Portobello Books, or consult the 'Lost British Colonial Papers' by the Foreign and Commonwealth Office, oversesreview.blogspot.co.uk/lost-british-colonial-papers-made.html.

[30] Evans, R. (2011) 'Learn for the right reasons', *Guardian*, 27 August.

[31] DfES (Department for Education and Skills) (2002) *Languages for life: A strategy for England*, London: DfES.

[32] Nuffield Foundation (2000) *Languages: The next generation*, http://www.nuffieldfoundation.org/nuffield-languages-inquiry-and-nuffield-languages-programme.

[33] Burstall, C. (1975) 'Primary French in the balance', *Educational Research*, vol 17, no 3, pp 193–8.

[34] 'El Sistema: changing lives through music', *CBS News Sixty Minutes*, http://www.cbsnews.com/stories/2008/04/11/60minutes/main4009335.shtml.

[35] Acceptance speech by José Antonio Abreu at the 2001 Right Livelihood Award Presentation, http://www.rightlivelihood.org/abreu.html.

[36] See http://makeabignoise.org.uk/sistema-scotland/board-members/.

[37] See article by Ed Vulliamy (2010) *Guardian*, 13 October, www.guardian.co.uk/2010/oct/0/britain-children-orchestra-sistema

[38] White, J. (2012) 'Towards a new ABC of curriculum-making: a reply to John Hopkin', *Forum*, vol 54, no 2, pp 305–12.

[39] Boyer, C. (1991) *A history of mathematics*, Oxford: Wiley.

[40] Gray, J. (2012) 'Wellbeing matters too', *Research Intelligence*, no 117, p 30.

[41] Pring, R. (2013) *Must secondary education for all be but a dream?*, London: Routledge, p 188.

Chapter 3

[1] See http://www.greatkat.com/03/madamecurie.html.

[2] Berners-Lee, T. and Fischetti, M. (1999) *Weaving the web: The original design and ultimate destiny of the World Wide Web by its inventor*, Windsor: Orion Business.

[3] Other kinds of practical abilities, equally important though they may be, are beyond the scope of this book.

[4] According to Mackintosh, the term 'IQ' derived from the German *intelligenz-quotient* and was used by William Stern in 1912 as a method of scoring children's intelligence tests. See Mackintosh, N. (1998) *IQ and human intelligence*, Oxford: Oxford University Press.

[5] Binet, A. (1903) *Experimental study of intelligence*, Paris: Schleicher.

[6] White, J. (2006) *Intelligence, destiny and education: The ideological roots of intelligence testing*, London: Routledge.

[7] Murdoch, S. (2007) *IQ: A smart history of a failed idea*, Hoboken, NJ: John Wiley and Sons Inc.

[8] Burt, C. (1933) *How the mind works*, London: Allen and Unwin, pp 28-9.

[9] Scarr, S. (1994) 'Burt, Cyril L.', in R. Sternberg (ed) *Encyclopaedia of intelligence*, New York: Macmillan.

[10] Sternberg, R. and Salter, W. (1982) *Handbook of human intelligence*, Cambridge, UK: Cambridge University Press.

[11] Gottfredson, L. (1997) 'Intelligence and social policy', *Intelligence*, vol 24, no 1, pp 1–12.

[12] Moseley, D., Baumfield, V., Elliott, J., Gregson, M., Higgins, S., Miller, J. and Newton, D. (2005) 'De Bono's lateral and parallel thinking tools', in D. Moseley (ed) *Frameworks for thinking*, Cambridge, UK: Cambridge University Press.

[13] See, for instance, Mayer, J., Carusso, D. and Salovey, P. (2000) 'Emotional intelligence meets traditional standards for an intelligence', *Intelligence*, vol 27, no 4, pp 267–98.

[14] Goleman, D. (1995) *Emotional intelligence: Why it can matter more than IQ*, New York: Bantam Books.

[15] Gardner, H. (1999) *Intelligence reframed: Multiple intelligences for the 21st century*, New York: Basic Books.

[16] This approach has also been severely criticised in, for instance, White, J. (1998) *Do Howard Gardner's multiple intelligences add up?* London: Institute of Education, University of London.

[17] See, for instance, Sternberg, R. and Grigorenko, E. (1997) *Intelligence, heredity and environment*, Cambridge, UK: Cambridge University Press.

[18] Gardner, H. (1997) 'The case of Mozart', in *Extraordinary Minds*, London: Weidenfeld and Nicolson.

[19] Laurance, J. (2006) 'Length of a woman's ring finger reveals her sporting ability', *Independent*, 28 September.

[20] See Gladwell, M. (2008) *Outliers: The story of success*, London: Allen Lane; Syed, M. (2010) *Bounce: How champions are made*, London: Fourth Estate.

[21] James, O. (2010) *How not to f*** them up*, London: Vermilion.

[22] According to the American National Institute of Neurological Disorders and Stroke information page in February 2011: 'Attention deficit-hyperactivity disorder (ADHD) is a neurobehavioral disorder that affects 3–5 percent of all American children. It interferes with a person's ability to stay on a task and to exercise age-appropriate inhibition (cognitive alone or both cognitive and behavioral). Some of the warning signs of ADHD include failure to listen to instructions, inability to organize oneself and school work, fidgeting with hands and feet, talking too much, leaving projects, chores and homework unfinished, and having trouble paying attention to and responding to details. There are several types of ADHD: a predominantly inattentive subtype, a predominantly hyperactive-impulsive subtype, and a combined subtype. ADHD is usually diagnosed in childhood, although the condition can continue into the adult years.'

[23] Sternberg, R. and Grigorenko, E. (eds) (1997) *Intelligence, heredity and environment,* Cambridge University Press: Cambridge; Kang, M., Hsu, M., Krajbich, I., Loewenstein, G., McClure, S., Wang, J. and Camerer, C. (2009) 'The wick in the candle of learning: epistemic curiosity activates reward circuitry and enhances memory', *Psychological Science*, vol 20, no 8, pp 963–73.

[24] See Cofer, C. and Appley, M. (1967) *Motivation: Theory and research*, New York, London, Sydney: John Wiley and Sons; Bandura, A. (1997) *Self-efficacy: The exercise of control*, New York: Freeman.

[25] Knox, R. (1950) *Enthusiasm*, Oxford: The Clarendon Press; Wesley, J. 'The nature of enthusiasm', in T. Jackson (1872) *The Sermons of John Wesley*, Nampa, ID: Wesley Center for Applied Theology, Northwest Nazarene University.

[26] Garmezy, N. (1991) 'Resiliency and vulnerability to adverse developmental outcomes associated with poverty', *American Behavioural Scientist*, vol 34, no 4, pp 416–30; Rutter, M. (2008) 'Developing concepts in developmental psychopathology', in J. Hudziak (ed) *Developmental psychopathology and wellness: Genetic and environmental influences*, Washington, DC: American Psychiatric Publishing.

[27] See OECD (2010) *PISA 2009 Results, What students know and can do: student performance in reading, mathematics and science*, Paris: OECD.

[28] Rutter, M. (2006) 'Implications of resilience concepts for scientific understanding', *Annals of the New York Academy of Sciences*, no 1094, pp 1–12.

[29] Chua, A. (2011) *Battle hymn of the tiger mother*, New York: Penguin Press.

[30] See, for instance, the way Chomsky distinguishes between 'competence' (idealised capacity) and 'performance' (actual utterances) in Chomsky, N. (1965) *Aspects of the theory of syntax*, Cambridge, MA: MIT Press.

[31] Ramsden, S., Richardson, F., Josse, G., Thomas, M., Ellis, C., Shakeshaft, C., Seghier, M. and Price, C. (2011) 'Verbal and non-verbal intelligence changes in the teenage brain', *Nature*, published online 19 October 2011, www.nature.com/nature/journal/v479/n7371/full/nature10514.html

[32] What statisticians term 'the standard deviation'.

[33] The BBC has broadcast a series of programmes in which the American writer Garrison Keillor describes life in a fictional town called Lake Wobegon.

[34] A common pattern of scores occurs on many statistical measures. This is known as a 'normal distribution'. The pattern resembles an upside-down U-shape (often called a bell curve) with the largest number of cases occurring in the centre of the curve and a declining but similar numbers of positive and negative cases at the 'thin ends' of the curve. Such patterns are found in the distribution of height, weight and many other human attributes, as well as in many natural phenomena.

[35] Jensen, A. (1969) 'How much can we boost IQ and scholastic achievement?', *Harvard Educational Press*, vol 39, no 1, pp 1–123; Gould, S. (1996) *The mismeasure of man* (2nd edn), New York: W.W. Norton and Co; Herrnstein, R. and Murray, C. (1994) *The bell curve: Intelligence and class structure in American life*, New York: Free Press; Wilson, W.J. (1987) *The truly disadvantaged: The inner city, the underclass and public policy*, Chicago: University of Chicago Press.

[36] European test producers' group (2011) *The A–Z of testing*, http://www.etpg.org/G-IOFTESTING.htm.

[37] Gladwell, M. (2008) *Outliers: The story of success*, London: Allen Lane.

[38] Syed, M. (2010) *Bounce: How champions are made*, London: Fourth Estate.

[39] Syed, M. (2010) *Bounce: How champions are made*, London: Fourth Estate, p 7.

[40] Collini, S. (2010) 'Social mobility: the playing field fallacy', *Guardian*, 23 August, Collini, S. (2007) *Common reading: Critics, historians, publics*, Oxford: Oxford University Press.

[41] Nash, P. (1976) *Teacher expectations and pupil learning*, London: Routledge and Kegan Paul.

[42] Rosenthal, R. and Jacobson, L. (1968) *Pygmalion in the classroom: Teacher expectation and pupils' intellectual development*, New York: Holt, Rinehart & Winston.

[43] Rhem, J. (1999) Online National Teaching and Learning Forum, no 8, p 2, www.ntlf.com/article-directory/editorsnote.aspx.

[44] Crawford, C., Dearden, L. and Greaves, E. (2011) 'Does when you are born matter? The impact of month of birth on children's cognitive and non-cognitive skills in England', A report to the Nuffield Foundation, London: Institute for Fiscal Studies.

[45] Gladwell, M. (2008) *Outliers: The story of success*, London: Allen Lane.

Chapter 4

[1] Abbott, J. (1994) *Learning makes sense*, Letchworth: Education 2000, p vii.

[2] The Effective Provision of Pre-School Education (EPPE) Project, *Research Report from Key Stage 3 Phase*, https.//www.education.gov.uk/publications/.

[3] Ryan, A. (1995) *John Dewey and the high tide of American liberalism*, New York: W.W. Norton.

[4] Roberts, P. (2000) *Education, literacy and humanization: Exploring the work of Paulo Freire*, Westport, CT: Bergin and Garvey.

[5] Lillard, A. (2005) *Montessori: The science behind the genius*, Oxford: Oxford University Press.

[6] Kolb, D. and Fry, R. (1975) 'Toward an applied theory of experiential learning', in C. Cooper (ed) *Theories of group process*, London: John Wiley.

[7] Kwok, J. (2010) *Girl in translation*, London: Penguin, p 1.

[8] Richardson, H. (2011) 'Slow starting pupils don't catch up, league tables how', BBC news online, www.bbc.co.uk/news/education-16186158

[9] Watson, J. (1913) 'Psychology as the behaviourist views it', *Psychological Review*, vol 20, pp 158–77.

[10] Skinner. B.F. (1968) *Technology of teaching*, East Norwalk, CT: Appledore-Century-Crofts.

[11] Todes, D. (1997) 'Pavlov's physiological factory', *Isis*, vol 88, *The History of Science society*, pp 205–46.

[12] Daniels, H. (ed) (1996) *An introduction to Vygotsky*, London: Routledge.

[13] Chaiklin, S. (2003) *Vygotsky's educational theory in cultural context*, Cambridge, UK: Cambridge University Press.

[14] Those interested should consult 'Genetic epistemology', in *The theory in practice (TIP) guide* by G. Kearsley. This is part of InstructionalDesign.org, http://www.instructionaldesign.org/index.html.

[15] Piaget, J. (1953) *The origin of intelligence in the child*, New York: Routledge and Kegan Paul.

[16] Ryan, A. (1995) *John Dewey and the high tide of American liberalism*, New York: W.W. Norton.

[17] Smith, M. (2001) *Kurt Lewin: Groups, experiential learning and action research*, Infed, http://www.infed.org/thinkers/et-lewin.htm.

[18] Olson, D. (2007) 'Jerome Bruner', in *Continuum library of educational thought*, London: Continuum.

[19] Duffy, T. and Jonassen, D. (eds) (1992) *Constuctivism and the technology of instruction: A conversation*, Hillsdale, NJ: Lawrence Erlbaum Associates.

[20] Bereiter, C. and Scandamalia, M. (1989) 'Intentional learning as a goal of instruction', in L. Resnick (ed) *Knowing, learning and instruction: essays in honour of Robert Glaser*, New York: Routledge.

[21] Baron-Cohen, S. (1991) 'Do people with autism understand what causes emotion?' *Child Development*, vol 62, no 2, pp 385–95.

[22] Kolb, D., Boyatzís, R. and Mainemelis, K. (1999) 'Experiental learning theory: previous research and new directions', in R.J. Sternberg and L.F. Zhang (eds) *Perspectives on cognitive learning and thinking styles*, NJ: Lawrence Erlbaum, p 4.

[23] Smith, M. (2001) *David A. Kolb on experiential learning*, http://www.infed.org/biblio/b-explrn.htm.

[24] A Learning Style questionnaire has been developed by Peter Honey and Alan Mumford. This is widely used as an employment tool in the UK – see Ipsos MORI 1999 poll, http://www.ipsosmori.com/researchpublications/researcharchive.aspx?keyword=Learning.

[25] Leite, W., Marilla, S. and Yuying, S. (2009) *Attempted validation of the scores of the VARK: Learning styles inventory with multitrait–multimethod confirmatory factor analysis models*, London: Sage Publications, p 2.

[26] See, for instance, Henry, J. (2007) 'Professor pans "learning style" teaching method', *Telegraph*, 29 July; Coffield, F., Moseley, D., Hall, E. and Ecclestone, K. (2004) *Learning styles and pedagogy in post-16 learning: A systematic and critical review*, London: Learning and Skills Research Centre; Hargreaves, D., Beere, J., Swindells, M., Wise, D., Desforges, C., Goswami, U. and Wood, D. (2005) *About learning: Report of the Learning Working Group*, London: Demos.

[27] Edleman, G. (1992) *Bright air, brilliant fire: On the matter of the mind*, New York, NY: Basic Books, p xiii.

[28] As argued by Sylvester, R. (1996) 'Recent cognitive science developments pose major educational challenges', *Education 2000 News*, June.

[29] Stanford Encyclopaedia of Philosophy, http://plato.stanford.edu/about.html.

[30] See http://www.ibnalhaytham.net/.

[31] See http://www.davinciandthebrain.org/neuro.jsp.

[32] See http://www.nobelprize.org/nobel_prizes/medicine/laureates/1906/cajal-bio.html.

[33] Carter, R. (2007) 'Architecture and the brain', in J. Eberhard (ed) *Architecture and the brain: A new knowledge base from neuroscience*, New York: Greenway Communications, p 1.

[34] McNeil, F. (1999) 'Brain research and learning: an introduction', *Research Matters*, no 10, p 2, London: Institute of Education.

[35] Laurillard, D. (1995) 'Multimedia and the changing experience of the learner', *British Journal of Educational Technology*, vol 26, no 3, pp 179–89.

[36] Moss, G., Jewitt, C., Levačič, R., Armstrong, V., Cardini, A.., Castle, F., Allen, B., Jenkins, A. and Hancock, M. with High, S. (2007) *The interactive whiteboards, pedagogy and pupil performance evaluation: An evaluation of the Schools Whiteboard Expansion (SWE) Project*, London: London Challenge.

[37] Department for Children, Schools and Families and British Educational Communications and Technology Agency (2007) *Evaluation of the DCSF Primary Schools Whiteboard Expansion Project*, London: DCSF.

[38] Buckingham, D. (2007) *Beyond technology: Children's learning in the age of digital culture*, Cambridge: Polity Press, p 13.

[39] Mitra, S., Dangwal, R., Chatterjee, S., Jha, S., Bisht, R. and Kapur, P. (2005) 'Acquisition of computing literacy on shared public computers: Children and the "hole in the wall"', *Australian Journal of Educational Technology*, vol 21, no 3, pp 407–26.

[40] Vezzosi, A. (1997) *Leonardo da Vinci: Renaissance man*, London: Thames and Hudson.

[41] Haughton, H., Phillips, A. and Summerfield, G. (1994) *John Clare in context*, Cambridge UK: Cambridge University Press.

[42] Shawn, A. (2002) *Arnold Schoenberg's journey*, New York: Farrar Straus and Giroux.

[43] Interested readers should consult some of the many publications from anthropology, linguistics, computer science, neuroscience and psychology such as Johnson-Laird, P. (1980) 'Mental models in cognitive science', *Cognitive Science*, vol 4, no 1, pp 71–115. For a specifically pedagogical reference see Moore, A. (2000) *Teaching and learning: Pedagogy, curriculum and culture*, London: Routledge Falmer.

[44] Baker, M. (2012) 'It's the non-core bits of the curriculum that stay with you for life', *Guardian*, 19 June.

Chapter 5

[1] Waugh, E. (1928) *Decline and fall*, London: Penguin Classics.

[2] Those interested in the history of the teaching profession in England should consult Aldrich, R. (1998) 'Teacher training in London', in R. Floud and S. Glynn (eds) *London Higher: The establishment of higher education in London*, London: Athlone Press.

[3] The full text is available at http://www.educationengland.org.uk/documents/james/.

[4] See the archived material on the GTC in the Institute of Education, http://www.ioe.ac.uk/services/64986.html.

[5] The Teaching Agency website, http://www.education.gov.uk/aboutdfe/executiveagencies/b0077806/teaching-agency/the-teaching-agency.

[6] Teach Direct website, http://www.teachdirect.co.uk/login/index.php.

[7] Teach First website, http://www.teachfirst.org.uk/AboutUs/.

[8] Institute of Education (2012) 'Government's decision on unqualified teachers contradicts its own White Paper', press release, 31 July.

[9] DfE (2010) *The Importance of Teaching: The Schools White Paper*, London: The Stationery Office, Cm 7980.

[10] See speech by Michael Gove at the National College Annual Conference, 17 June 2010, www.education.gov.uk/inthe news/speeches/a0061371/michael-gove-to-the-national-college-annual-conference-birmingham.

[11] Gilbert, F. (2012) 'This proposal is an outrage', *Guardian*, 28 July.

[12] Schleicher, A. (2012) 'You must emulate and innovate to keep pace', *Times Educational Supplement*, 16 November.

[13] Marland, M. (1975) *The craft of the classroom*, Oxford: Heinemann Education Publishing.

[14] See Ofsted website, http://www.goodpractice.ofsted.gov.uk/

[15] Mortimore, P. (1999) *Understanding pedagogy and its impact on learning*, London: Paul Chapman Publishing.

[16] DfE (2011) *Teachers' standards*, https://www.education.gov.uk/publications/standard/SchoolsSO/Page1/DFE-00066-2011.

[17] Association of Teachers and Lecturers (2011) *Response to the DfE Review of Teachers' Standards*, http://www.atl.org.uk/Images/ATLTeachingStandardsResponseFinal.pdf.

[18] McCourt, F. (2005) *Teacher man*, London: Fourth Estate, p 19.

[19] OECD (2012) *Education at a glance*, Paris: OECD, Chart D3.1. The figures have been changed from US dollars to pounds sterling.

[20] Institute of Education (2014) 'International survey offers wealth of new information on England's secondary schools', London: Institute of Education, 25 June, http://www.ioe.ac.uk//100850.html.

[21] OECD (2012) *Education at a glance*, Paris: OECD, Chart D4.2.

[22] Mortimore, P., Mortimore, J. and Thomas, H. (1994) *Managing associate staff: Innovation in primary and secondary schools*, London: Paul Chapman Publishing.

[23] Webster, R., Blatchford, P. and Russell, A. (2012) *The guide on the side: Realising the value of teaching assistants*, Abingdon, Oxon: Routledge.

[24] OECD (2012) *Education at a glance*, Paris: OECD, Table D2.1.

[25] Mortimore, P. and Blatchford, P. (1993) 'The issue of class size', *National Commission Briefings*, London: Heinemann; Krueger, A. (2003) 'Economic considerations and class size', *Economic Journal*, Royal Economic Society, vol 113 (485) pp 34–63.

[26] Blatchford, P. (2003) *The class size debate: Is small better?*, Maidenhead: Open University Press.

[27] Husbands, C. (2014) 'TALIS: A complex and realistic picture of teachers and teaching around the world', IoE blog, http://ioelondonblog.wordpress.com.

[28] Carlsen, W. (1991) 'Questioning in classrooms: a sociolinguistic perspective', *Review of Education Research*, vol 61, no 2, pp 157–78; Rosenshine, B. and Meister, C. (1994) 'Reciprocal teaching; a review of the research', *Review of Education Research*, vol 64, no 4, pp 478–530.

[29] Paul, R. and Elder, L. (2006) *The art of Socratic questioning*, Dillon Beach, CA: Foundation for Critical Thinking.

[30] Russell, W. (2011) Personal communication.

[31] Collins, N. (2012) 'Sir John Gurdon, Nobel Prize winner was "too stupid" for science at school', *Telegraph*, 8 October.

[32] Gipps, C. (1994) *Beyond testing: Towards a theory of educational assessment*, London: Routledge.

[33] See history of pupil profiling for background information, http://www.heacademy.ac.uk/assets/documents/resources/heca/heca_ra01.pdf.

[34] Spark, M. (1961) *The prime of Miss Jean Brodie*, London: Macmillan.

[35] John Keating, star of Peter Weir's 1989 film *Dead Poets Society*.

[36] Lawes, S. (2011) 'Schools of the future: what is education for?' Birmingham Salon – a public forum for debate, www.birminghamsalon.org/

[37] McKinsey Education (2009) *Shaping the future: How good education systems can become great in the decade ahead*, Report on the International Education Round Table, Singapore.

[38] Chapman, J. (2012) 'Bad teachers should be sacked in weeks', *Mail Online*, 13 January.

[39] Shaw, G.B. (1903) 'Maxims for revolutionists', New York: W.W. Norton and Company.

[40] Camus, A. (1957) Letter to his teacher on receiving the news that he had been awarded the Nobel Prize for literature, in O. Todd (1997) *Albert Camus: A life*, New York, NY: Alfred A. Knopf, Inc.

Chapter 6

[1] Education Otherwise, http://www.education-otherwise.net/.

[2] MacGregor, N. (2010) *A history of the world in 100 objects*, London: Allen Lane.

[3] Clements, J. (2008) *Confucius: A biography*, Stroud, England: Sutton Publishing.

[4] Cherniss, H. (1945) *The riddle of the early academy*, Cambridge, UK: Cambridge University Press.

[5] Barnes, J. (1995) 'Life and work', in *The Cambridge Companion to Aristotle*, Cambridge, UK: Cambridge University Press.

[6] Gillard, D. (2011) *Education in England: A brief history*, www.educationengland.org.uk/history.

[7] Wiborg, S. (2009) *Education and social integration*, Basingstoke: Palgrave Macmillan.

[8] Gillard, D. (2011) *Education in England: A brief history*, www.educationengland.org.uk/history.

[9] HM Government (1944) The Education Act (Butler Act).

[10] Ministry of Education (1945) *The Nation's Schools*, explained that the new 'modern' schools would be for working-class children 'whose future employment will not demand any measure of technical skill or knowledge', quoted in Benn, C. and Chitty, C. (1996) *Thirty years on: Is comprehensive education alive and well or struggling to survive?* London: David Fulton Publishers.

[11] Gillard. D. (2011) *Education in England: A brief history*, www.educationengland.org.uk/history.

[12] Gillard, D. (2011) *Education in England: A brief history*, www.educationengland.org.uk/history.

[13] See *Observer*, 11 November 2011.

[14] Benn, M. (2011) *School wars: The battle for Britain's education*, London: Verso.

[15] DfE (2012a) *Schools, pupils and their characteristics*, www.gov.uk/government/publications/schools-pupils-and-their-characteristics-January-2013.

[16] Alston, C. (1989) *Transition into the secondary school*, London: ILEA Research and Statistics.

[17] DfE (2012b) *The school census and Edubase*, www.education.gov.uk/rsgateway/schoolcensus.shtml.

[18] Grant-maintained schools database at the National Archives, http://www.nationalarchives.gov.uk/catalogue/displaycataloguedetails.asp?CATLN=3&CATID=60004&SearchInit=4&SearchType=6&CATREF=ED+278&j=1.

[19] Those interested should visit the Headmasters' and Headmistresses' Conference website, http://www.hmc.org.uk/hmc6.htm.

[20] Beacon status was a government designation used between 1998 and 2005. Designated schools were funded to build partnerships with schools defined as failing, or in special measures, in order to improve their performance.

[21] See the DfE website, http://www.education.gov.uk/schools/leadership/typesofschools/technical.

[22] See the DfE website, http://www.education.gov.uk/schools/leadership/typesofschools/technical.

[23] Swedish National Agency for Education (2007) *The Swedish education system,* Stockholm: SNAE.

[24] Center for Research on Education Outcomes (CREDO) (2009) *Multiple choice: Charter school performance in 16 states*, Stanford, CA: Stanford University.

[25] www.newschoolsnetwork.org/understanding-free-schools/free-school-facts-and-figures

[26] See the DfE website, www.education.gov.uk/schools/leadership/typesofschools/a00210474/uts.

[27] DfE (2010) *The Importance of Teaching: The Schools White Paper*, Cm 7980, London: The Stationery Office, Cm 7980.

[28] Clifton, J. (2011) 'International comparisons can be instructive if used properly – but, on this too, England is lagging behind', *Times Educational Supplement*, 15 July.

[29] Lawn, M. and Grek, S. (2012) *Europeanizing education: Governing a new policy space*, Oxford: Symposium Books, p 19.

[30] Center for Research on Education Outcomes (CREDO), (2009) *Multiple choice: Charter school performance in 16 states,* Stanford, CA: Stanford University, http://credo.stanford.edu.

[31] Imsen, G., Blossing, U. and Moos, L. (eds) (forthcoming) *A school for all encounters neo-liberal policy*, London: Springer.

[32] Known in Denmark as an STX school.

[33] Known in Denmark as an HTX school.

[34] Known in Denmark as an HHX school.

[35] Frandsen, J., Gjesing, K. and Haue, H. (forthcoming) *More than a school: An introduction to the Danish efterskole.*

[36] PISA is discussed in Chapter Eleven.

[37] Sahlberg, P. (2011) *Finnish lessons: What can the world learn from educational change in Finland?* New York: Teachers' College, Columbia University, p 39.

[38] Sahlberg, P. (2011) *Finnish lessons: What can the world learn from educational change in Finland?* New York: Teachers' College, Columbia University, p 39.

[39] Moos, L. (2013) *Transnational influences on values and practices in Nordic education*, London: Springer.

[40] Gopinathan, S. (1996) 'Globalisation, the state and education policy in Singapore', *Asia Pacific Journal of Education*, vol 16, no 1, pp 74–87.

[41] Singapore Ministry of Education (2012) *Our education system*, Singapore: Ministry of Education.

[42] Eurydice (2010) *National system overviews of education systems – Spain*, Brussels: European Commission.

[43] See 'Recommendation on special education in the schools of the Federal Republic of Germany' (*Empfehlungen zur sonderpädagogischen Förderung in den Schulen in der Bundesrepublik Deutschland*, Decision of 6 May 1994), http://www.european-agency.org/country-information/germany/national-overview/special-needs-education-within-the-education-system.

[44] Neill, A.S. (1996) *Summerhill School: A new view of childhood*, New York: St. Martin's Griffin.

[45] Russell, W., recounted on Radio 4 programme 'With great pleasure', personal communication, 3 November 2011.

[46] Those wishing to see a film of A.S. Neill at the school can view the 1964 film *Here and now: Summerhill Freedom School*, East Anglian Film Archive, Leiston, Suffolk, http://www.eafa.org.uk/default.aspx.

[47] Stronach, I. (2012) '(B)othering education: an autobiography of alternatives', *Other Education: The Journal of Educational Alternatives*, vol 1, no 1, pp 171–4.

[48] Twain, M. (1898) *Mark Twain's notebook*, New York: Harper and Brothers.

[49] McCourt, F. (2005) *Teacher man*, London: Fourth Estate, p 255.

[50] Chatzitheochari, S., Parsons, S. and Platt, L. (2014) *Bullying victimisation among disabled children and young people: Evidence from two British longitudinal studies*, London: Institute of Education, http://www.cls.ioe.ac.uk/childhooddisability.

[51] Lawson, D. and Silver, H. (1973) *A social history of education in England*, London: Methuen.

[52] *Evening Standard*, 17 October 2011, p 29.

[53] Elton Report (1989) *Discipline in Schools*, London: Her Majesty's Stationery Office, p 11.

[54] Steer Report (2005) *Learning behaviour: The report of the Practitioners' Group on school behaviour and discipline*, London: Department for Education and Skills, p 52.

[55] Letter from Alan Steer to Secretary of State, 6 February 2009.

[56] Ofsted (2011) *Annual Report 2010–11*, London: Ofsted, p 12.

[57] Institute of Education (2014) 'International survey offers wealth of new information on England's secondary schools', London: Institute of Education, 25 June, http://www.ioe.ac.uk//100850.html.

[58] 'The tempest', posted on 28 September 2012, http://themusingsofaheadteacher.wordpress.com/2012/09/28/the-tempest/.

[59] Dobson, J. (2008) 'Pupil mobility, choice and the secondary school market: assumptions and realities', *Educational Review*, vol 60, no 3, pp 299–314.

[60] DfE (2012a) *Schools, pupils and their characteristics*, www.education.gov.uk/researchandstatistics/datasets/a00209478/schl-pupil-charac-jan-2012

[61] Mortimore, P., Davies, J., Varlaam, A. and West, A. with Devine, P. and Mazza, J. (1983) *Behaviour problems in schools: An evaluation of support centres*, Beckenham: Croom Helm.

[62] See, for instance, Dawkins, R. (1976) *The selfish gene*, Oxford: Oxford University Press.

[63] Adrenalin – a natural stimulant manufactured in the kidney and carried in the bloodstream, which controls the heart rate, http://www.ch.ic.ac.uk/rzepa/mim/drugs/html/adrenaline_text.htm.

[64] Ofsted (2003) *The education of six year olds in England, Denmark and Finland: An international comparative study*, London: Ofsted.

[65] Beckett, F. (2011) 'Take-your- pick schools, with do-it-all heroes', *New Statesman*, 15 September.

[66] Rutter, M., Maughan, B., Mortimore, P. and Ouston, J. (1979) *Fifteen thousand hours: Secondary schools and their effects on children*, London: Open Books.

[67] See for instance: Mortimore, P. (1998) 'The vital hours: reflecting on research on schools and their effects', in A. Hargreaves, A. Lieberman, M. Fullan and D. Hopkins (eds) *International handbook of educational change*, Dordrecht, Netherlands: Kluwer Academic Publishers.

[68] Sammons, P. (2007) *School effectiveness and equity – making connections: A literature review*, London: Council for British Teachers Education Trust.

[69] Mortimore, P., Sammons, P., Stoll, L., Lewis, D. and Ecob, R. (1988) *School matters: The junior years*, London: Paul Chapman Publishing.

[70] Mortimore, P. (1998) *The road to improvement: Reflections on school effectiveness*, Lisse, Netherlands: Svets and Zeitlinger.

[71] See, for instance, White, J. and Barber, M. (1997) *Perspectives on school effectiveness and school improvement*, London: Institute of Education.

[72] A term coined by the French sociologist Pierre Bourdieu in his discussion of the types of 'capital' that people own and that parents can endow on their children in addition to straightforward economic capital. Bourdieu distinguishes between 'social capital' – membership of supportive groups or networks of friends; 'symbolic capital' – honours, recognition or fame; and 'cultural capital' – positive attitudes towards learning and knowledge of how the education system works. See Bourdieu, P. and Passeron, J. (1990) *Reproduction in education, society and culture*, London: Sage Publications.

[73] National Equality Panel (2010) *An anatomy of economic inequality in the UK*, London: Government Equalities Office.

[74] According to The System for Teacher and Student Advancement (TAP) website, value-added analysis is a statistical technique 'that uses student achievement data over time to measure the learning gains students make. This methodology offers a way to estimate the impact schools and teachers have on student learning isolated from other contributing factors such as family characteristics and socioeconomic background. In other words, value-added analysis provides a way to measure the effect a school or teacher has on student academic performance over the course of a school year or another period of time' (http://www.tapsystem.org/policyresearch/policyresearch.taf?page=valueadded).

[75] See, for instance, Gorard, S. (2006) 'Value-added is of little value', *Journal of Educational Policy*, vol 21, no 2, pp 235–43.

[76] Paton, G. (2011) 'More children being sent to private tutors, says Sutton Trust', *Telegraph*, 5 September.

[77] Bray, M. (2011) *Confronting the shadow education system: What government policies for what private tutoring?*, Paris: IIER/UNESCO Publishing.

[78] Reported by Tania Branigan, *Guardian*, 29 July 2012.

[79] Maddern, K. (2012) 'How the poorest school beat the odds', *Times Educational Supplement*, 26 October.

[80] OECD (2012) *Schooling for tomorrow: Scenarios*, Paris: OECD.

[81] See Hutmacher, W., Cochrane, D. and Bottani, N. (eds) (2001) *In pursuit of equity in education*, New York: Springer.

[82] Schleicher, A. (2012) 'You must emulate and innovate to keep pace', *Times Educational Supplement*, 16 November.

[83] Barker, E. (1953) *Father of the man*, London, Oxford: Oxford University Press.

Chapter 7

[1] The Exeter experiment is noted in Gillham, B. (1977) 'The reluctant beneficiaries: the teacher and the public examination system', *British Journal of Educational Studies*, vol 25, no 1, pp 50–62.

[2] See Mortimore, J., Mortimore, P. and Chitty, C. (1986) *Secondary school examinations: The helpful servant not the dominating master*, London: Bedford Way Papers.

[3] See the Revised Code of 1862 ('Lowe's Code') in Gillard, D. (2011) *Education in England: A brief history*, www.educationengland.org.uk/history.

[4] See the DfE website, http://www.education.gov.uk/childrenandyoungpeople/earlylearningandchildcare/a0068102/early-years-foundation-stage-eyfs.

[5] It was part of a set of three levels. The others were Advanced Level (A level) for 18-year-olds and Scholarship Level (S level) for academic high-flyers wanting to enter the more prestigious universities.

[6] The CSE was the product of a recommendation from the 1954 Crowther Committee, made a reality by the 1960 Beloe Report. The first examinations were offered 1965 to give time for it to bed down before the change to compulsory school attendance.

[7] Jones, K. (2003) *Education in Britain: 1944 to the present*, Cambridge, UK: Polity Press, quoted in Gillard, D. (2011) *Education in England: A brief history*, www.educationengland.org.uk/history, http://www.educationengland.org.uk/history/px/dailymirror.JPG.

[8] Joint Council for Qualifications (2012) *GCSEs*, www.jcq.org.uk/examination-results/gcses.

[9] See the QCA's guide, *GCSEs – the official student guide to the system*, www.qca.org.uk/GCSE/.

[10] These include: Assessment and Qualifications Alliance (web.aqa.org.uk); Oxford, Cambridge and Royal Society of Arts Examinations (www.OCR.org.uk); Edexcel – owned by Pearsons, a large international publishing company (www.edexel.com); Welsh Joint Examination Committee (www.WJEC.co.uk) and the Council for the Curriculum, Examinations and Assessment of Northern Ireland (www. council-for-the-curriculum-examinations-and-assesment-ccea.html).

[11] Ofqual is the regulator of qualifications, examinations and assessments in England, www.ofqual.gov.uk/

[12] See www.ofqual.gov.uk.

[13] Reported in *Guardian*, 23 October 2012.

[14] Those interested in the normal distribution curve should consult 'Maths is fun', www.mathsisfun.com/data/standard-normal-distribution.html.

[15] 'Only brightest students to take new EBacc', *Telegraph*, 8 October 2012, www.telegraph.co.uk/education/educationnews/9590878/Only-brightest-students-to-take-new-EBacc.html.

[16] Rosen, M. (2012) 'Letter from a curious parent', *Guardian*, 3 July.

[17] House of Commons Education Committee (2013) *From GCSEs to EBCs: The government's proposals for reform,* Eighth Report of Session 2012–13, London: The Stationery Office.

[18] Walker, P. (2013) 'Michael Gove warned by exams watchdog to rethink EBacc', *Guardian*, 5 December.

[19] Oral statement to Parliament on education reform by Michael Gove, www.gov.uk/government/organisations/department-for-education.

[20] Stewart, W. (2013) 'It's GCSEs, but not as we know them', *Times Educational Supplement*, 14 June.

[21] Curriculum 2000 changed A levels into a set of six modules, with half taken at the end of the first year, at age 17, and the next three a year later, at age 18. Vocational subjects, such as art and design, applied business studies, and business and science, were also added to the potential mix.

[22] Machin, S. and Vignoles, A. (2006) *Education policies in the UK*, London: Centre for the Economics of Education, London School of Economics.

[23] DfES/Welsh Office (1988) *Advancing A Levels: Report of a Committee appointed by the Secretary of State for Education and Science and the Secretary of State for Wales* (The Higginson Report), London: HMSO.

[24] Tomlinson, M. (2004) *Final Report of the Working Group on 14–19 Reform*, London: DfE.

[25] Wolf, A. (2011) *Review of vocational education: The Wolf Report*, www.education.gov.uk/publications/.

[26] Excerpt from Michael Gove's letter to Ofqual, www.bbc.co.uk/news/education-17588292.

[27] Marshall, B. and Brown, M. (2012) personal communication.

[28] Gopal, P. (2012) 'A version of class war', *Guardian*, 4 April.

[29] Paton, G. (2013) 'Russell Group invited to 'review new A-level exams', *Telegraph*, 14 June.

[30] Lowe was condemned by a resolution of MPs. He was later cleared of editing HMI Reports but was not reinstated in this post. He went on to serve, among other positions, as Chancellor of the Exchequer.

[31] Dunford, J. (1999) *Her Majesty's Inspectorate of schools: Standard bearers or turbulent priests?* London: Woburn Press.

[32] DfES/Welsh Office (1982) *Study of HM Inspectorate in England and Wales* (Rayner Report), London: HMSO.

[33] Thomas, G. (1998) 'A brief history of the genesis of the new schools' inspection system', *British Journal of Educational Studies*, vol 46, no 4, pp 415–27.

[34] The Education (Schools) Act 1992 established the Office of Her Majesty's Chief Inspector (Ofsted) as a non-ministerial department of state. It is explicitly named as Ofsted in the Education and Inspections Act 2006.

[35] Hackett, G. (1999) 'MPs angered by support for Woodhead', *Times Educational Supplement*, 30 July.

[36] Harvey Goldstein and I wrote a critique of an Ofsted Report concerned with reading in the inner city and Chris Woodhead and I engaged in a somewhat heated argument about it on the BBC *Today* programme in October 1996.

[37] Ofsted (2012) *Annual report of Her Majesty's Inspector of Education, Children's Services and Skills*, London: The Stationery Office.

Chapter 8

[1] White, J. (2007) *What schools are for and why*, IMPACT Paper no 14, Philosophy of Education Society of Great Britain, p 1.

[2] Reported in Alexander, R. (2010) *Children, their world, their education*, London: Routledge.

[3] http://www.parliament.uk/about/living-heritage/transformingsociety/livinglearning/school/overview/1870educationact/.

[4] Butler, R.A. (1943) Speech to House of Commons, 29 July, *Hansard*, vol 391, cc1, 825–928.

[5] HM Government (1988) *Education Reform Act*, London: Stationery Office.

[6] Dearing, R. (1993) *The National Curriculum and its assessment: Final Report*, London: School Curriculum and Assessment Authority.

[7] DfEE (Department for Education and Employment) (1997) *Excellence in Schools, White Paper*, Cm 3681, London: HMSO.

[8] Qualifications and Curriculum Authority (2007) *The National Curriculum at Key Stages 3 and 4*, London: QCA.

[9] DfE (2010) *The Importance of Teaching: The Schools White Paper*, Cm 7980, London: The Stationery Office.

[10] See Norwegian Ministry of Education Act, 17 July 1998, amended 25 June 2010.

[11] See Alexander, R. (2010) *Children, their world, their education*, London: Routledge. On page 197 he sets out 12 aims for primary education. These include distinct

aims for 'the individual', 'self, others and the wider world' and 'learning, knowing and doing'. For an assessment of White's views see Bloom, A. (2007) 'A curriculum out of time', *Times Educational Supplement*, 23 February.

[12] Mortimore, J. and Blackstone, T. (1982) *Disadvantage and education*, London: Heinemann Educational Books.

[13] See www.educationengland.org.uk/documents/taylor/.

[14] See www.education.gov.uk/leadership/governance/.

[15] 'Tougher tests planned for trainee teachers', *The Times*, 26 October 2012.

[16] Ofsted (2010) *The Annual Report of Her Majesty's Chief Inspector of Education, Children's Services and Skills 2009/10*, London: Ofsted, p 32.

[17] 'Former superhead to appear in court', *Times Educational Supplement*, 26 October 2012.

[18] Stewart, W. (2012) 'Financial malpractice rife in schools, says council', *Times Educational Supplement*, 31 August.

[19] Ofsted (2010) *The Annual Report of Her Majesty's Chief Inspector of Education, Children's Services and Skills 2009/10*, London: Ofsted, p 32.

[20] Ipsos/MORI (1963–2011) *Veracity index*, with Royal College of Physicians.

[21] For a description of pupil profiles in the 1970s see Burgess, T. and Adams, E. (1980) *Outcomes of education*, London: Macmillan; Scottish Council for Research in Education (1977) *Pupils in profile*, London: Hodder and Stoughton; and Swales, T. (1979) 'Record of personal achievement', Schools Council Pamphlet 16, London: Schools Council.

[22] DfEE (1999) *Citizenship – The National Curriculum*, https://www.education.gov.uk/publications/eOrderingDownload/QCA-99-470.pdf .

[23] See the In Harmony Project website, www.ihse.org.uk.

[24] OECD (2009) *Doing better for children*, Paris: OECD, fig 2.13.

[25] See the Forest School website, http://www.forestry.gov.uk/website/pdf.nsf/pdf/SERG_Forest_School_research_summary.pdf/$FILE/SERG_Forest_School_research_summary.pdf.

[26] Programme for International Student Assessment (PISA) (2009) *What students know and can do*, vol 1, Paris: OECD.

[27] See the direct.gov website, http://www.direct.gov.uk/en/Parents/Preschooldevelopmentandlearning/NurseriesPlaygroupsReceptionClasses/DG_173054.

[28] Hutchings, J., Bywater, T., Daley, D., Gardner, F., Whitaker, C., Jones, K., Eames, C. and Edwards, R. (2007) 'Parenting intervention in Sure Start services for children at

risk of developing conduct disorder: pragmatic randomised controlled trial', *British Medical Journal*, vol 334 (7595), pp 678–82.

[29] See http://www.dur.ac.uk/research/directory/view/?mode=project&id=11.

[30] National Evaluation of Sure Start Team (2008) *The impact of Sure Start on local programmes and three year-olds and their families*, http://www.ness.bbk.ac.uk/impact/documents/42.pdf.

Chapter 9

[1] Chantrill, C. (2012) 'UK public spending since 1900', www.ukpublicspending.co.uk/spending_brief.php.

[2] Treasury Estimates for 2013–14, https://www.gov.uk/government/uploads/system/uploads/attachment_data/file/197737/intro_mainsupplyestimates_201314.pdf.

[3] Chowdry, H. and Sibieta, L. (2011) *Trends in education and school spending*, London: Institute for Fiscal Studies.

[4] See BBC News report for details of the scheme, http://news.bbc.co.uk/1/hi/education/3638739.stm.

[5] See the Wikipedia entry on EMAs, http://en.wikipedia.org/wiki/Education_Maintenance_Allowance.

[6] Wainwright, O. (2012) 'Holland Park School opts for corporate vision with £80m building', www.guardian.co.uk/artanddesign/2012/oct/28/holland-park-school-building?INTCMP=SRCH

[7] Her Majesty's Inspectors (1978) *Primary education in England: A survey by HM Inspectors of Schools*, London: HMSO.

[8] Central Advisory Council for Education (England) (1967) *Children and their primary schools* (The Plowden Report), London: HMSO. The Council, chaired by Bridget Plowden, carried out a three-year investigation into primary education. The Report was seen as child-centred because it considered issues such as the relationship between schools and homes, nursery education, corporal punishment and the need for positive discrimination in favour of the most disadvantaged. It also recommended the use of primary school buildings out of school hours and increasing the number of male primary teachers.

[9] First used in 1960 by Lord Eccles, Minister of Education, according to Gillard, D. (1988) *The National Curriculum and the role of the primary teacher in curriculum development*, www.educationengland.org.uk/articles/07ncteacher.html.

[10] DfES (Department of Education and Science) (1977) *Curriculum 11–16* (HMI 'Red Book'), London: HMSO.

[11] Hirst, P. (1974) *Knowledge and the curriculum*, London: Routledge and Kegan Paul.

[12] Lawton, D. (1980) 'Common curriculum or core curriculum?', *International Journal of Research and Method in Education*, vol 3, no 1, pp 5–10.

[13] Reported in Graham, D. and Tytler, D. (1993) *A lesson for us all: The making of the National Curriculum*, London: Routledge.

[14] Dearing, R. (1993) *The National Curriculum and its assessment*, London: DfES, HMSO.

[15] See report from Democratic Life website, www.democraticlife.org.uk/curriculum-review/national-curriculum-review-summary-terms-of-reference-and-timeframe/.

[16] For the full report see https://www.education.gov.uk/publications/eOrderingDownload/NCR-Expert%20Panel%20Report.pdf.

[17] Institute of Education (2012) 'Curriculum adviser says Gove's proposals are "fatally flawed"', press release, 12 June.

[18] Pollard, A. (2012) quoted by Jeevan Vasagar in 'Expert adviser attacks Gove's new curriculum', *Guardian*, 13 June.

[19] DfE (2013) *Draft National Curriculum programmes of study*, www.education.gov.uk/schools/teachingandlearning/curriculum/nationalcurriculum2014/.

[20] www.gov.uk/government/collections/nationalcurriculum.

[21] Mansell, W. (2007) *Education by numbers*, London: Politico.

[22] House of Commons Children, Schools and Families Committee (2008) *Testing and Assessment: Third Report of Session 2007–08*, London: The Stationery Office.

[23] Black, P., Gardner, J. and Wiliam, D. (2007) *Evidence provided to the House of Commons Children, Schools and Families Committee*, London: The Stationery Office.

[24] House of Commons Children, Schools and Families Committee (2008) *Testing and Assessment: Third Report of Session 2007–08*, London: The Stationery Office.

[25] Readers wanting more details of the 2012 GCSE episode should consult the *Times Educational Supplements* for autumn 2012.

[26] Shepherd, J. (2012) 'GCSE and A-levels are easier, Ofqual finds', *Guardian*, 1 May.

[27] House of Commons Education Committee (2012) *Chief Regulator of Qualifications and Examinations: Eighth Report of Session 2010–12*, London: The Stationery Office.

[28] Tattersall, K. (2012) 'An exam that will define failure, not success', *Guardian*, 18 September.

[29] See, for example, Stobart, G. (2008) *Testing times*, London: Routledge.

[30] Martini, R., Mortimore, P. and Byford, D. (1985) 'Some O levels are more equal than others', *Times Educational Supplement*, 28 June.

[31] Vasagar, J. and Booth, R. (2012) 'Teachers and pupils furious after sudden change in exam gradings', *Guardian*, 24 August.

[32] Michael Gove, quoted on BBC News, 3 September 2012, news.bbc.co.uk/today/hi/today/newsid_9748000/9748283.stm

[33] This was set in 2004 by ministry officials at 20% of pupils getting five A*–C GCSEs (English and maths not included); in 2006 it rose to 25%; in 2007 it rose to 30% getting five A*–C GCSEs including English and maths. In 2010, the Coalition government raised it to 35% getting five A*–C GCSEs including English and maths, combined with the majority of pupils making above-average progress from Key Stage 2 to Key Stage 4. The 35% 'floor' will increase. In 2012, it will rise to 40% and by the end of the Parliament it will rise to 50%.

[34] For an interesting discussion of this issue see Hattersley, R. (2005) 'Looking out for number one', *Education Guardian*, 22 February.

[35] See Mansell, W. (2007) *Education by numbers*, London: Politico.

[36] Newell, C. and Watt, H. (2011) 'Exam boards: "We're cheating, we're telling you the question cycle"', *Telegraph*, 7 December.

[37] *Times Educational Supplement* (2012) 'From the Editor', 24 August.

[38] See the discussion in: Symposium on Sustainable Schools (2014) 'Exam reform – unresolved issues: the risks and effects in focus', Symposium on Sustainable Schools.

[39] These included special agreement schools' secondary classes in elementary schools, permitted by the 1938 Education Act.

[40] Rogers, S. (2012) 'Data blog: how many poor children go to faith schools', 5 March, http://www.guardian.co.uk/news/datablog/2012/mar/05/faith-schools-admissions?INTCMP=SRCH.

[41] Allen, R. and West, A. (2011) 'Why do faith secondary schools have advantaged intakes? The relative importance of neighbourhood characteristics, social background and religious identification amongst parents', *British Educational Research Journal*, vol 37, no 4, pp 691–712.

[42] Shepherd, J. (2012) 'Faith schools and free school meals: case studies', *Guardian*, 5 March.

[43] Ward, H. (2012) 'Catch-up lessons are going down', *Times Educational Supplement*, 21 September.

[44] Rosen, M. (2012) 'Out of the toy cupboard', *New Statesman*, 5 March.

[45] In 1998 the National Literacy Strategy developed the literacy hour for primary schools. It was a daily English lesson that was structured in a specific way. The lesson began with clear objectives. For the first half pupils were taught as a whole class, reading together, extending their vocabulary, looking at the phonetics of words and being taught grammar, punctuation and spelling. This teacher-led part of the

hour was interactive, with the teacher modelling what the pupils had to do and the pupils increasingly joining in the activity, so that they had the confidence to work on their own in the second half of the lesson. Then they worked in groups or individually, with the teacher focusing on one group. The lesson ended with feedback from the children on what they had been doing in relation to the objectives of the lesson. See the National Literacy Trust information, www.literacytrust.org.uk/reading_connects/resources/331_the_literacy_hour_in_primary_schools.

[46] See, for instance, Rosen, C. and Rosen, H. (1973) *The language of primary school children*, Harmondsworth: Penguin; Meek, M. (1982) *Learning to read*, London: Bodley Head; Waterland, L. (1985) *Read with me: An apprenticeship approach to reading*, Stroud: Thimble Press; DfEE (1998) *The National Literacy strategy framework for teaching*, Sudbury: DfEE Publications; Rose, J. (2006) *Independent review of the teaching of early reading*, Nottingham: DfES Publications; Wyse, D. and Styles, M. (2007) 'Synthetic phonics and the teaching of reading: the debate surrounding England's "Rose Report"', *Literacy*, vol 41, no 1, pp 35–42.

[47] See Johnston, R. and Watson, J. (2005) 'A seven year study of the effects of synthetic phonics teaching on reading and spelling attainment', *Insight*, no 17, Edinburgh: Scottish Government, www.scotland.gov.uk/Publications/2005/02/20682/52383.

[48] National Institute of Child Health and Human Development (2000) *Report of the National Reading Panel, Teaching Children to Read: An evidence based assessment of the scientific research literature on reading and its implications for reading instruction: Reports of the subgroups*, NIH Publication no. 00-4754, Washington, DC: US Government Printing Office; Australian Department of Education Science and Training (2005) *Teaching reading: Report and recommendations, National enquiry into the teaching of literacy*, Barton, Australia: Department of Education, Science and Training.

[49] Committee of Enquiry (1975) *A language for life* (The Bullock Report) London: HMSO, p 32.

[50] Berliner, W. (2005) 'War of words', Education *Guardian*, 5 April.

[51] Wyse, D. and Parker, C. (2012) *The early literacy handbook*, London: Practical Preschool Books.

[52] Krashen, S. (2012) 'Wide reading is key', *Guardian*, 31 July.

[53] See http://timssandpirls.bc.edu/pirls2011/

[54] Elliott, A. (2012) 'Twenty years inspecting English schools – Ofsted 1992–2012', *Rise Review*, November.

[55] Ofsted also 'regulates and inspects childcare and children's social care, and inspects the Children and Family Court Advisory Support Service, initial teacher training, work-based learning and skills training, adult and community learning and education and training in prisons and other secure establishments. Ofsted assesses council children's services and inspects safeguarding, child protection, and services for looked after children' (Ofsted, https://www.education.gov.uk/publications/eOrderingDownload/120010.pdf).

[56] *Guardian*, 24 January 2012, p 32.

[57] Central Government Supply Estimates 2013–14. Main Supply Estimates 18 April 2013, https://www.gov.uk/government/uploads/system/uploads/attachment_data/file/229061/1074.pdf.

[58] Smith, E. (2012) *Luck: What it means and why it matters*, London: Bloomsbury.

[59] Wilby, P. (2012) 'Aside from football, sport in Britain is still a game for the elite', *Guardian*, 1 August.

[60] DfES (2003) *Full-service extended schools planning documents*, London: The Stationery Office.

[61] See, for instance, Dryfoos, J. (1995) 'Full service schools: revolution or fad?', *Journal of Research on Adolescence*, vol 5, no 2, pp 147–72.

[62] Rée, H. (1973) *Educator extraordinary: The life and achievements of Henry Morris, 1889–1961*, London: Longman.

Chapter 10

[1] Kogan, M. (1971) *The politics of education*, Harmondsworth: Penguin.

[2] See http://www.educationengland.org.uk/documents/robbins/.

[3] See http://www.educationengland.org.uk/documents/bullock/.

[4] See http://www.educationengland.org.uk/documents/warnock/.

[5] National Commission on Education (1993) 1. *Learning to succeed*. 2. *Briefings*. 3. *Insight*, London: William Heinemann.

[6] Alexander, R. (2010) *Children, their world, their education*, Abingdon, Oxon: Routledge.

[7] Clark, L. (2009) 'Children should start school at six says Cambridge review of primary education', *Mail Online*, 16 October.

[8] See Boston, J., Martin, J., Pallot, J. and Walsh, P. (1996) *Public management: The New Zealand model*, Auckland and Oxford: Oxford University Press; Karlsen, G. (2010) 'Friedman's ideas based on his book "Capitalism and Freedom" (1962, 2002)', paper presented at NordNet Seminar, Oslo, September; Le Grand, J. (2003) *Motivation, agency and public policy: Of knights and knaves, pawns and queens*, Oxford: Oxford University Press.

[9] Le Grand, J. (2003) *Motivation, agency and public policy: Of knights and knaves, pawns and queens*, Oxford: Oxford University Press.

[10] Jones, B. (2012) 'First "free" sixth form oversubscribed', *Guardian*, 5 March, notes that 'the London Academy of Excellence will be housed in former council offices

for Newham children's services and is drawing on the staff of its partner schools. ... Eton will supply an English teacher.'

[11] Wilkinson, R. and Pickett, K. (2009) *The spirit level: Why more equal societies almost always do better*, London: Allen Lane.

[12] Reay, D., Crozier, G. and James, D. (2011) *White middle-class identities and urban schooling*, Basingstoke: Palgrave Macmillan, p 7.

[13] Warwick Mansell (2011) reported that net financial benefits to schools becoming academies could be as much as £500,000 per year, 'Schools cash in on academy status', *Guardian*, 26 April.

[14] See Downes, P. (2011) 'I can't believe what is happening to the English education system', *Forum*, vol 53, no 3, pp 357–66. In this he reports a converted academy annually receiving more than £400,000 above the costs of its conversion.

[15] DfES, source quoted by Sutcliffe, J. (2001) *Times Educational Supplement*, 13 April, p 20.

[16] Pollack, A. (2004), cited in Ball, S. (2007) *Education PLC: Understanding private sector participation in public sector education*, Abingdon: Routledge.

[17] UNISON (2005) *The business of education*, http://www.unison.org.uk/acrobat/B1956.pdf.

[18] Benn, C. and Simon, B. (1970) *Half way there: Report on the British comprehensive system*, London: McGraw Hill.

[19] Millar, F. (2012) 'Time to debunk some myths about schools', *Guardian*, 10 April.

[20] Benn, M. (2011) *School wars: The battle for Britain's education*, London: Verso.

[21] Adapted by M. Strathern from Goodhart, C. (1984) *Monetary theory and practice: The UK experience*, London: Macmillan, p 96, http://www.atm.damtp.cam.ac.uk/mcintyre/papers/LHCE/goodhart.html.

[22] Buchanan, D. and Storey, J. (2010) 'Don't stop the clock: manipulating hospital waiting lists', *Journal of Health Organization and Management*, vol 24, no 4, pp 343–60.

[23] See Maclure, S. (1965) *Educational documents, Volume II*, Abingdon: Routledge.

[24] Morris, E. (2000), quoted by Liz Lightfoot, 'Labour praises ethos of private schools', *Telegraph*, 30 September.

[25] Bell, D. (2003) 'Standards and inspections in independent schools', Brighton College Conference on Independent Schools, reprinted in *Guardian*, 29 April.

[26] Fitz, J., Edwards, T. and Whitty, G. (1986) 'Beneficiaries, benefits and costs: an investigation of the Assisted Places Scheme', *Research Papers in Education*, vol 1, no 3, pp 169–93.

[27] Murray, J. (2012) 'They sat and talked to me about my child', *Guardian*, 24 July.

[28] National Centre for Social Research (2011) *British Social Attitudes Survey 28*, London: National Centre for Social Research.

[29] For examples of such dilemmas see Reay, D., Crozier, G. and James, D. (2011) *White middle-class identities and urban schooling*, Basingstoke: Palgrave Macmillan.

[30] National Centre for Social Research (2011) *British Social Attitudes Survey 28*, London: National Centre for Social Research.

[31] National Centre for Social Research (2011) *British Social Attitudes Survey 28*, London: National Centre for Social Research.

[32] Benn, M. (2011) *School wars: The battle for Britain's education*, London: Verso.

[33] Benn, M. and Millar, F. (2006) *A comprehensive future: Quality and equality for all our children*, London: Compass.

[34] Elliott, A. (2007) *State schools since the 1950s*, London: Trentham Books.

[35] Jackson, B. and Marsden, D. (1962) *Education and the working class*, Harmondsworth: Penguin.

[36] Barker, B. (2012) 'Grammar schools: brief flowering of social mobility?', *Forum*, vol 54, no 3, pp 429–47.

[37] Hillgate Group (1994) *The reform of British education*, London: Claridge Press.

[38] Benn, M. and Millar, F. (2006) *A comprehensive future: Quality and equality for all our children*, London: Compass

[39] Benn, M. and Millar, F. (2006) *A comprehensive future: Quality and equality for all our children*, London: Compass, p 13.

[40] Egan, M. and Bunting, B. (1991) 'The effects of coaching on 11+ scores', *British Journal of Educational Psychology*, vol 61, no 1, pp 85–91.

[41] Bunting, B. and Mooney, E. (2001) 'The effects of practice and coaching on test results for educational selection at eleven years of age', *Educational Psychology*, vol 21, no 3, pp 243–53.

[42] See the full Buckinghamshire Report, www.elevenplusexams.co.uk/forum/11plus/viewtopic.php?t=19691.

[43] Vernon, P.E. (ed) (1957) *Secondary school selection: A British Psychological Society Enquiry*, London: Methuen.

[44] Griffiths, J. (2003) *NFER the first fifty years 1946–1996*, Slough: NFER.

[45] Ramsden, S., Richardson, F., Josse, G., Thomas, M., Ellis, C., Shakeshaft, C., Seghier, M. and Price, C. (2011) 'Verbal and non-verbal intelligence changes in the teenage brain', *Nature*, published online 19 October, www.nature.com/nature/journal/v479/n7371/full/nature10514.html

[46] Danish Technological Institute (2005) *Explaining student performance, A study undertaken for the European Commission*, Copenhagen: Danish Technological Institute.

[47] Hutton, W. (2012) 'Born poor? Bad luck, you have won last prize in the lottery of life', *Observer*, 15 July.

[48] *Hansard*, 26 April 2011, cc 289W.

[49] *The grammar school: A secret history*, broadcast in two parts on BBC4 on 5 and 12 January 2012.

[50] Burgess, S., Dickson, M. and Macmillan, L. (2014) *Selective schooling systems increase inequality*, London: Institute of Education.

[51] Streaming is a form of grouping pupils according to their perceived overall ability in school work. Each stream remains together for all subjects.

[52] Setting is a form of grouping pupils according to their perceived ability in different subjects. Pupils can, in theory, be in different sets for different subjects.

[53] Speech to a Conservative audience in Tooting, South London, reported by Helene Mulholland, *Education Guardian*, 18 June 2007.

[54] Harlen, W. and Malcolm, H. (1999) 'Setting and streaming: A research review', *SCRE Publication 143*, Edinburgh: The Scottish Council for Research in Education.

[55] Lacey, C. (1975) 'De-streaming in a pressurised academic environment', in S.J. Eggleston (ed) *Contemporary research in the sociology of education*, London: Methuen; Boaler, J., William, D. and Brown, M. (2000) 'Experiences of ability grouping – disaffection, polarisation and the construction of failure', *British Educational Research Journal*, vol 28, no 5, pp 631–48; Ireson, J. and Hallam, S. (2001) *Ability grouping in education*, London: Paul Chapman Publishing; Gamoran, A. (2002) *Standards, inequality and ability grouping in schools*, CES Briefing, no 25, Edinburgh: Centre for Educational Sociology, Scottish Council for Educational Research, www.leeds.ac.uk/educol/documents/163446.pdf.

[56] Field, S., Kuczera, M. and Pont, B. (2007) 'No more failures: ten steps to equity in education', *Education and training policy*, Paris: OECD.

[57] OECD (2012) *Equity and quality in education: Supporting disadvantaged students and schools*, Paris: OECD.

[58] Laukkanen, R. (2006) 'Finnish strategy for high-level education for all', paper presented at Conference on Educational Systems and the Challenge of Improving Results, University of Lausanne, 15–16 September.

[59] OECD (2010) *PISA 2009 Results: What students know and can do, Volumes I–V*, Paris: OECD.

[60] HM Government (2005) *Higher standards, better schools for all*, White Paper, Cm 6677, London: HMSO.

[61] Data taken from http://www.barnardos.org.uk/what_we_do/our_work/child_poverty/child_poverty_what_is_poverty/child_poverty_statistics_facts.htm.

[62] Bertelsmann Stiftung (2011) 'Strong variations in social justice within the OECD', www.bertelsmann-stiftung.de/cps/rde/xchg/bst_engl/hs.xsl/nachrichten_110193.htm.

[63] Wilkinson, R. and Pickett, K. (2009) *The spirit level: Why more equal societies almost always do better*, London: Allen Lane.

[64] DCSF (2003) *Every child matters*, Green Paper, Cm 5860, London: DCSF.

[65] UNICEF (2012) 'Measuring child poverty', *Innocenti Research Centre Report Card 10*, Florence: Unicef Innocenti Research Centre.

[66] UNICEF (2007) 'Child poverty in perspective', *Innocenti Research Centre Report Card 7*, Florence: Innocenti Research Centre.

[67] Ipsos MORI/UNICEF (2011) *Child well-being in UK, Spain and Sweden: The role of inequality and materialism: A qualitative study*, London: UNICEF.

[68] UNICEF (2013) 'Child well-being in rich countries', *Innocenti Research Centre Report Card 11*, Florence: Innocenti Research Centre.

[69] Bradshaw, J. and Richardson, D. (2009) 'An index of child well-being in Europe', *Child Indicators Research*, vol 2, no 3, pp 319–51.

[70] See The Children's Society website entry on 'well-being', www.childrenssociety.org.uk/well-being-1; and Layard, R. and Dunn, J. (2009) *A good childhood: Searching for values in a competitive age*, London: Children's Society.

[71] The Children's Society (2012) *The Good Childhood Report: A review of our children's well-being*, London: Children's Society, www.childrenssociety.org.uk/well-being.

[72] Howard League for Penal Reform (2008) *Punishing children: A survey of criminal responsibility and approaches across Europe*, London: Howard League.

[73] Pring, R. (2013) *Must secondary education for all be but a dream?*, London: Routledge p 69.

[74] Extract taken from the Nuffield Foundation, Longman Resource Centre: 'The Certificate of Secondary Education (CSE) had been introduced in 1965 to provide a leaving certificate for the majority of students in schools who did not take GCSE O-levels. There were five pass grades (one to five). Grade One was recognised as equivalent to a pass at O-level. CSE and O-levels merged into the GCSE qualification in 1985. There were two popular CSE Modes: Mode 1 – a syllabus and examinations controlled externally by one of 14 regional CSE Boards and Mode 3 – a syllabus and examinations devised locally, by teachers in one or more schools, with external moderation. The course team argued that, at least at first, Mode 3 examining was particularly suitable for Secondary Science because it made it easier for teachers to ensure that their students were tested in ways that

reflected the objectives of the teaching' (www.nationalstemcentre.org.uk/elibrary/resource/2138/examining-at-cse-level).

Chapter 11

[1] White, J. (2005) *Towards an aims led curriculum*, London: QCA, http://dera.ioe.ac.uk/9704/1/11482_john_white_towards_an_aims_led_curr.pdf.

[2] See Deem, R., Brehony, K. and Heath, S. (1995) *Active citizenship and the governing of schools*, Buckingham: Open University Press.

[3] For an interesting discussion of the impact of extra resources see Pugh, G., Mangan, J. and Gray, J. (2011) 'Do increased resources increase educational attainment during a period of rising expenditure?', *British Educational Research Journal*, vol 37, no 1, pp 163–89.

[4] Downes, P. (2011) 'I can't believe what is happening to the English education system', *Forum*, vol 53, no 3, pp 357–66.

[5] HM Treasury (2011) *Treasury Minutes: Government responses on the Fourteenth to the Eighteenth Reports from the Committee of Public Accounts Session 2010–11* (March), London: Department for Education, Cm 8042, www.hm-treasury.gov.uk/d/minutes_14_18_reports.

[6] Vaughan, R. (2012) 'Because they're worth it', *Times Educational Supplement*, 2 November.

[7] See DfE, www.education.gov.uk/schools/adminandfinance/schoolscapital/buildingsanddesign/baseline.

[8] *BBC News*, 6 December 2011, www.bbc.co.uk/news/education-16050321.

[9] HEFCE (Higher Education Funding Council for England) (2010) *Trends in young peoples' participation in higher education: Core results for England*, Swindon: HEFCE.

[10] Figure cited in Baker, M. (2012) 'The shortage of primary places is a car crash', *Guardian*, 17 January.

[11] The examination results cut-off used by the ministry to close or reorganise a school – see discussion and note 33 in Chapter Nine.

[12] UK Parliament (2003) 'Individual Learning Accounts', *Select Committee on Public Accounts Tenth Report*, www.publications.parliament.uk/pa/cm200203/cmselect/cmpubacc/544/54403.htm.

[13] *Guardian*, 23 May 2014.

[14] See ATL (Association of Teachers and Lecturers) (2012) 'The middle tier – a view from the profession', ATL Policy Papers, www.atl.org.uk/Images/Middle%20tier%20doc.pdf.

[15] Crawford, C. (2014) *The link between secondary school characteristics and university participation and outcomes*, London: DfE.

[16] DfE (2013) *Phonics screening check and National Curriculum Assessments at Key Stage 1 in England*, London: DfE.

[17] This is an oversimplification. The TGAT report, produced by a group chaired by an expert in assessment from King's College, was ground breaking but necessarily complicated (Black, P. (1988) *Task Group on Assessment and Testing*, TGAT, London: King's College). I sat on the first working party set up to implement its recommendations and the task was extremely difficult. Since then there have been many modifications to both the teacher assessment and the testing.

[18] See definitions and explanations of common statistical terms in About.com Psychology, http://psychology.about.com/od/mindex/g/mean.htm.

[19] This is a new agency created by the DfE in 2012, http://www.education.gov.uk/aboutdfe/armslengthbodies/b00198511/sta.

[20] DfE (2012b) *National Curriculum Assessments at Key Stage 2 in England*, London: DfE.

[21] This is the most suitable comparison I could make because of a change in the formats of the data between 2011 and 2012.

[22] See DfE (2012) *GCSE (results provisional) sfr25/2012ks3*, London: DfE; and Paton, G. (2012) 'Academy schools inflate results with easy qualifications', *Telegraph*, 3 February.

[23] Patrick, H. (1996) 'Comparing public examination standards over time', paper presented at British Educational Research Association (BERA) conference, Birkbeck College, London.

[24] Barton, G. (2012) 'Flippancy makes exam system look even less credible', *Times Educational Supplement*, 14 September.

[25] A number of writers have focused on this issue. See Hörmann, B. (2009) 'Disappearing students: PISA and students with disability', in S. Hopmann and G. Brinek (eds) *PISA according to PISA*, Vienna: University of Vienna, http://www.univie.ac.at/pisaaccordingtopisa/pisazufolgepisa.pdf.

[26] Brown, M. (1998) 'The tyranny of the international horse race', in R. Slee and G. Weiner with S. Tomlinson (eds) *School effectiveness for whom*, London: Falmer Press.

[27] These points are made in Mortimore, P. (2009) 'Alternative models for analysing and representing countries' performance in PISA', paper commissioned by Education International Research Institute, Brussels: Education International.

[28] See oecdpisaletter.org.

[29] PIRLS is coordinated by the International Association for the Evaluation of Educational Achievement (IEA), http://timssandpirls.bc.edu/index.html.

[30] Mullis, I., Martin, M., Minnich, C., Stanco, G., Arora, A., Centurino, V. and Castle, C. (eds) (2012) *TIMSS 2011 Encyclopaedia: Education policy and curriculum in mathematics and science* (vols 1–2), Chestnut Hill, MA: Boston College.

[31] Mullis, I.V.S., Martin, M.O., Foy, P. and Arora, A. (2012) *2011 International results in mathematics*, Boston, MA: Timms and PIRLS International Study Center, Lynch School of Education, Boston College.

[32] PISA (2006) *Technical report*, Paris: OECD, p 20.

[33] PISA (2006) *Technical report*, Paris: OECD, p 22.

[34] See the letter of 3 October 2012 from Andrew Dilnot, Chair of the UK Statistics Authority on the fullfact.org website, http://fullfact.org/articles/statistics_watchdog_education_international_school_league_table_28392.

[35] See the comment by fullfact.org, http://fullfact.org/articles/statistics_watchdog_education_international_school_league_table-28392.

[36] Jerrim, J. (2012) 'England's plummeting PISA test scores between 2000 and 2009: is the performance of our secondary school pupils really in relative decline?' London: Institute of Education, www.ioe.ac.uk/newsEvents/60021.html.

[37] Schleicher, A. (2012) 'You must emulate and innovate to keep pace', *Times Educational Supplement*, 16 November.

[38] Over 100 in a school career, according to Marshall, B. (2005) 'Testing, testing, testing', in E. Wragg (ed) *Letters to the Prime Minister*, London: New Vision Group.

[39] House of Commons Children, Schools and Families Committee (2008) *Testing and Assessment: Third Report of Session 2007–08*, London: The Stationery Office.

[40] Mansell, W. (2007) *Education by numbers*, London: Politico.

[41] Schleicher, A. (2012) 'You must emulate and innovate to keep pace', *Times Educational Supplement*, 16 November.

[42] See the comment by Fullfact.org, http://fullfact.org/articles/statistics_watchdog_education_international_school_league_table-28392.

[43] Institute of Education (2014) 'International survey offers wealth of new information on England's secondary schools', London: Institute of Education, 25 June, http://www.ioe.ac.uk//100850.html.

Chapter 12

[1] Forster, E.M. (1909) *The machine stops*, Gloucester: Dodo Press.

[2] *Observer* (2011) 'Education reform: we need transparency not ideological zeal', 18 December.

[3] O'Shaughnessy, J. (2012) 'Competition meets collaboration: helping school chains address England's long tail of educational failure', London: Policy Exchange.

[4] Tomlinson, G. and Maud, J. (1951) Report of the Ministry of Education, quoted in Editorial, *Forum*, vol 53, no 3, pp 335–6.

[5] Labour Party (2014) *Review of education structures, functions and the raising of standards for all: Putting students and parents first* (The Blunkett Report), London: Labour Party.

[6] See Marmot, M., Rose, G., Shipley, M. and Hamilton, P. (1978) 'Employment grade and coronary heart disease in British civil servants', *Journal of Epidemiology and Community Health*, vol 32, no 4, pp 244–9.

[7] DES (Department for Education and Science) (1973) *Teacher education and training* (The James Report), London: DES.

[8] Mortimore, P. (2009) *Learning to be leaders of learning: Pitfalls seen by an English eye*, paper presented at the KL Partnerskab om Folkeskolen, Odense, Denmark, 24 February.

[9] Gurría, A. (2012) *Inequality*, address to the Chinese Academy of Governance by the Secretary General of the OECD, Beijing, People's Republic of China, 19 March.

[10] Yarker, P. (2011) *Crown Woods: Death of a comprehensive*, www.workersliberty.org/story/2011/08/02/crown-woods-death-comprehensive.

Chapter 13

[1] Bassey, M. (2012) 'Proposal for a national education service for primary and secondary education', www.free-school-from-government-control.com.

[2] O'Grady, S. (2012) 'Childcare costs parents quarter of their earnings', *Daily Express*, 2 July.

[3] Cooke, G. and Henehan, K. (2012) *Double Dutch: The case against deregulation and demand-led funding in childcare*, London: Institute for Public Policy Research.

[4] Jiménez, M. (2009) 'Early education's top model: Finland', *Toronto Globe and Mail*, 16 June.

[5] Toynbee, P. (2012) 'A strategy for growth must include childcare for all', *Guardian*, 14 February.

[6] For more information see www.education.gov.uk/childrenandyoungpeople/earlylearningandchildcare/delivery/education/a0068102/early-years-foundation-stage-eyfs.

[7] Ben-Galim, D. (2011) 'Making the case for universal childcare', London: Institute for Public Policy Research.

[8] Effective Provision of Pre-School Education Project (2002) 'Measuring the impact of pre-school on children's cognitive progress over the pre-school period', Technical Paper 8a, London: Institute of Education.

[9] Alexander, R. (2010) *Children, their world, their education*, London: Routledge.

[10] Glatter, R. (2012) 'Towards whole system improvement', *Forum*, vol 54, no 3, pp 411–16.

[11] Jenkins, S. (2012) 'This bid to force all schools into line will end in failure', *Guardian*, 28 November.

[12] Jenkins, S. (2012) 'This bid to force all schools into line will end in failure', *Guardian*, 28 November.

[13] See the DfE information on these posts – www.regionalschoolscommissioner.com/sections/about_the_org.

[14] Millar, F. (2012) 'We aren't going to surrender', *Guardian*, 19 June.

[15] LGA (Local Government Association) (2012) *Get in on the Act, Briefing on the Health and Social Care Act 2012*, London: LGA.

[16] Kluger, R. (1975) *Simple justice: The history of Brown v Board of Education and Black America's struggle for equality*, New York: Harper and Row.

[17] See Wikipedia article 'Desegregation bussing in the United States', En.wikipedia.org/wiki/desegregation_housing

[18] Allen, R., Burgess, S. and McKenna, L. (2010) *The early impact of Brighton and Hove's school admission reforms*, London: Institute of Education; Bristol: Centre for Market and Public Organisation, University of Bristol.

[19] See OECD (2010) *PISA 2009 results: What students know and can do*, Paris: OECD.

[20] Cho, S. (2011) 'Centralised national drive with advanced ICT infrastructure for preparation of Korean school teachers', paper given at the Comparative and International Education Society Conference, Montreal, Canada, 2 May.

[21] Interviews taken from the film *Lessons from Alberta* (2011), Evans Woolfe Media.

[22] The Sutton Trust (2012) *Democratising entry to independent day schools*, www.suttontrust.com/public/documents/1open-access-report-march-2012-final.pdf.

[23] Wilby, P. (2012) 'My idea to break the stranglehold of the public school gang', *Guardian*, 18 September.

[24] Barker, I. (2012) 'Private schools – Liverpool College and King's School, Tynemouth – give up on selection in bid to beat recession', *Times Educational Supplement*, 12 October.

[25] Dr Jonathan Romain, quoted in Paton, G. (2012) 'Selection by religion should be banned in state schools', *Telegraph*, 12 November.

[26] Stobart, G. (2008) *Testing times: The uses and abuses of assessment*, Oxford: Routledge, p 186.

[27] *Times Educational Supplement*, 9 February 2007, p 13.

[28] Huxley, A. (1932) *Brave new world*, London: Chatto and Windus.

[29] Wolf, A. (2011) *Review of vocational education*, London: DfE.

[30] Stobart, G. (2008) *Testing times: The uses and abuses of assessment*, Oxford: Routledge, p 186.

[31] Schleicher, A. (2012) 'You must emulate and innovate to keep pace', *Times Educational Supplement*, 16 November.

[32] Tomlinson, M. (2004) *Final Report of the Working Group on 14–19 Reform*, London: DfE.

[33] Ofsted (2012) *Annual report of Her Majesty's Inspector of Education, Children's Services and Skills*, London: The Stationery Office.

[34] Ofsted's formal status is as a non-ministerial government department.

[35] Weston, P. (1999) *Homework: Learning from practice*, London: Ofsted.

[36] Cummings, C., Dyson, A. and Todd, L. (2011) *Beyond the school gates: Can full service and extended schools overcome disadvantage?* Abingdon, Oxon: Routledge.

[37] See the Law Commission website, www.justice.gov.uk/about/law-comm.

[38] White, J. (2011) *The invention of the secondary curriculum*, New York: Palgrave Macmillan, p 142.

[39] Rosen, M. (2012) 'Letter from a curious parent', *Guardian*, 7 February.

[40] Mortimore, J., Mortimore, P. and Chitty, C. (1986) *Secondary school examinations: The helpful servant, not the dominating master*, London: Institute of Education.

[41] Wilby, P. (2012) 'For-profit schools would be no more virtuous than other private-sector firms', *Guardian*, 30 July.

[42] Mansell, W. (2012) 'The only way is Pearson', *Guardian*, 17 July.

[43] Ravitch, D., quoted in Mansell, W. (2012) 'The only way is Pearson', *Guardian*, 17 July.

Chapter 14

[1] For an analysis of this see Dorling, D. (2010) *Injustice: Why social inequality persists*, Bristol: The Policy Press.

[2] Raphael, D. and Macfie, A. (1976) 'Introduction', in D. Raphael and A. Macfie (eds) *Adam Smith, The theory of moral sentiments*, Oxford: Oxford University Press.

[3] See Leader, Z. (2000) (ed) *The letters of Kingsley Amis*, London: Harper Collins.

[4] Schleicher, A. (2012) 'You must emulate and innovate to keep pace', *Times Educational Supplement*, 16 November.

[5] Benn, M. (2011) *School wars: The battle for Britain's education*, London: Verso.

[6] Fielding, M. and Moss, P. (2011) *Radical education and the common school*, London: Routledge.

[7] White, J. (2011) *The invention of the secondary curriculum*, New York: Palgrave Macmillan.

[8] Pring, R. (2013) *Must secondary education for all be but a dream?*, London: Routledge.

[9] Reay, D., Crozier, G. and James, D. (2011) *White middle-class identities and urban schooling*, Basingstoke: Palgrave Macmillan.

[10] Ball, S. (2008) *The education debate*, Bristol: The Policy Press.

[11] Dorling, D. (2010) *Injustice: Why social inequality persists*, Bristol: The Policy Press.

[12] Thane, P. (2010) *Unequal Britain*, London: Continuum.

[13] Wilkinson, R. and Pickett, K. (2009) *The spirit level: Why more equal societies almost always do better*, London: Allen Lane.

[14] Millar, F. (2012) 'Labour needs to step up to the plate, fast', *Guardian*, 11 September.

[15] Adonis, A. (2012) *Education, education, education: Reforming England's schools*, London: Biteback Publishing.

[16] Adonis, A. (2012) *Education, education, education: Reforming England's schools*, London: Biteback Publishing, p xii.

[17] Marland, M. (1975) *The craft of the classroom*, London: Heinemann Educational.

[18] Adonis, A. (2012) *Education, education, education: Reforming England's schools*, London: Biteback Publishing, p 150.

[19] Sahlberg, P. (2011) *Finnish lessons: What can the world learn about educational change in Finland?*, New York and London: Teachers College Press.

[20] London Citizens, see www.citizensuk.org.

[21] Pirie, M. (2012) *Think tank: The story of the Adam Smith Institute*, London: Biteback Publishing.

Afterword

[1] Labour Party (2014) *Review of education structures, functions and the raising of standards for all: Putting students and parents first* (The Blunkett Report), London: Labour Party.

[2] Jenkins, S. (2014) 'Whitehall meddling is only ever bad news for education'. *Guardian*, 11 June.

[3] 'The Trojan horse' is the title given to an unsigned and undated letter – suspected of being a hoax – circulated among Birmingham school governors in March 2014. This letter, alleged to be from Islamists, suggested ways to take over control of schools in the city and in Bradford. The minister ordered Ofsted to investigate 21 schools and set up a further inquiry to be undertaken by a former police expert in terrorism, prompting criticism of promoting a witch hunt. Ofsted declared six schools to be inadequate (five were academies answering directly to the minister, some of which had formerly been rated as 'outstanding'). The affair was the subject of public arguments between the minister and the Home Secretary. For further discussion see the article by Oliver Wright in *The Independent* on Tuesday, 17 June, http://www.independent.co.uk/news/education/education-news/exclusive-fresh-doubt-over-michael-goves-version-of-trojan-horse-affair-9524627.html, or that by Tim Brighouse in the *Guardian* on the same day, https://www.google.co.uk/webhp?sourceid=chrome-instant&ion=1&espv=2&ie=UTF-8#q=Birmingham+Trojan+Horse+affair&tbm=nws, or for a fuller account, the Editorial in *School Leadership Today*, vol 6.1 – 'Gove and Wilshaw will rue Operation Trojan Donkey' – http://www.independent.co.uk/news/education/education-news/trojan-horse-row-qa-everything-you-need-to-know-about-alleged-plot-by-fundamentalist-muslims-to-take-over-schools-in-birmingham.

[4] The validity of such a choice of values – and the right to claim them as particularly British – has been questioned by a number of commentators. For a particularly astute critique, see: Rosen, M. (2014) 'Letter from a curious parent', *Guardian*, 1 July.

[5] Oxfam (2014) *The Inequality World Cup*, Report, 11 July, http://www.oxfam.org.uk/what-we-do/issues-we-work-on/inequality-world-cup.

[6] Education Committee (2014) *Underachievement in education by white working class children,* Report Number 1, London: Stationery Office, 11 June.

[7] Norton, J. (2014) 'Fine parents who don't read to their children, says Ofsted head (and Sir Michael Wilshaw also wants to punish those who miss school events)', Mail Online, 17 June, http://www.dailymail.co.uk/news/article-2659781/Fine-parents-dont-read-children-says-Ofsted-head-Sir-Michael-Wilshaw-wants-punishments-miss-school-events.html.

[8] Wilshaw, M. (2014) Address at Sunday Times Wellington Education Festival, 22 June.

[9] Institute of Education (2014) 'International survey offers wealth of new information on England's secondary schools', London: Institute of Education, 25 June, http://www.ioe.ac.uk//100850.html.

[10] Institute of Education (2014) 'International survey offers wealth of new information on England's secondary schools', London: Institute of Education, 25 June, http://www.ioe.ac.uk//100850.html.

[11] Bennett, A. (2014) 'Fair play', *London Review of Books* vol 36, no 12, pp 29-30.

References

Abbott, J. (1994) *Learning makes sense*, Letchworth: Education 2000.

Adonis, A. (2012) *Education, education, education: Reforming England's schools,* London: Biteback Publishing.

Aldrich, R. (1998) 'Teacher training in London', in R. Floud and S. Glynn (eds) *London Higher: The establishment of higher education in London*, London: Athlone Press.

Alexander, R. (2010) *Children, their world, their education*, London: Routledge.

Allen, R. and West, A. (2011) 'Why do faith secondary schools have advantaged intakes? The relative importance of neighbourhood characteristics, social background and religious identification amongst parents', *British Educational Research Journal*, vol 37, no 4, pp 691–712.

Allen, R., Burgess, S. and McKenna, L. (2010) *The early impact of Brighton and Hove's school admission reforms*, London: Institute of Education; Bristol: Centre for Market and Public Organisation, University of Bristol.

Aristotle (c 350 BC) *Politics, Book 8, Part 2* (trans B. Jowett), The Internet Classics Archive, http://classics.mit.edu/Aristotle/politics.8.eight.html.

Association of Teachers and Lecturers (2011) *Response to the DfE Review of Teachers' Standards*, http://www.atl.org.uk/Images/ATLTeachingStandardsResponseFinal.pdf.

ATL (Association of Teachers and Lecturers) (2012) 'The middle tier – a view from the profession', ATL Policy Papers, www.atl.org.uk/Images/Middle%20tier%20doc.pdf.

Australian Department of Education Science and Training (2005) *Teaching reading: Report and recommendations, National enquiry into the teaching of literacy,* Barton, Australia: Department of Education, Science and Training.

Baker, M. (2012) 'It's the non-core bits of the curriculum that stay with you for life', *Guardian*, 19 June.

Baker, M. (2012) 'The shortage of primary places is a car crash', *Guardian*, 17 January.

Ball, S. (2007) *Education PLC: Understanding private sector participation in public sector education,* Abingdon: Routledge.

Ball, S. (2008) *The education debate*, Bristol: The Policy Press.

Bandura, A. (1997) *Self-efficacy: The exercise of control*, New York: Freeman.

Barber, L. (2009) 'My harsh lesson in love and life', *Observer*, 7 June.

Barker, B. (2012) 'Grammar schools: brief flowering of social mobility?', *Forum*, vol 54, no 3, pp 429–47.

Barker, E. (1953) *Father of the man*, London, Oxford: Oxford University Press.

Barker, I. (2012) 'Private schools – Liverpool College and King's School, Tynemouth – give up on selection in bid to beat recession', *Times Educational Supplement*, 12 October.

Barnes, J. (1995) 'Life and work', in *The Cambridge Companion to Aristotle*, Cambridge, UK: Cambridge University Press.

Barnes, J. (2011) *Sense of an ending*, London: Jonathan Cape.

Baron-Cohen, S. (1991) 'Do people with autism understand what causes emotion?', *Child Development*, vol 62, no 2, pp 385–95.

Bassey, M. (2012) 'Proposal for a national education service for primary and secondary education', www.free-school-from-government-control.com.

Beckett, F. (2011) 'Take-your- pick schools, with do-it-all heroes', *New Statesman*, 15 September.

Bell, D. (2003) 'Standards and inspections in independent schools', Brighton College Conference on Independent Schools, reprinted in *Guardian*, 29 April.

Ben-Galim, D. (2011) 'Making the case for universal childcare', London: Institute for Public Policy Research.

Benn, C. and Chitty, C. (1996) *Thirty years on: Is comprehensive education alive and well or struggling to survive?*, London: David Fulton Publishers.

Benn, C. and Simon, B. (1970) *Half way there: Report on the British comprehensive system*, London: McGraw Hill.

Benn, M. (2011) *School wars: The battle for Britain's education*, London: Verso.

Benn, M. and Millar, F. (2006) *A comprehensive future: Quality and equality for all our children*, London: Compass.

Bennett, A. (2014) 'Fair play', *London Review of Books*, vol 36, no 12, pp 29-30.

Bereiter, C. and Scandamalia, M. (1989) 'Intentional learning as a goal of instruction', in L. Resnick (ed) *Knowing, learning and instruction: Essays in honour of Robert Glaser*, New York: Routledge.

Berliner, W. (2005) 'War of words', *Education Guardian*, 5 April.

Berners-Lee, T. and Fischetti, M. (1999) *Weaving the web: The original design and ultimate destiny of the World Wide Web by its inventor*, Windsor: Orion Business.

Bertelsmann Stiftung (2011) 'Strong variations in social justice within the OECD', http://www.bertelsmann-stiftung.de/cps/rde/xchg/bst_engl/hs.xsl/nachrichten_110193.htm.

Binet, A. (1903) *Experimental study of intelligence*, Paris: Schleicher.

Black, P. (1988) *Task Group on Assessment and Testing*, TGAT, London: King's College.

Black, P., Gardner, J. and Wiliam, D. (2007) *Evidence provided to the House of Commons Children, Schools and Families Committee*, London: The Stationery Office.

Blatchford, P. (2003) *The class size debate: Is small better?*, Maidenhead: Open University Press.

Bloom, A. (2007) 'A curriculum out of time', *Times Educational Supplement*, 23 February

Bloom, A. (2007) 'Me level 4, you level 2 = end of friendship', *Times Educational Supplement*, 9 February, p 13.

Boaler, J., William, D. and Brown, M. (2000) 'Experiences of ability grouping – disaffection, polarisation and the construction of failure', *British Educational Research Journal*, vol 28, no 5, pp 631–48.

Boston, J., Martin, J., Pallot, J. and Walsh, P. (1996) *Public management: The New Zealand model*, Auckland and Oxford: Oxford University Press

Bourdieu, P. and Passeron, J. (1990) *Reproduction in education, society and culture*, London: Sage Publications.

Boyer, C. (1991) *A history of mathematics*, Oxford: Wiley.

Bradshaw, J. and Richardson, D. (2009) 'An index of child well-being in Europe', *Child Indicators Research*, vol 2, no 3, pp 319–51.

Bray, M. (2011) *Confronting the shadow education system: What government policies for what private tutoring?*, Paris: IIER/UNESCO Publishing.

Brown, M. (1998) 'The tyranny of the international horse race', in R. Slee and G. Weiner with S. Tomlinson (eds) *School effectiveness for whom*, London: Falmer Press.

Buchanan, D. and Storey, J. (2010) 'Don't stop the clock: manipulating hospital waiting lists', *Journal of Health Organization and Management*, vol 24, no 4, pp 343–60.

Buckingham, D. (2007) *Beyond technology: Children's learning in the age of digital culture*, Cambridge: Polity Press

Buckinghamshire Report (2009), www.elevenplusexams.co.uk/forum/11plus/viewtopic.php?t=19691.

Bunting, B. and Mooney, E. (2001) 'The effects of practice and coaching on test results for educational selection at eleven years of age', *Educational Psychology*, vol 21, no 3, pp 243–53.

Burgess, S., Dickson, M. and Macmillan, L. (2014) *Selective schooling systems increase inequality*, London: Institute of Education.

Burgess, T. and Adams, E. (1980) *Outcomes of education*, London: Macmillan.

Burstall, C. (1975) 'Primary French in the balance', *Educational Research*, vol 17, no 3, pp 193–8.

Burt, C. (1933) *How the mind works*, London: Allen and Unwin.

Butler, R.A. (1943) Speech to House of Commons, 29 July, *Hansard*, vol 391, cc1, 825–928.

Buxton, L. (1981) *Do you panic about maths?* London: Heinemann.

Kang, M., Hsu, M., Krajbich, I., Loewenstein, G., McClure, S., Wang, J. andCamerer, C. (2009) 'The wick in the candle of learning: epistemic curiosity activates reward circuitry and enhances memory', *Psychological Science*, vol 20, no 8, pp 963–73.

Camus, A. (1957) Letter to his teacher on receiving the news that he had been awarded the Nobel Prize for literature, in O. Todd (1997) *Albert Camus: A life*, New York, NY: Alfred A. Knopf, Inc.

Carlsen, W. (1991) 'Questioning in classrooms: a sociolinguistic perspective', *Review of Education Research*, vol 61, no 2, pp 157–78.

Carter, R. (2007) 'Architecture and the brain', in J. Eberhard (ed) *Architecture and the brain: A new knowledge base from neuroscience*, New York: Greenway Communications.

Center for Research on Education Outcomes (CREDO) (2009) *Multiple choice: Charter school performance in 16 states*, Stanford, CA: Stanford University, http://credo.stanford.edu.

Central Advisory Council for Education (England) (1967) *Children and their primary schools* (The Plowden Report), London: HMSO.

Chaiklin, S. (2003) *Vygotsky's educational theory in cultural context*, Cambridge, UK: Cambridge University Press.

Chantrill, C. (2012) 'UK public spending since 1900', www.ukpublicspending.co.uk/spending_brief.php.

Chapman, J. (2012) 'Bad teachers should be sacked in weeks', *Mail Online*, 13 January.

Chatzitheochari, S., Parsons, S. and Platt, L. (2014) *Bullying victimisation among disabled children and young people: Evidence from two British longitudinal studies*, London: Institute of Education, http://www.cls.ioe.ac.uk/childhooddisability.

Cherniss, H. (1945) *The riddle of the early academy*, Cambridge, UK: Cambridge University Press.

Cho, S. (2011) 'Centralised national drive with advanced ICT infrastructure for preparation of Korean school teachers', paper given at the Comparative and International Education Society Conference, Montreal, Canada, 2 May.

Chomsky, N. (1965) *Aspects of the theory of syntax*, Cambridge, MA: MIT Press.

Chomsky, N. (1979) *Language and responsibility*, Sussex: Harvester Press.

Chowdry, H. and Sibieta, L. (2011) *Trends in education and school spending*, London: Institute for Fiscal Studies.

Chua, A. (2011) *Battle hymn of the tiger mother*, New York: Penguin Press.

Churchill, W. (1930) *A roving commission: My early life*, London: Charles Scribner.

Clark, L. (2009) 'Children should start school at six says Cambridge review of primary education', *Mail Online*, 16 October.

Clements, J. (2008) *Confucius: A biography*, Stroud, England: Sutton Publishing.

Clifton, J. (2011) 'International comparisons can be instructive if used properly – but, on this too, England is lagging behind', *Times Educational Supplement*, 15 July.

Cobain, L. (2011) *Cruel Britannia: A secret history of torture*, London: Portobello Books

Cofer, C. and Appley, M. (1967) *Motivation: Theory and research*, New York, London, Sydney: John Wiley and Sons.

Coffield, F., Moseley, D., Hall, E. and Ecclestone, K. (2004) *Learning styles and pedagogy in post-16 learning: A systematic and critical review*, London: Learning and Skills Research Centre.

Collini, S. (2007) *Common reading: Critics, historians, publics*, Oxford: Oxford University Press.

Collini, S. (2010) 'Social mobility: the playing field fallacy', *Guardian*, 23 August.

Collins, N. (2012) 'Sir John Gurdon, Nobel Prize winner was "too stupid" for science at school', *Telegraph*, 8 October.

Comenius, J. (1984) *The school of infancy*, ed E. McNeill Eller, Chapel Hill, NC: Carolina Press.

Committee of Enquiry (1975) *A language for life* (The Bullock Report), London: HMSO.

Cooke, G. and Henehan, K. (2012) *Double Dutch: The case against deregulation and demand-led funding in childcare*, London: Institute for Public Policy Research.

Crawford, C. (2014) *The link between secondary school characteristics and university participation and outcomes,* London: DfE.

Crawford, C., Dearden, L. and Greaves, E. (2011) 'Does when you are born matter? The impact of month of birth on children's cognitive and non-cognitive skills in England', A report to the Nuffield Foundation, London: Institute for Fiscal Studies.

Csikszentmihalyi, M. (1990) *Flow: The psychology of optimal experience*, New York: Harper and Row.

Cummings, C., Dyson, A. and Todd, L. (2011) *Beyond the school gates: Can full service and extended schools overcome disadvantage?*, Abingdon, Oxon: Routledge.

Daniels, H. (ed) (1996) *An introduction to Vygotsky*, London: Routledge.

Danish Technological Institute (2005) *Explaining student performance, A study undertaken for the European Commission*, Copenhagen: Danish Technological Institute.

Dawkins, R. (1976) *The selfish gene*, Oxford: Oxford University Press.

DCSF (Department for Children, Schools and Families) (2003) *Every child matters,* Green Paper, Cm 5860, London: DCSF.

DCSF and British Educational Communications and Technology Agency (2007) *Evaluation of the DCSF Primary Schools Whiteboard Expansion Project*, London: DCSF.

Dearing, R. (1993) *The National Curriculum and its assessment: Final Report*, London: School Curriculum and Assessment Authority.

Deem, R., Brehony, K. and Heath, S. (1995) *Active citizenship and the governing of schools*, Buckingham: Open University Press.

DES (Department for Education and Science) (1973) *Teacher education and training* (The James Report), London: DES.

DfE (Department for Education) (2010) *The Importance of Teaching: The Schools White Paper*, Cm 7980, London: The Stationery Office.

DfE (2011) *Teachers' standards*, https://www.education.gov.uk/publications/standard/SchoolsSO/Page1/DFE-00066-2011.

DfE (2012) *National Curriculum Assessments at Key Stage 2 in England*, London: DfE.

DfE (2012) *Phonics screening check and National Curriculum Assessments at Key Stage 1 in England*, London: DfE.

DfE (2012) *Schools, pupils and their characteristics*, www.gov.uk/government/publications/schools-pupils-and-their-characteristics-January-2013..

DfE (2012) *The school census and Edubase*, www.education.gov.uk/rsgateway/schoolcensus.shtml.

DfE (2013) *Draft National Curriculum programmes of study*, www.education.gov.uk/schools/teachingandlearning/curriculum/nationalcurriculum2014./

DfEE (Department for Education and Employment) (1997) *Excellence in Schools, White Paper*, Cm 3681, London: HMSO.

DfEE (1998) *The National Literacy strategy framework for teaching*, Sudbury: DfEE Publications.

DfEE (1999) *Citizenship – The National Curriculum*, https://www.education.gov.uk/publications/eOrderingDownload/QCA-99-470.pdf

DfES (Department of Education and Science) (1977) *Curriculum 11–16* (HMI 'Red Book'), London: HMSO.

DfES (Department for Education and Skills) (2002) *Languages for life: A strategy for England*, London: DfES.

DfES (2003) *Full-service extended schools planning documents*, London: The Stationery Office.

DfES/Welsh Office (1982) *Study of HM Inspectorate in England and Wales* (Rayner Report), London: HMSO.

DfES/Welsh Office (1988) *Advancing A Levels: Report of a Committee appointed by the Secretary of State for Education and Science and the Secretary of State for Wales* (The Higginson Report), London: HMSO.

Dobson, J. (2008) 'Pupil mobility, choice and the secondary school market: assumptions and realities', *Educational Review*, vol 60, no 3, pp 299–314.

Dorling, D. (2010) *Injustice: Why social inequality persists*, Bristol: The Policy Press.

Downes, P. (2011) 'I can't believe what is happening to the English education system', *Forum*, vol 53, no 3, pp 357–66.

Dryfoos, J. (1995) 'Full service schools: revolution or fad?', *Journal of Research on Adolescence*, vol 5, no 2, pp 147–72.

Duffy, T. and Jonassen, D. (eds) (1992) *Constuctivism and the technology of instruction: A conversation*, Hillsdale, NJ: Lawrence Erlbaum Associates.

Dunford, J. (1999) *Her Majesty's Inspectorate of schools: Standard bearers or turbulent priests?*, London: Woburn Press.

Edleman, G. (1992) *Bright air, brilliant fire: On the matter of the mind*, New York, NY: Basic Books.

Education Committee (2014) *Underachievement in education by white working class children*, Report Number 1, London: Stationery Office, 11 June.

Effective Provision of Pre-School Education Project (2002) 'Measuring the impact of pre-school on children's cognitive progress over the pre-school period', Technical Paper 8a, London: Institute of Education.

Effective Provision of Pre-School Education (EPPE) Project, *Research Report from Key Stage 3 Phase*, https.//www.education.gov.uk/publications/.

Egan, M. and Bunting, B. (1991) 'The effects of coaching on 11+ scores', *British Journal of Educational Psychology*, vol 61, no 1, pp 85–91.

Einstein, A. (1931) *Cosmic religion: With other opinions and aphorisms*, New York: Dover Publications.

Elliott, A. (2007) *State schools since the 1950s*, London: Trentham Books.

Elliott, A. (2012) 'Twenty years inspecting English schools – Ofsted 1992–2012', *Rise Review*, November.

Elton Report (1989) *Discipline in schools*, London: Her Majesty's Stationery Office

European Organisation for Nuclear Research (2011) 'The Large Hadron Collider', press release, 21 September, http://press.web.cern.ch/public/en/LHC/LHC-en.html.

Eurydice (2010) *National system overviews of education systems – Spain*, Brussels: European Commission.

European test producers' group (2011) *The A–Z of testing*, www.etpg.org/G-IOFTESTING.htm.

Evans, R. (2011) 'Learn for the right reasons', *Guardian*, 27 August.

Field, S., Kuczera, M. and Pont, B. (2007) 'No more failures: ten steps to equity in education', *Education and training policy*, Paris: OECD.

Fielding, M. and Moss, P. (2011) *Radical education and the common school,* London: Routledge.

Fitz, J., Edwards, T. and Whitty, G. (1986) 'Beneficiaries, benefits and costs: an investigation of the Assisted Places Scheme', *Research Papers in Education*, vol 1, no 3, pp 169–93.

Flavell, J.H. (1976) 'Metacognitive aspects of problem solving', in L.B. Resnick (ed) *The nature of intelligence*, Hillsdale, NJ: Erlbaum Associates.

Foreign and Commonwealth Office, 'Lost British Colonial Papers', oversesreview.blogspot.co.uk/lost-british-colonial-papers-made.html.

Forster, E.M. (1909) *The machine stops*, Gloucester: Dodo Press.

Frandsen, J., Gjesing, K. and Haue, H. (forthcoming) *More than a school: An introduction to the Danish efterskole.*

Gamoran, A. (2002) *Standards, inequality and ability grouping in schools*, CES Briefing no 25, Edinburgh: Centre for Educational Sociology, Scottish Council for Educational Research, www.leeds.ac.uk/educol/documents/163446.pdf.

Gardner, H. (1997) 'The case of Mozart', in *Extraordinary minds*, London: Weidenfeld and Nicolson.

Gardner, H. (1999) *Intelligence reframed: Multiple intelligences for the 21st century,* New York: Basic Books.

Garmezy, N. (1991) 'Resiliency and vulnerability to adverse developmental outcomes associated with poverty', *American Behavioural Scientist*, vol 34, no 4, pp 416–30

Germer, C., Siegel, R. and Fulton, P. (eds) (2013) *Mindfulness and psychotherapy,* New York: Guilford Press.

Gilbert, F. (2012) 'This proposal is an outrage', *Guardian*, 28 July.

Gillard, D. (1988) 'The National Curriculum and the role of the primary teacher in curriculum development', www.educationengland.org.uk/articles/07ncteacher.html.

Gillard, D. (2011) 'Education in England: A brief history', www.educationengland.org.uk/history.

Gillham, B. (1977) 'The reluctant beneficiaries: the teacher and the public examination system', *British Journal of Educational Studies*, vol 25, no 1, pp 50–62.

Gipps, C. (1994) *Beyond testing: Towards a theory of educational assessment,* London: Routledge.

Gladwell, M. (2008) *Outliers: The story of success*, London: Allen Lane.

Glatter, R. (2012) 'Towards whole system improvement', *Forum*, vol 54, no 3, pp 411–16.

Goleman, D. (1995) *Emotional intelligence: Why it can matter more than IQ*, New York: Bantam Books.

Goodhart, C. (1984) *Monetary theory and practice: The UK experience*, London: Macmillan.

Gopal, P. (2012) 'A version of class war', *Guardian*, 4 April.

Gopinathan, S. (1996) 'Globalisation, the state and education policy in Singapore', *Asia Pacific Journal of Education*, vol 16, no 1, pp 74–87.

Gorard, S. (2006) 'Value-added is of little value', *Journal of Educational Policy*, vol 21, no 2, pp 235–43.

Gottfredson, L. (1997) 'Intelligence and social policy', *Intelligence*, vol 24, no 1, pp 1–12.

Gould, S. (1996) *The mismeasure of man* (2nd edn), New York: W.W. Norton and Co.

Graham, D. and Tytler, D. (1993) *A lesson for us all: The making of the National Curriculum*, London: Routledge.

Gray, J. (2012) 'Wellbeing matters too', *Research Intelligence*, no 117, p 30.

Green, A. (1997) *Education, globalisation and the nation state*, London: Macmillan.

Greene, G. (1955) *The quiet American*, London: Heinemann.

Greene, G. (1966) *The Comedians*, London: Bodley Head.

Griffiths, J. (2003) *NFER the first fifty years 1946–1996*, Slough: NFER.

Gurría, A. (2012) *Inequality*, address to the Chinese Academy of Governance by the Secretary General of the OECD, Beijing, People's Republic of China, 19 March.

Hackett, G. (1999) 'MPs angered by support for Woodhead', *Times Educational Supplement*, 30 July.

Hargreaves, D., Beere, J., Swindells, M., Wise, D., Desforges, C., Goswami, U. and Wood, D. (2005) *About learning: Report of the Learning Working Group,* London: Demos.

Harlen, W. and Malcolm, H. (1999) 'Setting and streaming: A research review', SCRE Publication 143, Edinburgh: The Scottish Council for Research in Education.

Hattersley, R. (2005) 'Looking out for number one', *Education Guardian*, 22 February.

Haughton, H., Phillips, A. and Summerfield, G. (1994) *John Clare in context,* Cambridge UK: Cambridge University Press.

Hawking, S. and Penrose, R. (1996) *The nature of space and time*, Princeton, NJ: Princeton University Press.

HEFCE {Higher Education Funding Council for England) (2010) *Trends in young peoples' participation in higher education: Core results for England*, Swindon: HEFCE.

Henry, J. (2007) 'Professor pans "learning style" teaching method', *Telegraph*, 29 July.

Her Majesty's Inspectors (1978) *Primary education in England: A survey by HM Inspectors of Schools*, London: HMSO.

Herrnstein, R. and Murray, C. (1994) *The bell curve: Intelligence and class structure in American life*, New York: Free Press.

Higgins, C. (2011) 'Historians say Michael Gove risks turning history lessons into propaganda classes', *Guardian*, 17 August.

Hillgate Group (1994) *The reform of British education*, London: Claridge Press.

Hirst, P. (1974) *Knowledge and the curriculum*, London: Routledge and Kegan Paul.

HM Government (1944) *The Education Act* (Butler Act).

HM Government (2005) *Higher standards, better schools for all*, White Paper, Cm 6677, London: HMSO.

HM Treasury (2011) *Treasury Minutes: Government responses on the Fourteenth to the Eighteenth Reports from the Committee of Public Accounts Session 2010–11 (March)*, London: Department for Education, Cm 8042, www.hm-treasury.gov.uk/d/minutes_14_18_reports.

HM Treasury (2012) *Public expenditure statistical analysis (PESA) report*, London: HM Treasury.

Hörmann, B. (2009) 'Disappearing students: PISA and students with disability', in S. Hopmann and G. Brinek (eds) *PISA according to PISA*, Vienna: University of Vienna, www.univie.ac.at/pisaaccordingtopisa/pisazufolgepisa.pdf.

House of Commons Children, Schools and Families Committee (2008) *Testing and Assessment: Third Report of Session 2007–08*, London: The Stationery Office.

House of Commons Education Committee (2012) Chief Regulator of Qualifications and Examinations: Eighth Report of Session 2010–12, London: The Stationery Office.

House of Commons Education Committee (2013) *From GCSEs to EBCs: The government's proposals for reform*, Eighth Report of Session 2012–13, London: The Stationery Office.

Howard League for Penal Reform (2008) *Punishing children: A survey of criminal responsibility and approaches across Europe*, London: Howard League.

Hutchings, J., Bywater, T., Daley, D., Gardner, F., Whitaker, C., Jones, K., Eames, C. and Edwards, R. (2007) 'Parenting intervention in Sure Start services for children at risk of developing conduct disorder: pragmatic randomised controlled trial', *British Medical Journal*, vol 334 (7595), pp 678–82.

Hutmacher, W., Cochrane, D. and Bottani, N. (eds) (2001) *In pursuit of equity in education,* New York: Springer.

Hutton, W. (2012) 'Born poor? Bad luck, you have won last prize in the lottery of life', *Observer*, 15 July.

Huxley, A. (1932) *Brave new world*, London: Chatto and Windus.

Institute of Education (2012) 'Curriculum adviser says Gove's proposals are "fatally flawed"', press release, 12 June.

Institute of Education (2012) 'Government's decision on unqualified teachers contradicts its own White Paper', press release, 31 July.

Institute of Education (2014) 'International survey offers wealth of new information on England's secondary schools', London: Institute of Education, 25 June, http://www.ioe.ac.uk//100850.html.

Ipsos MORI/UNICEF (2011) *Child well-being in UK, Spain and Sweden: The role of inequality and materialism: a qualitative study*, London: UNICEF.

Ireson, J. and Hallam, S. (2001) *Ability grouping in education*, London: Paul Chapman Publishing.

Jackson, B. and Marsden, D. (1962) *Education and the working class,* Harmondsworth: Penguin.

James, O. (2010) *How not to f*** them up*, London: Vermilion.

Jenkins, S. (2012) 'Gove's centralism is not so much socialist as Soviet', *Guardian*, 12 October.

Jenkins, S. (2012) 'This bid to force all schools into line will end in failure', *Guardian*, 28 November.

Jenkins, S. (2014) 'Whitehall meddling is only ever bad news for education'. Guardian, 11 June.

Jensen, A. (1969) 'How much can we boost IQ and scholastic achievement?', *Harvard Educational Press*, vol 39, no 1, pp 1–123.

Jerrim, J. (2012) 'England's plummeting PISA test scores between 2000 and 2009: is the performance of our secondary school pupils really in relative decline?', London: Institute of Education, www.ioe.ac.uk/newsEvents/60021.html.

Jiménez, M. (2009) 'Early education's top model: Finland', *Toronto Globe and Mail*, 16 June.

Johnson-Laird, P. (1980) 'Mental models in cognitive science', *Cognitive Science*, vol 4, no 1, pp 71–115.

Johnston, R. and Watson, J. (2005) 'A seven year study of the effects of synthetic phonics teaching on reading and spelling attainment', *Insight*, no 17, Edinburgh: Scottish Government, www.scotland.gov.uk/Publications/2005/02/20682/52383.

Joint Council for Qualifications (2012) *GCSEs*, www.jcq.org.uk/examination-results/gcses.

Jones, B. (2012) 'First "free" sixth form oversubscribed', *Guardian*, 5 March.

Jones, K. (2003) *Education in Britain: 1944 to the present*, Cambridge, UK: Polity Press.

Kang, M., Hsu, M., Krajbich, I., Loewenstein, G., McClure, S., Wang, J. and Camerer, C. (2009) 'The wick in the candle of learning: epistemic curiosity activates reward circuitry and enhances memory', *Psychological Science*, vol 20, no 8, pp 963–73.

Karlsen, G. (2010) 'Friedman's ideas based on his book "Capitalism and Freedom" (1962, 2002)', paper presented at NordNet Seminar, Oslo, September.

Kluger, R. (1975) *Simple justice: The history of Brown v Board of Education and Black America's struggle for equality*, New York: Harper and Row.

Knox, R. (1950) *Enthusiasm*, Oxford: The Clarendon Press.

Kogan, M. (1971) *The politics of education*, Harmondsworth: Penguin.

Kolb, D. and Fry, R. (1975) 'Toward an applied theory of experiential learning', in C. Cooper (ed) *Theories of group process*, London: John Wiley.

Kolb, D., Boyatzís, R. and Mainemelis, K. (1999) 'Experiental learning theory: previous research and new directions', in R.J. Sternberg and L.F. Zhang (eds) *Perspectives on cognitive learning and thinking styles*, NJ: Lawrence Erlbaum.

Krashen, S. (2012) 'Wide reading is key', *Guardian*, 31 July.

Krueger, A. (2003) 'Economic considerations and class size', *Economic Journal*, Royal Economic Society, vol 113 (485) pp 34–63.

Kwok, J. (2010) *Girl in translation*, London: Penguin.

Labour Party (2014) *Review of education structures, functions and the raising of standards for all: Putting students and parents first* (The Blunkett Report), London: Labour Party

Lacey, C. (1975) 'De-streaming in a pressurised academic environment', in S.J. Eggleston (ed) *Contemporary research in the sociology of education*, London: Methuen.

Laukkanen, R. (2006) 'Finnish strategy for high-level education for all', paper presented at Conference on Educational Systems and the Challenge of Improving Results, University of Lausanne, 15–16 September.

Laurance, J. (2006) 'Length of a woman's ring finger reveals her sporting ability', *Independent*, 28 September.

Laurillard, D. (1995) 'Multimedia and the changing experience of the learner', *British Journal of Educational Technology*, vol 26, no 3, pp 179–89.

Lawes, S. (2011) 'Schools of the future: what is education for?', Birmingham Salon – a public forum for debate, www.birminghamsalon.org/

Lawn, M. and Grek, S. (2012) *Europeanizing education: Governing a new policy space*, Oxford: Symposium Books.

Lawson, D. and Silver, H. (1973) A social history of education in England, London: Methuen.

Lawton, D. (1980) 'Common curriculum or core curriculum?', *International Journal of Research and Method in Education*, vol 3, no 1, pp 5–10.

Layard, R. (2009) 'This is the greatest good', *Guardian*, 13 September, www.guardian.co.uk.

Layard, R. (2011) *Happiness: Lessons from a new science* (revised edn), London: Penguin.

Layard, R. and Dunn, J. (2009) *A good childhood: Searching for values in a competitive age*, London: Children's Society.

Leader, Z. (ed) (2000) *The letters of Kingsley Amis*, London: Harper Collins.

Le Grand, J. (2003) *Motivation, agency and public policy: Of knights and knaves, pawns and queens*, Oxford: Oxford University Press.

Leite, W., Marilla, S. and Yuying, S. (2009) *Attempted validation of the scores of the VARK: Learning styles inventory with multitrait–multimethod confirmatory factor analysis models*, London: Sage Publications.

LGA (Local Government Association) (2012) *Get in on the Act, Briefing on the Health and Social Care Act 2012*, London: LGA.

Lightfoot, L. (2000) 'Labour praises ethos of private schools', *Telegraph*, 30 September.

Lillard, A. (2005) *Montessori: The science behind the genius*, Oxford: Oxford University Press.

Lowe, R. (1862) Statement to the House of Commons, quoted in Johnson, B. (1956) 'The development of English education 1856–1882', MEd thesis, University of Durham.

MacGregor, N. (2010) *A history of the world in 100 objects*, London: Allen Lane.

Machin, S. and Vignoles, A. (2006) *Education policies in the UK*, London: Centre for the Economics of Education, London School of Economics.

Mackintosh, N. (1998) *IQ and human intelligence*, Oxford: Oxford University Press.

Maclure, S. (1965) *Educational documents, Volume II,* Abingdon: Routledge.

Maddern, K. (2012) 'How the poorest school beat the odds', *Times Educational Supplement*, 26 October.

Maguire, E., Gadian, D., Johnsrude, I., Good, C., Ashburner, J., Frackowiak, R. and Frith, C. (2000) 'Navigation-related structural change in the hippocampi of taxi drivers', *Proceedings of the National Academy of Sciences of the United States of America*, published online before print, 14 March 2000, doi: 10.1073/pnas.070039597, http://www.pnas.org/content/97/8/4398.short.

Mansell, W. (2007) *Education by numbers*, London: Politico.

Mansell, W. (2011) 'Schools cash in on academy status', *Guardian*, 26 April.

Mansell, W. (2012) 'The only way is Pearson', *Guardian*, 17 July.

Marland, M. (1975) *The craft of the classroom*, Oxford: Heinemann Education Publishing.

Marmot, M., Rose, G., Shipley, M. and Hamilton, P. (1978) 'Employment grade and coronary heart disease in British civil servants', *Journal of Epidemiology and Community Health*, vol 32, no 4, pp 244–9.

Marshall, B. (2005) 'Testing, testing, testing', in E. Wragg (ed) *Letters to the Prime Minister*, London: New Vision Group.

Martini, R., Mortimore, P. and Byford, D. (1985) 'Some O levels are more equal than others', *Times Educational Supplement*, 28 June.

Maslow, A. (1943) 'A theory of human motivation', *Psychological Review*, vol 50, no 4, pp 370–96.

Mayer, J., Carusso, D. and Salovey, P. (2000) 'Emotional intelligence meets traditional standards for an intelligence', *Intelligence*, vol 27, no 4, pp 267–98.

McCourt, F. (2005) *Teacher man*, London: Fourth Estate.

McKinsey Education (2009) *Shaping the future: How good education systems can become great in the decade ahead*, Report on the International Education Round Table, Singapore.

McNeil, F. (1999) 'Brain research and learning: an introduction', *Research Matters*, no 10, p 2, London: Institute of Education.

Meek, M. (1982) *Learning to read*, London: Bodley Head.

Millar, F. (2012) 'Labour needs to step up to the plate, fast', *Guardian*, 11 September.

Millar, F. (2012) 'Time to debunk some myths about schools', *Guardian*, 10 April.

Millar, F. (2012) 'We aren't going to surrender', *Guardian*, 19 June.

Moseley, D., Baumfield, V., Elliott, J., Gregson, M., Higgins, S., Miller, J. and Newton, D. (2005) 'De Bono's lateral and parallel thinking tools', in D. Moseley (ed) *Frameworks for thinking*, Cambridge, UK: Cambridge University Press.

Moss, G., Jewitt, C., Levacic, R., Armstrong, V., Cardini, A.., Castle, F., Allen, B., Jenkins, A. and Hancock, M. with High, S. (2007) *The interactive whiteboards, pedagogy and pupil performance evaluation: An evaluation of the Schools Whiteboard Expansion (SWE) Project*, London: London Challenge.

Mullis, I.V.S., Martin, M.O., Foy, P. and Arora, A. (2012) *2011 International results in mathematics*, Boston, MA: Timms and PIRLS International Study Center, Lynch School of Education, Boston College.

Mullis, I., Martin, M., Minnich, C., Stanco, G., Arora, A., Centurino, V. and Castle, C. (eds) (2012) *TIMSS 2011 Encyclopaedia: Education policy and curriculum in mathematics and science* (vols 1–2), Chestnut Hill, MA: Boston College.

Murdoch, S. (2007) *IQ: A smart history of a failed idea*, Hoboken, NJ: John Wiley and Sons Inc.

Murray, J. (2012) 'They sat and talked to me about my child', *Guardian*, 24 July.

Nash, P. (1976) *Teacher expectations and pupil learning*, London: Routledge and Kegan Paul.

National Centre for Social Research (2011) *British Social Attitudes Survey 28*, London: National Centre for Social Research.

National Commission on Education (1993) *1. Learning to succeed. 2. Briefings. 3. Insight,* London: William Heinemann.

National Equality Panel (2010) *An anatomy of economic inequality in the UK*, London: Government Equalities Office.

National Evaluation of Sure Start Team (2008) *The impact of Sure Start on local programmes and three year-olds and their families*, www.ness.bbk.ac.uk/impact/documents/42.pdf.

National Institute of Child Health and Human Development (2000) *Report of the National Reading Panel, Teaching Children to Read: An evidence based assessment of the scientific research literature on reading and its implications for reading instruction: Reports of the subgroups*, NIH Publication No 00-4754, Washington, DC: US Government Printing Office.

Neill, A.S. (1996) *Summerhill School: A new view of childhood*, New York: St. Martin's Griffin.

Newell, C. and Watt, H. (2011) 'Exam boards: "We're cheating, we're telling you the question cycle"', *Telegraph*, 7 December.

Norton, J. (2014) 'Fine parents who don't read to their children, says Ofsted head (and Sir Michael Wilshaw also wants to punish those who miss school events)', Mail Online, 17 June, http://www.dailymail.co.uk/news/article-2659781/Fine-parents-dont-read-children-says-Ofsted-head-Sir-Michael-Wilshaw-wants-punishments-miss-school-events.html.

Nuffield Foundation (2000) *Languages: The next generation*, www.nuffieldfoundation.org/nuffield-languages-inquiry-and-nuffield-languages-programme.

Observer (2011) 'Education reform: we need transparency not ideological zeal', 18 December.

OECD (2009) *Doing better for children,* Paris: OECD.

OECD (2010) *PISA 2009 Results, What students know and can do,* Vols I–V, Paris: OECD.

OECD (2012) *Education at a glance,* Paris: OECD.

OECD (2012) *Equity and quality in education: Supporting disadvantaged students and schools*, Paris: OECD.

OECD (2012) *Schooling for tomorrow: Scenarios,* Paris: OECD.

Office for National Statistics (2011) 'Initial investigation into Subjective Wellbeing', Opinions Survey, 1 December.

Ofsted (2003) *The education of six year olds in England, Denmark and Finland: An international comparative study*, London: Ofsted.

Ofsted (2010) *The Annual Report of Her Majesty's Chief Inspector of Education, Children's Services and Skills 2009/10*, London: Ofsted,

Ofsted (2011) *Annual Report 2010–11*, London: Ofsted.

Ofsted (2012) *Annual report of Her Majesty's Inspector of Education, Children's Services and Skills*, London: The Stationery Office.

O'Grady, S. (2012) 'Childcare costs parents quarter of their earnings', *Daily Express*, 2 July.

Olson, D. (2007) 'Jerome Bruner', in *Continuum library of educational thought,* London: Continuum.

Orwell, G. (1948) *Nineteen eighty-four*, London: Penguin.

O'Shaughnessy, J. (2012) 'Competition meets collaboration: helping school chains address England's long tail of educational failure', London: Policy Exchange.

Oxfam (2014) *The Inequality World Cup, Report*, 11 July, http://www.oxfam.org.uk/what-we-do/issues-we-work-on/inequality-world-cup

Paton, G. (2011) 'More children being sent to private tutors, says Sutton Trust', *Telegraph*, 5 September

Paton, G. (2012) 'Academy schools inflate results with easy qualifications', *Telegraph*, 3 February.

Paton, G. (2012) 'Selection by religion should be banned in state schools', *Telegraph*, 12 November.

Paton, G. (2013) 'Russell Group invited to "review new A-level exams"', *Telegraph*, 14 June.

Patrick, H. (1996) 'Comparing public examination standards over time', paper presented at British Educational Research Association (BERA) conference, Birkbeck College, London.

Paul, R. and Elder, L. (2006) *The art of Socratic questioning*, Dillon Beach, CA: Foundation for Critical Thinking.

Piaget, J. (1953) *The origin of intelligence in the child,* New York: Routledge and Kegan Paul.

Piaget, J. and Inhelder, B., trans H. Weaver (1969) *The psychology of the child*, New York: Basic Books.

Pirie, M. (2012) *Think tank: The story of the Adam Smith Institute*, London: Biteback Publishing.

PISA (2006) *Technical report*, Paris: OECD.

Prange, K. (2004) 'Bildung: a paradigm regained?', *European Educational Research Journal*, vol 3, no 2, pp 501–9.

Pring, R. (2013) *Must secondary education for all be but a dream?*, London: Routledge.

Programme for International Student Assessment (PISA) (2009) *What students know and can do*, vol 1, Paris: OECD.

QCA (Qualifications and Curriculum Authority) *GCSEs – the official student guide to the system*, www.qca.org.uk/GCSE/.

QCA (2007) *The National Curriculum at Key Stages 3 and 4*, London: QCA

Ramsden, S., Richardson, F., Josse, G., Thomas, M., Ellis, C., Shakeshaft, C., Seghier, M. and Price, C. (2011) 'Verbal and non-verbal intelligence changes in the teenage brain', *Nature*, published online 19 October, www.nature.com/nature/journal/v479/n7371/full/nature10514.html.

Raphael, D. and Macfie, A. (1976) 'Introduction', in D. Raphael and A. Macfie (eds) *Adam Smith, The theory of moral sentiments*, Oxford: Oxford University Press.

Reay, D., Crozier, G. and James, D. (2011) *White middle-class identities and urban schooling*, Basingstoke: Palgrave Macmillan.

Rée, H. (1973) *Educator extraordinary; the life and achievements of Henry Morris, 1889–1961*, London: Longman.

Rees, M. (2011) 'Educating Einsteins', *Guardian*, 20 September.

Rhem, J. (1999) Online National Teaching and Learning Forum, no 8, p 2, www.ntlf.com/article-directory/editorsnote.aspx.

Richardson, H. (2011) 'Slow starting pupils don't catch up, league tables how', BBC News Online, www.bbc.co.uk/news/education-16186158.

Roberts, P. (2000) *Education, literacy and humanization: Exploring the work of Paulo Freire*, Westport, CT: Bergin and Garvey.

Rogers, S. (2012) 'Data blog: how many poor children go to faith schools', 5 March, www.guardian.co.uk/news/datablog/2012/mar/05/faith-schools-admissions?INTCMP=SRCH.

Rose, J. (2006) *Independent review of the teaching of early reading*, Nottingham: DfES Publications.

Rosen, C. and Rosen, H. (1973) *The language of primary school children*, Harmondsworth: Penguin.

Rosen, M. (2012) 'Letter from a curious parent', *Guardian*, 3 July.

Rosen, M. (2012) 'Letter from a curious parent', *Guardian*, 7 February.

Rosen, M. (2012) 'Out of the toy cupboard', *New Statesman*, 5 March.

Rosen, M. (2014) 'Letter from a curious parent', *Guardian*, 1 July

Rosenshine, B. and Meister, C. (1994) 'Reciprocal teaching; a review of the research', *Review of Education Research*, vol 64, no 4, pp 478–530.

Rosenthal, R. and Jacobson, L. (1968) *Pygmalion in the classroom: Teacher expectation and pupils' intellectual development*, New York: Holt, Rinehart & Winston.

Rutter, M. (2006) 'Implications of resilience concepts for scientific understanding', *Annals of the New York Academy of Sciences*, no 1094, pp 1–12.

Rutter, M. (2008) 'Developing concepts in developmental psychopathology', in J. Hudziak (ed) *Developmental psychopathology and wellness: Genetic and environmental influences*, Washington, DC: American Psychiatric Publishing.

Rutter, M., Maughan, B., Mortimore, P. and Ouston, J. (1979) *Fifteen thousand hours: Secondary schools and their effects on children*, London: Open Books.

Ryan, A. (1995) *John Dewey and the high tide of American liberalism*, New York: W.W. Norton and Company.

Sahlberg, P. (2011) *Finnish lessons: What can the world learn from educational change in Finland?*, New York: Teachers' College, Columbia University

Sammons, P. (2007) *School effectiveness and equity – making connections: A literature review*, London: Council for British Teachers Education Trust.

Scarr, S. (1994) 'Burt, Cyril L.', in R. Sternberg (ed) *Encyclopaedia of intelligence*, New York: Macmillan.

Schleicher, A. (2012) 'You must emulate and innovate to keep pace', *Times Educational Supplement*, 16 November.

Scottish Council for Research in Education (1977) *Pupils in profile*, London: Hodder and Stoughton

Seldon, A. (2011) 'Toby Young has a point', *Guardian*, 3 September.

Shaw, G.B. (1903) 'Maxims for revolutionists', New York: W.W. Norton and Company.

Shawn, A. (2002) *Arnold Schoenberg's journey*, New York: Farrar Straus and Giroux.

Shepherd, J. (2012) 'Faith schools and free school meals: case studies', *Guardian*, 5 March.

Shepherd, J. (2012) 'GCSE and A-levels are easier, Ofqual finds', *Guardian*, 1 May.

Singapore Ministry of Education (2012) *Our education system*, Singapore: Ministry of Education.

Skinner. B.F. (1968) *Technology of teaching*, East Norwalk, CT: Appledore-Century-Crofts.

Smith, E. (2012) *Luck: What it means and why it matters*, London: Bloomsbury.

Smith, L. (ed) (1996) *Critical readings on Piaget*, London: Routledge.

Smith, M. (2001) *David A. Kolb on experiential learning*, www.infed.org/biblio/b-explrn.htm.

Smith, M. (2001) *Kurt Lewin: Groups, experiential learning and action research*, Infed, www.infed.org/thinkers/et-lewin.htm

Spark, M. (1961) *The prime of Miss Jean Brodie*, London: Macmillan.

Steer Report (2005) *Learning behaviour: The report of the Practitioners' Group on school behaviour and discipline*, London: Department for Education and Skills.

Sternberg, R. and Grigorenko, E. (eds) (1997) *Intelligence, heredity and environment,* Cambridge, UK: Cambridge University Press.

Sternberg, R. and Salter, W. (1982) *Handbook of human intelligence*, Cambridge, UK: Cambridge University Press.

Stewart, W. (2012) 'Financial malpractice rife in schools, says council', *Times Educational Supplement*, 31 August.

Stewart, W. (2013) 'It's GCSEs, but not as we know them', *Times Educational Supplement*, 14 June.

Stiglitz, J., Sen, A. and Fitoussi, J. (2009) *Report by the Commission on the Measurement of Economic Performance and Social Progress*, www.stiglitz-sen-fitoussi.fr.

Stobart, G. (2008) *Testing times: The uses and abuses of assessment*, London: Routledge.

Stronach, I. (2012) '(B)othering education: an autobiography of alternatives', *Other Education: The Journal of Educational Alternatives*, vol 1, no 1, pp 171–4.

The Sutton Trust (2012) *Democratising entry to independent day schools*, www.suttontrust.com/public/documents/1open-access-report-march-2012-final.pdf.

Swales, T. (1979) 'Record of personal achievement', Schools Council Pamphlet 16, London: Schools Council.

Swedish National Agency for Education (2007) *The Swedish education system*, Stockholm: SNAE.

Syed, M. (2010) *Bounce: How champions are made*, London: Fourth Estate.

Sylvester, R. (1996) 'Recent cognitive science developments pose major educational challenges', *Education 2000 News*, June.

Symposium on Sustainable Schools (2014) 'Exam reform – unresolved issues: the risks and effects in focus', Symposium on Sustainable Schools.

Tattersall, K. (2012) 'An exam that will define failure, not success', *Guardian*, 18 September.

Thane, P. (2010) *Unequal Britain*, London: Continuum.

Thomas, G. (1998) 'A brief history of the genesis of the new schools' inspection system', *British Journal of Educational Studies*, vol 46, no 4, pp 415–27.

Times Educational Supplement (2012) 'From the Editor', 24 August.

Todes, D. (1997) 'Pavlov's physiological factory', *Isis*, vol 88, The History of Science Society, pp 205–46.

Tomlinson, M. (2004) *Final Report of the Working Group on 14–19 Reform*, London: DfE.

Toynbee, P. (2012) 'A strategy for growth must include childcare for all', *Guardian*, 14 February.

Twain, M. (1898) *Mark Twain's notebook*, New York: Harper and Brothers.

UK Parliament (2003) 'Individual Learning Accounts', *Select Committee on Public Accounts Tenth Report*, www.publications.parliament.uk/pa/cm200203/cmselect/cmpubacc/544/54403.htm.

UNICEF (2007) 'Child poverty in perspective', *Innocenti Research Centre Report Card 7*, Florence: Innocenti Research Centre.

UNICEF (2012) 'Measuring child poverty', *Innocenti Research Centre Report Card 10*, Florence: Unicef Innocenti Research Centre.

UNICEF (2013) 'Child well-being in rich countries', *Innocenti Research Centre Report Card 11*, Florence: Innocenti Research Centre.

UNISON (2005) *The business of education*, www.unison.org.uk/acrobat/B1956.pdf.

Vasagar, J. (2012) 'Expert adviser attacks Gove's new curriculum', *Guardian*, 13 June.

Vasagar, J. and Booth, R. (2012) 'Teachers and pupils furious after sudden change in exam gradings', *Guardian*, 24 August.

Vaughan, R. (2012) 'Because they're worth it', *Times Educational Supplement*, 2 November.

Vernon, P.E. (ed) (1957) *Secondary school selection: A British Psychological Society Enquiry*, London: Methuen.

Vezzosi, A. (1997) *Leonardo da Vinci: Renaissance man*, London: Thames and Hudson.

Vulliamy, E. (2010) 'Strings attached: what the Venezuelans are doing for British kids', *Guardian*, 13 October, www.guardian.co.uk/2010/oct/0/britain-children-orchestra-sistema.

Walker, P. (2012) 'Michael Gove warned by exams watchdog to rethink EBacc', *Guardian*, 5 December.

Ward, H. (2012) 'Catch-up lessons are going down', *Times Educational Supplement*, 21 September.

Watson, J. (1913) 'Psychology as the behaviourist views it', *Psychological Review*, vol 20, pp 158–77.

Waterland, L. (1985) *Read with me: An apprenticeship approach to reading*, Stroud: Thimble Press.

Waugh, E. (1928) *Decline and fall*, London: Penguin Classics.

Webster, R., Blatchford, P. and Russell, A. (2012) *The guide on the side: Realising the value of teaching assistants*, Abingdon, Oxon: Routledge.

Wesley, J. 'The nature of enthusiasm', in T. Jackson (1872) *The Sermons of John Wesley*, Nampa, ID: Wesley Center for Applied Theology, Northwest Nazarene University.

Weston, P. (1999) *Homework: Learning from practice*, London: Ofsted.

White, J. (1998) *Do Howard Gardner's multiple intelligences add up?*, London: Institute of Education, University of London.

White, J. (2005) *Towards an aims led curriculum*, London: QCA, http://dera.ioe.ac.uk/9704/1/11482_john_white_towards_an_aims_led_curr.pdf.

White, J. (2006) *Intelligence, destiny and education: The ideological roots of intelligence testing*, London: Routledge.

White, J. (2007) *What schools are for and why*, IMPACT Paper no 14, Philosophy of Education Society of Great Britain.

White, J. (2011) *The invention of the secondary curriculum*, New York: Palgrave Macmillan.

White, J. (2012) 'Towards a new ABC of curriculum-making: a reply to John Hopkin', *Forum*, vol 54, no 2, pp 305–12.

White, J. and Barber, M. (1997) *Perspectives on school effectiveness and school improvement*, London: Institute of Education.

Wiborg, S. (2009) *Education and social integration*, Basingstoke: Palgrave Macmillan

Wilby, P. (2012) 'Aside from football, sport in Britain is still a game for the elite', *Guardian*, 1 August.

Wilby, P. (2012) 'For-profit schools would be no more virtuous than other private-sector firms', *Guardian*, 30 July.

Wilby, P. (2012) 'My idea to break the stranglehold of the public school gang', *Guardian*, 18 September.

Wilkinson, R. and Pickett, K. (2009) *The spirit level: Why more equal societies almost always do better*, London: Allen Lane.

Wilson, W.J. (1987) *The truly disadvantaged: The inner city, the underclass and public policy*, Chicago: University of Chicago Press.

Wolf, A. (2011) *Review of vocational education: The Wolf Report*, London: DfE, https://www.education.gov.uk/publications/.

Wyse, D. and Parker, C. (2012) *The early literacy handbook*, London: Practical Preschool Books.

Wyse, D. and Styles, M. (2007) 'Synthetic phonics and the teaching of reading: the debate surrounding England's "Rose Report"', *Literacy*, vol 41, no 1, pp 35–42.

Yarker, P. (2011) *Crown Woods: Death of a comprehensive*, www.workersliberty.org/story/2011/08/02/crown-woods-death-comprehensive.

Young, C., Wu, S. and Menon, V. (2012) 'The neurodevelopment basis of maths anxiety', *Psychological Science,* vol 23, no 5, pp 492–501.

Mitra, S., Dangwal, R., Chatterjee, S., Jha, S., Bisht, R. and Kapur, P. (2005) 'Acquisition of computing literacy on shared public computers: Children and the "hole in the wall"', *Australian Journal of Educational Technology*, vol 21, no 3, pp 407–26.

Moore, A. (2000) *Teaching and learning: Pedagogy, curriculum and culture*, London: Routledge Falmer.

Moos, L. (2013) *Transnational influences on values and practices in Nordic education*, London: Springer.

Mortimore, J. and Blackstone, T. (1982) *Disadvantage and education*, London: Heinemann Educational Books.

Mortimore, J., Mortimore, P. and Chitty, C. (1986) *Secondary school examinations: The helpful servant not the dominating master*, London: Bedford Way Papers.

Mortimore, P. (1998) *The road to improvement: Reflections on school effectiveness*, Lisse, Netherlands: Svets and Zeitlinger.

Mortimore, P. (1998) 'The vital hours: reflecting on research on schools and their effects', in A. Hargreaves, A. Lieberman, M. Fullan and D. Hopkins (eds) *International handbook of educational change*, Dordrecht, Netherlands: Kluwer Academic Publishers.

Mortimore, P. (1999) *Understanding pedagogy and its impact on learning*, London: Paul Chapman Publishing.

Mortimore, P. (2009) 'Alternative models for analysing and representing countries' performance in PISA', paper commissioned by Education International Research Institute, Brussels: Education International.

Mortimore, P. (2009) *Learning to be leaders of learning: Pitfalls seen by an English eye*, paper presented at the KL Partnerskab om Folkeskolen, Odense, Denmark, 24 February.

Mortimore, P. and Blatchford, P. (1993) 'The issue of class size', *National Commission Briefings*, London: Heinemann.

Mortimore, P., Davies, J., Varlaam, A. and West, A. with Devine, P. and Mazza, J. (1983) *Behaviour problems in schools: An evaluation of support centres*, Beckenham: Croom Helm.

Mortimore, P., Sammons, P., Stoll, L., Lewis, D. and Ecob, R. (1988) *School matters: The junior years*, London: Paul Chapman Publishing.

Mortimore, P., Mortimore, J. and Thomas, H. (1994) *Managing associate staff: Innovation in primary and secondary schools*, London: Paul Chapman Publishing.

Index

Page references for notes are followed by n

D

H

I

J

K

L

T

U

V

W

Y

Z